Praise for *Truth in*

"In his fine new book, McCraw takes us behind the scenes of the venerable (or failing, depending on your perspective) *New York Times*. A self-professed 'raving moderate,' McCraw is in prime position to provide this backstage view as he draws equally on his experience as a writer and a lawyer. He excels at both, explaining legal issues in lay terms and unspooling the stories that propel the book."
—Preet Bharara,
in *The New York Times Book Review*

"David McCraw is far more than a lawyer. He's an advocate, a sage, and a level-headed, witty partner who ensures that principled, hard-won journalism sees the light of day and is protected and defended after it's published. David is also one of the world's foremost proponents of the First Amendment and free expression—and our community is lucky to have him."
—Timothy L. O'Brien, executive editor of
Bloomberg Opinion and author of *TrumpNation*

"Arguably the best 25 behind-the-scenes stories from the *New York Times* newsroom since 9/11. Inarguably better than law school. To read about David McCraw's legal work is largely to envy his career."
—David G. Bradley, chairman of Atlantic Media

"Everyone in the business knows that David McCraw is the best friend a reporter can have. Brilliant, steadfast, and brave, he has made some of the best journalism done in my lifetime better, and, most importantly, possible. The audience, the authors, and the owners he has guided owe him."
—Lowell Bergman, Pulitzer Prize winner and distinguished chair in
Investigative Reporting at the University of California, Berkeley

"David McCraw's wise, witty, and consequential tale brings us into the often-harrowing challenges that beset the *Times* in the era of Wikileaks, the #MeToo movement, and 'fake news.' McCraw's unabashed love affair with the First Amendment shines a convincing light on the vital tie between our democracy and a free press—and on the ever-important role of its defenders."
—Karen Greenberg,
director of the Center on National Security at
Fordham University School of Law and author of *Rogue Justice*

"In *Truth in Our Times*, David McCraw, a wry Midwesterner with a gift for storytelling, deftly spells out the consequences for democracy when the

very idea of journalism is under attack. He gives us a compulsively readable account of the pressures under which the *Times* operates from his front-row perspective as a trusted counselor to the paper's reporters and executives. Without ever making himself a hero, his account forces us to confront the need to reassert the value of a free press at a time of growing darkness. Required reading for every American who cares about the future of our country."
—Susan Crawford,
author of *Captive Audience* and *Fiber*

"There are few more comforting and joyful words in journalism than 'Don't worry, David McCraw is here.' McCraw is a national treasure, the reason why so many great articles have appeared, and a legal and moral force for justice and truth."
—Charles Duhigg, Pulitzer Prize winner and
author of *The Power of Habit*

"McCraw guides us to the front lines of the fight for press freedom, bringing much-needed perspective to the dangers emanating from the current occupant of the White House. Through stories involving the toughest calls in journalism, he gives us an entertaining civics lesson in the First Amendment, deepening our understanding of how press freedoms have enriched our democracy."
—Andrew Longstreth,
in the *New York Law Journal*

"If the worst fears some have about the crumbling of American institutions were to come to be, this book would stand as a chronicle of what happened and how."
—Ashley Messenger, in the *MediaLawLetter*

"McCraw, the deputy general counsel of The New York Times, recounts 17 years of defending the First Amendment and the paper's legal integrity in this passionate memoir. Best known for a letter he wrote responding to a lawsuit threat from President Trump about a report detailing groping accusations against him from two women, McCraw colors his legalese with wit and levity. . . . News junkies will relish the insider access."
—*Publishers Weekly*

"A passionate, important defense of the First Amendment and its absolute necessity in a democracy."
—*Kirkus Reviews*

Truth
in Our

**Inside the Fight for Press Freedom
in the Age of Alternative Facts**

David E. McCraw

ST. MARTIN'S GRIFFIN
NEW YORK

Published in the United States by St. Martin's Griffin, an imprint of St. Martin's Publishing Group

www.stmartins.com

Library of Congress Cataloging-in-Publication Data

Names: McCraw, David Edward, author.
Title: Truth in our times : inside the fight to save press freedom in the age of alternative
    facts / David McCraw.
Description: First edition. | New York : All Points Books, 2019. | Includes index.
Identifiers: LCCN 2018045141| ISBN 9781250184429 (hardcover) |
    ISBN 9781250184436 (ebook)
Subjects: LCSH: Press law—United States. | Freedom of the press—United States. |
    Libel and slander—United States. | Press and politics—United States. |
    Fake news—United States. | New York Times Company—Trials, litigation, etc. |
    United States—Politics and government—21st century.
Classification: LCC KF2750 .M377 2019 | DDC 342.7308/53—dc23
LC record available at https://lccn.loc.gov/2018045141

ISBN 978-1-250-78247-2 (trade paperback)

Our books may be purchased in bulk for promotional, educational, or business use. Please contact your local bookseller or the Macmillan Corporate and Premium Sales Department at 1-800-221-7945, extension 5442, or by email at MacmillanSpecialMarkets@macmillan.com.

First St. Martin's Griffin Edition: 2021

10 9 8 7 6 5 4 3 2 1

Dedicated to the men and women of the *New York Times* newsroom. Miracle workers, every day.

CONTENTS

PREFACE

This book tracks a particularly unsettling period in American press freedom. It begins with the turbulent presidential campaign of 2016 and then follows the escalating hostilities between the press and the president through the first year and a half of the Trump administration. The administration's war with the press comes with no clock. By the time you read this, much more will have happened: new skirmishes with reporters, a scattershot barrage of "fake news" tweets, another round of calls for the scaling back of press freedom. But the events that unfolded in the last months of the campaign and the first months of the new administration were critical. It was in those days that each side, and America, came to understand what the terms of engagement were going to be—what shape the attack on the American press would take and how the press would respond.

I have spent a decade and a half as the newsroom lawyer for The New York Times. I set out with a modest objective for this book: to let readers look behind the scenes at some of the most consequential reporting done by *The New York Times* and to understand how, sometimes quietly and sometimes not, the law protected journalism, shaped it, and, in a more fundamental way, made it possible. I did not want this to be either an abstract treatise on the First Amendment (although the law is front and center throughout the book) or a blind rant about Trump (even though the president fares poorly in virtually every chapter, at least until Harvey Weinstein shows up). The reason for that is simple: America's tradition of press freedom will not survive if the First Amendment strikes people as abstract and disconnected from the real life of the country or nothing more than a vehicle for advancing some political agenda. In journalism, the First Amendment happens at ground level, empowering and illuminating choices that journalists make every day in their pursuit of the truth. That is the story told in these pages.

Not everything can be told here. I am a lawyer, and that means there are confidences that cannot be shared. I work with journalists doing cutting-edge reporting, and that means they have sources who have to be protected. I have played a pivotal role in the rescue of journalists when they have been kidnapped or detained overseas, and some of the details of what happened remain secret. But within those bounds, I have tried to honestly capture the real interplay between lawyers and journalists in the nation's most important newsroom. This is not a lawyer-as-hero book, as much as I wish it were. I was wrong about Trump for much too long. I held back at times when the press should have been making its case more forcefully, either in the court of public opinion or in a court of law. I misjudged how polarized America had become on the issue of press freedom.

For most of my time at the paper, to be a lawyer for The Times was to occupy a fairly tidy corner of the First Amendment world. People complained about stories, detected what they were sure was bias, challenged (sometimes correctly) our facts, and railed against our editorial positions. A few of them were even motivated to sue. But, even among our harshest critics, few people seemed to question that press freedom mattered, that we were all better off with a press that was free to report inconvenient truths, take on the government, and speak up about the excesses and missteps of powerful companies. Now we live in a time when the president demands that laws be changed to rein in First Amendment freedoms and denounces the press as the enemy of the people, a stain on society, traffickers in "fake news." The problem is not so much that he says all of that; the problem is how well it plays, delighting crowds that, in a frenzy, turn to jeer the assembled press corps covering the event.

In the days when I was completing this book, a gunman opened fire in the newsroom of a newspaper in Maryland, killing five people. The White House press secretary declined to say that the press was not the enemy of the people. One of the president's lawyers, Rudy Giuliani, went on national TV to declare "truth isn't truth." And the president himself asked the Department of Justice to open a criminal investigation to find out the identity of "Anonymous," a senior government official who had committed the "crime" of writing a *Times* op-ed capturing the president's erratic behavior, impetuous policy choices, and disregard for the rule of law.

Much of what follows here is not rendered in the dark colors of troubled times. The book is often irreverent, even funny (yes, even by a lawyer). Here's the thing: It's a joy to be a newspaper lawyer. Zany things happen, crazy people emerge from nowhere, and little is as intoxicating as being present at the moments that world-rattling journalism is taking form. Lawyering for a newspaper may not be a labor of love, but it's pretty close, and I have tried here to capture the spirit that animates the work.

None of which should distract anyone from the real point: bad things are happening to democracy, and we need to do something.

Truth in Our Times

Election Day

The failing @NYTimes has been wrong about me from the very beginning. Said I would lose the primaries, then the general election. FAKE NEWS!

—Donald Trump, Jan. 28, 2017

NOVEMBER 8, 2016: At 10:00 p.m. I made one last circuit of the newsroom. Our CEO, Mark Thompson, stood near the political desk, looking on with his wife and a small group of others connected somehow to The Times. Pennsylvania, Wisconsin, and Michigan remained in doubt, but the reality was sinking in: Donald Trump was on the verge of winning the American presidency. I have been in newsrooms on election night before. I know how it is supposed to be. The only thing that ever mattered was the horse race (think Gore-Bush) or the historic moment (think Obama-McCain). There was no investment in which candidate was winning—he (or she) was destined to disappoint in the long run—and the dominant emotion was a certain not-quite-cynical detachment amid the electric buzz of the vote count and projections and the anticipation of relief that the endless push of the campaign was finally over. Sure, you couldn't ignore the victories or the big-picture moments, and the day-after stories would be celebratory in their way—duly restrained but with a nod to victory itself, not unlike the next-day account of a Super Bowl or Game Seven of the World Series.

Capture the triumph for a night or relish the race too close to call. Leave the dancing and the crying for others, for believers. But this night was like no other election night. There had been an investment, not just journalistic but spiritual. Donald Trump had campaigned not just against Hillary Clinton but also against The New York Times and the mainstream American press. And his astonishing rise to the top of the Republican Party had been built on a near-daily attack on facts—on the very idea that facts mattered. For journalists, who approach truth like a secular religion and who had seen a thousand times before how a single true story could gut the political career of a lying politician, it had been a year of faith-shaking disbelief. A line had not just been crossed but obliterated. The shock was palpable as the numbers came in, laced for some with the fading hope for a different outcome among people who generally wanted nothing more than a story worth telling. And there was still a paper to put out, a reckoning to account for.

It was too much on an already long night. I slipped away. At the elevators, I ran into Sue Craig and a guy who was obviously not from The Times. Sue had broken one of the biggest stories of the campaign: she was the one who went to her mailbox one day in September and found pages from Donald Trump's tax returns in an envelope. She introduced me to her acquaintance. He had once worked for Trump. I didn't ask why he was there. Like me, Sue had decided to get away. "It's too weird here," she said. We all got on the elevator: Sue, who had written a devastating story about Trump; me, whose letter to Trump's lawyer had lit up the internet for a week in October; and one of Trump's guys. We rode in silence, a strange tableau on the strangest night of the year.

Fourteen hours earlier, as I came into the building, The Times security guards had called me over. They wanted to make sure I knew about the plans for the next morning. In the quirky ways that things happen at The Times, I had become the lawyer to see for all the things the security guys encountered—from the intruder who pilfered women's shoes to the anonymous letter weaponized with razor blades. The Times was printing thousands of extra newspapers, and tables were going to be set up outside for all the people who would be showing up to buy *The New York Times* for posterity's sake. (The headline, I learned later, was going to read "Madam President.") We had been caught flat-footed eight years earlier, when Barack Obama had made history. By the time I arrived for work early on the morning after the 2008 election, the line was already starting to snake down the sidewalk. Soon there were hundreds of Obama supporters who thought—why wouldn't they?—that the place to buy a copy of *The New York Times* was surely at The New York Times. Lots of things happen at The Times building; selling newspapers is not one of them. Employees were pressed into emergency duty to cart bundles of newspapers from The Times printing plant in Queens, and the long lines outside the building stretched on into the afternoon. But it was Obama's victory in 2012 that was on my mind this morning. I vote in a neighborhood that is predominately black and middle class. In 2012, following a drumbeat of stories about how Republicans hoped to suppress voter turnout, I walked into my polling place at a local school eight minutes after it opened. The line already extended back to the schoolhouse doors. "Did y'all sleep here?," a guy wanted to know as he stepped into the foyer. On this morning in 2016, I had arrived again before dawn. I was the only one in line at my precinct's table.

That all seemed like a strangely distant memory as midnight approached. I had made my escape from the building with Sue and the Trump guy. At home, I sat alone in the glow of the TV screen as the states that mattered fell into place for the Republicans. I turned it off. Donald Trump was about to become the president of the United States.

The next morning, in a light drizzle on a gray November day, the newspaper sales tables were set up outside the building as planned. No one stopped. The vendors sat idly amid the stacks. There was no "Madam President" front page. Instead, the headline read "Trump Triumphs," and the first two paragraphs of the lead story talked about how the vote "threatened convulsions throughout the country" and made an early mention of those who "had watched with alarm" the rise of Trump. Nearly half the country had voted for the man. I had just spent a weekend in October back in rural Illinois, in my hometown, and for a moment I allowed myself to see the coverage through the eyes of the rest of America, where, at least for this one night, his victory represented a certain kind of hope that change was going to come at last.

It wasn't that hard. I wasn't one of those people you saw around the building who were real Timesmen and Timeswomen, people you were certain had been destined for the place from the time they were in junior high. My path, from the small-town Midwest to a law degree at age 37 and, a decade later, to The New York Times, had never been foreordained.

On a Thursday morning in May 2002, I said goodbye to the guard at the New York Daily News building on 33rd Street in Manhattan and made my way 10 blocks north to start my new job as a lawyer for The New York Times. I had spent two years at the Daily News, a blue-collar tabloid struggling to survive in the gritty world of New York City journalism, telling the stories of cops and killers, intrigue at City Hall, sex romps gone bad, the slaughter of pedestrians on Queens Boulevard (aka the Boulevard of Death), the shifting fates of the New York Mets, the evil genius of George Steinbrenner, and the workaday indignities of the city's subways. It was only a quick 15-minute walk that separated the News's downmarket offices from the gothic temple that was The Times, a paper we loathed and resented and envied in more or less equal parts. When I occasionally showed up for news industry meetings at The Times, I would be led through a winding corridor where every wall was lined with outsized plaques, one for each of its dozens of Pulitzer Prize winners, every step seemingly a reminder of one's own unworthiness and lack of belonging.

Three decades earlier, as a brand-new journalism graduate from the University of Illinois, I had taken a job at the *Quad-City Times* in Davenport, Iowa. While I was there, the city council decided to hire a New York City police official as the new chief of police. Our city editor placed a call to one of the clerks who ran the "morgue" at The New York Times, that ancient catacomb in which a team was employed to clip each day's newspaper and carefully place the articles into drawers of endless filing cabinets, stored away forever for future research. The editor from Davenport was hoping to find a little background on the new chief.

"Hello," he said, "my name is Mike McGreevy, and I am the city editor at the *Quad-City Times* in Davenport, Iowa."

"I couldn't be more impressed," the clerk said.

To me, a small-town kid from Illinois working as a journalist in a small city in Iowa, a million light-years from New York, that said it all, what it was like to be The New York Times. When I tell this story later to colleagues at The Times, they invariably say the place isn't like that now, and they are right, and maybe it was never really so offhanded in its arrogance, although no one ever doubts the story happened.

And for all of the paper's deeply held tradition, the narrative of my time at The Times was a narrative of change. The day I walked through the door on 43rd Street in 2002, the company owned 20 newspapers in places from Santa Rosa, California, and Gadsden, Alabama, to Boston and Paris. It had TV stations around the Midwest and the South. The Times website, nytimes.com, had been in existence for six years, but the heartbeat of The New York Times remained the thunder of printing presses and the sound of newspaper bundles hitting sidewalks. As it had been for decades, the paper was a singular voice in American journalism, setting the agenda for hundreds of smaller news outlets. The business of being an in-house media lawyer had changed little over the preceding decades. I vetted stories for legal problems, oversaw a handful of libel lawsuits, and answered reporters' questions about newsgathering. Interesting work, and The Times provided a platform like no other for lawyering as well as for journalism.

By the time Donald Trump made his improbable run for president, much of that had changed. The Times had exited the broadcast industry and sold off all of its other newspapers. It was in an existential fight to remain a relevant and powerful global news provider while reinventing itself as a digital publisher in a media ecosystem marked by ruthless competition for ad dollars, an explosion of pitchfork partisanship, and a head-spinning cultural war over the very nature of truth. Governments had long embraced secrecy but, post-9/11, in a nation unnerved by terrorism, the expanding national security state erected endless barriers for journalists trying to cover the inner workings of government and America's global ambitions. That rising tide of secrecy was met by leaks of startling proportion and audacity. WikiLeaks was able to make hundreds of thousands of pages of secret government documents available instantly and globally. Edward Snowden walked away with more data than it was possible to quantify. It was no longer the world of Daniel Ellsberg and the Pentagon Papers.

The work of reporters was changing as well. Tweeting became both a form of journalism and, as a president with a cell phone would prove, the subject of journalism. The grim reality of foreign correspondents' new place in the world was horrifyingly captured by the video of James Foley being beheaded by ISIS in Syria. Reporters, once viewed by all sides as honest brokers in a conflict zone, had become soft targets.

Those same disruptive forces transformed what it meant to be a lawyer for The Times. With no training and no warning, I became the go-to person when our journalists were kidnapped, hurt in war zones, or detained by hostile governments. I spent every day for seven months working to free a reporter after he was kidnapped in Afghanistan in 2008. Three months after his return, it started all over again with a phone call on a Saturday morning as I walked across a grocery store parking lot: two more journalists had been kidnapped by the Taliban. Even my core work pivoted. As secrecy spread across every level of government, we doubled down on trying to unlock the information that the government did not want us to see. Over the course of a decade, I brought dozens of suits seeking government documents hidden from view. I stood with our editors when they decided to publish classified information that shed light on the surveillance of Americans and the government's misconduct and its misguided policies abroad. As The Times became a true global news source, libel suits were brought against us in Greece and China, Iraq and Indonesia, India and France. And it was all happening as the sheer pace of journalism accelerated in a way that was unimaginable a decade before—unrelenting deadlines around the clock, with fewer editing hands touching copy as stories were instantly launched to an audience that was everywhere. We were sued over a tweet in 2011. Law, ever slow to change and deeply bound by tradition and form, was plunged headfirst into its own uncharted digital future.

How much my world had changed had become self-evident in the fever pitch of the 2016 presidential campaign. One morning in October I wrote a letter to Donald Trump's lawyers defending our story about two women who said Trump had groped them. In ways, it was not so different from dozens of lawyer letters I had written before to those unhappy with what The Times had done. Only this one landed in the white heat of the campaign, and it pointedly suggested that Trump's reputation, at least when it came to the treatment of women, was so tarnished it could be tarnished no more. It ended with an invitation to the candidate to sue us if he really believed the First Amendment didn't protect The Times. Because his letter had been published online, we too launched ours onto the internet, where it was swept up in the cascading tide of social media. Millions of people on Twitter and Facebook and whoknowswhat .com read it and passed it on, over and over again. It became, thanks to the internet and the singular stature of The New York Times, an artifact of the 2016 campaign, a 17-sentence defense of press freedom and the right of women to stand up to the powerful. Old-school lawyering met its social media moment.

That digital flash moment had pretty much dimmed by the morning after the election, as I made my way to The Times Legal Department, as if it were just another day at the office, which it certainly wouldn't be. I couldn't help but think about what the press had learned over the course of a bruising campaign, what it needed to be now as it stepped forward into the uncertainties of a Trump presidency. Whatever your politics were, it was impossible not to understand that we had become a country of breach, divided in fundamental ways. There was a time, 50 years ago, when a free press had helped heal a country torn by racism and inequality and the war in Vietnam by staying loyal to the truth, reporting the hard facts, and forcing America to confront its worst demons.

But this time? Could the press play that role again, could it be the honest broker that never lost sight of the public's best interest? Or had something fundamental changed in the nature of the American public, or in the nature of the American press, or in the symbiotic relationship between the two?

Wherever we were going, the one thing you knew for certain was that the central player in whatever narrative was to come would be Trump himself. He was unlike any politician America had ever seen before. Trump talked unscripted to reporters more than any president in recent history, yet he savagely lashed out at the press in public. He demanded that the laws of libel be changed so it would be easier for people like him to sue. He egged on crowds to jeer the working journalists at his rallies. Articles that challenged his leadership, his ethics, his honesty, or his popularity were denounced as fake news. In Trump's world, there were "alternative facts" when the truth became too inconvenient. All the things I had believed to be self-evident about the place of press freedom in America—its value, its necessity, its centrality to democracy—were under siege and no longer seemed so certain. There was a war going on for the hearts and minds of the American people, and like it or not, America's press was pinned down in the middle of it.

It was a hell of a time to be a lawyer for The New York Times.

2

Reckless Disregard

My lawyers want to sue the failing @nytimes so badly for irresponsible intent. I said no (for now), but they are watching. Really disgusting.
—Donald Trump, Sept. 17, 2016

Oh good. So you are against a free press. You thin skinned manchild. Maybe they should sue you for defamation.
—Response from a Twitter user

THE EMAIL POPPED up in my inbox on November 3, with just days to go before the election. "David, hi, I'm a contributing editor at *New York* magazine, and I'd like to write a short piece on your lawyer-letter-heard-'round-the-world for our annual Reasons to Love New York issue. Would you have time next week for an interview?"

Letter heard 'round the world? The piece would write itself. Times lawyer writes letter to Trump lawyer. Letter goes viral. Sanity is restored, Trump loses, Times lawyer ends up among the icons in Reasons to Love New York. I made an appointment to see the writer on November 9. That would be the right time to do such a thing, the morning after the election of Hillary Rodham Clinton.

A certain awkwardness ensued when the appointed hour came. "I guess yesterday kind of killed this story," I offered. The writer was not so easily deterred. As we sat in my office and talked, it was clear he was looking for the thread that would pull the piece together, that money quote from the barricades, me with a lawyerly pitchfork standing lonely guard on the First Amendment in the first hours of the political Armageddon. I could sense his disappointment. I told him I thought it was too early to say what might happen. Trump scoring political points at the media's expense in campaign rallies was one thing; waging a for-real war on the press from the White House was another. The laws protecting the press were strong and resilient. Reporters weren't going to back down. The public understood the need for a free and independent press. Sure, leak investigations that went after reporters' sources were a concern—it was the one place where the legal protections were inadequate—but even there the big confrontations between the government and the press had been the exception rather than the rule. "We'll just have to see," I said.

He wanted to know what my family thought, a fairly transparent attempt, in my mind, to find out whether there was somebody sane at home who didn't share my disturbingly mushy views about the impending Trump disaster and might be able to set me straight. I rambled on about the trip I had just taken to Illinois, to my tiny hometown in the center of the state, about being surrounded by Trump voters, about understanding Trump's appeal to the people I grew up with, about how I thought everything was going to work out OK because even in a divided nation freedom of speech was one of those issues that liberals and conservatives could agree on. He stopped taking notes. I walked him to the elevator.

When *New York* magazine published the Reasons to Love New York issue, there was a theme of sorts. (*No. 3:* Because Our Streets Defy Dictators . . . *No. 4:* Because We Know Where Trump Lives . . . *No. 47:* Because Hillary Clinton Thought Brooklyn Could Be the Capital of America . . .) I was—no surprise—not among them, but there was at least this: *No. 22:* Because since Trump's election . . .

180,000 people bought *New York Times* subscriptions, ten times the normal rate.

The interview was no fluke. All around me people were talking about the Trump election as the end of press freedom as we know it, or maybe the end of freedom, or, in some corners of the Upper West Side of New York, maybe just the end. I was not there. Those of us who spend our days in the world of media law and press freedom and journalism are always a little too ready to crank up the First Amendment Outrage Machine at the first sign of trouble. I believed we all needed to take a deep breath, wait for something real to happen (besides Trump's loopy rants about changing the libel laws so he could get more money), and react in a measured and appropriate way. There was a reason one of my young colleagues called me a "raving moderate."

In the election's wake, Emily Bazelon, the talented legal affairs writer at *The Times Magazine*, was doing a piece on some troubling press-law cases. The story would appear later under the headline "Billionaires vs. the Press in the Era of Trump." It was a sharp-eyed look at lawsuits being brought with open wallets by right-wing aristocrats eager to take on the press. There was the Idaho billionaire Frank VanderSloot, who unrelentingly went after the left-leaning magazine *Mother Jones* over its portrayal of his involvement in a gay-rights controversy. And there was Peter Thiel, the Silicon Valley billionaire who secretly financed Hulk Hogan's successful invasion-of-privacy suit against Gawker after the snarky website posted outtakes from a video showing Hogan having sex with his best friend's wife. And there was Trump himself, who directly or through his companies had been the proud plaintiff in seven suits involving libel or similar claims, all losers (to put it in Trumpian terms) except for the one in which the defendant failed to show up. (When Emily asked for comment from Trump for the article, Hope Hicks, his aide, responded, "Mr. Trump is focused on the issues that were the cornerstones of his campaign as well as appointing a cab-

inet to achieve his ambitious agenda. Best, Hope.") Emily's thinking was encapsulated in the subhead her magazine piece carried:
"A small group of superrich Americans—the president-elect among
them—has laid the groundwork for an unprecedented legal assault
on the media. Can they succeed?"

Not long after Trump's victory, I read a prepublication draft of
Emily's story as I waited at LaGuardia for a flight to Boston. I told her
I thought that she was . . . well . . . wrong. "I fundamentally disagree
with the premise of the piece—I don't see a trend and I don't see
much of a threat, not compared, say, to what was going on in 1964."

Yes, in the months to come, it would be cringe-inducing whenever I went back to read that email. Few things in life are worse than
retroactive embarrassment. But the email pretty much nailed how
I missed out for so long on what was really going on: I was thinking like a lawyer. And 1964 was the year when the U.S. Supreme
Court had decided *New York Times v. Sullivan*, setting new legal
barriers for powerful people who wanted to use libel suits to punish the press and silence their critics. For America's fat cats and plutocrats, the libel game was being shut down. *Sullivan* pretty much
guaranteed that Donald Trump, perpetually unhappy about his
press coverage, would spend large chunks of his adult life storm-
ing around his empire threatening libel suits that he would never
bring and couldn't win.

In the years since *Sullivan*, the media—not the Donald Trumps
of the world—had won. Repeatedly. Decisively. Consistently. Media
lawyers and their journalist clients had spent most of the last three
decades consolidating victories, not fighting rearguard actions to
save press freedom from the well-heeled and well-placed.

Sullivan had begun a revolution. It was a 9–0 smackdown of
plaintiffs who saw libel suits as a legal extortion racket to be used
to silence publishers. L. B. Sullivan, the plaintiff, was a commissioner overseeing the police in Birmingham, Alabama, and therefore a man ideally positioned to do what he could to set back racial

justice by a few decades. Commissioner Sullivan sued The Times for libel for publishing an ad from supporters of Martin Luther King. The ad called out the violence being visited upon civil rights protesters in the South, in particular the police misconduct during a demonstration at a college in Birmingham. Sullivan claimed that the ad had besmirched his good name, and he persuaded an Alabama jury—not that this was hard—to hit The New York Times with a $500,000 verdict in his favor. There was nothing particularly special about Sullivan. He was just one of dozens of tinhorn Southern power brokers who at that time were bringing libel suits against publishers and broadcasters from the North because they wouldn't shut up about the evils of segregation and the criminal behavior of public officials in the Jim Crow South.

Never mind that the ad never mentioned Sullivan. Never mind that few people in Sullivan's hometown could honestly say they had ever laid eyes on the ad. The Times was not exactly Alabama's go-to newspaper of choice: Only 35 copies of the paper with the ad had been delivered to Montgomery County. Never mind that folks who held Commissioner Sullivan in high esteem probably didn't have their opinions altered on the say-so of an ad placed in The New York Times by a bunch of civil rights types. Truth be told, it probably polished his image to be denounced by rabble-rousing civil rights leaders and their pointy-headed Northern pals.

No matter. Sullivan's lawyers strung together a series of statements that they considered untrue: the protesters had not sung "My Country 'Tis of Thee" (it was the national anthem), the police had not created a ring around the university campus (they were deployed nearby), King had not been arrested seven times (it was only four), nine students had not been expelled for leading a demonstration at the state capitol (the expulsion came because they demanded service at the lunch counter in the Montgomery County Courthouse). That was sufficient to get Sullivan a $500,000 verdict in Montgomery.

By the time the case reached the Supreme Court, the justices had seen enough. "This technique for harassing and punishing a free press—now that it has shown to be possible—is by no means limited to cases with racial overtones; it can be used in other fields where public feelings may make local as well as out-of-state newspapers easy prey for libel verdict seekers," one of the justices wrote. The court famously held that henceforth public officials would need to show that the publisher acted with "actual malice"—reckless disregard of the truth—in publishing a story if they hoped to win a libel suit. Just getting something wrong would not be enough to leave news organizations open to crushing libel verdicts. Plaintiffs like Sullivan would need to show that journalists had entertained substantial doubt about the truth and then published the article anyway.

The message to journalists coming out of Washington that day may not have been immediately clear—the case involved an advertisement after all—but it soon became unmistakable: the truth may not set you free, but the actual malice standard will. The court wanted journalists to stop working in fear, afraid that one error in a story that offended the powerful could spell financial doom for their employer. That era ended on March 9, 1964, the day *Sullivan* was handed down.

Over the next two decades, the Supreme Court repeatedly stared down challenges brought by those who wanted to punish the press for doing nothing more than printing the truth. It freed a Virginia paper of a criminal penalty that had been imposed when reporters published—truthfully—that a judge was under investigation. It found that the First Amendment protected a West Virginia publisher that reported the name of a juvenile offender, a name reporters had obtained by simply interviewing people. It defended a tiny Florida newspaper's right to print the name of a sexual assault victim after learning of the case from an official police report.

When I first came to The Times in 2002, I was invited by Glenn

Kramon, the editor of the business section, to meet with his staff. He introduced me by saying that at other newspapers the legal department was where stories went to die, but at The Times it was different. At The Times, the lawyers worked to make sure stories got into print. I was too green to know whether that was true or whether Glenn was essentially assuring his department that I would never ever be a legal pest. It is true, though: the overarching message to journalists from the Supreme Court was to be brave, take chances, pursue the hard ones. With the press having been set free by law by the highest court in the land, something goes seriously amiss when it is media lawyers who become the voices of fear and hedging heard in journalists' ears.

Years ago, over coffee and cookies at a conference, an FBI agent wanted to know, and not in a nice way, whether I had the cushiest job in all of law. "So how does it work: your reporters ask if they can do something, and you say 'yes'?" That's pretty much it, I said between bites of cookie. That's actually pretty much how it is supposed to be.

Of course, there's more to it. The law doesn't give journalists a free pass, but it is a system built on imbalance instead of balance, a collective American understanding that the price of freedom is a tolerance of a certain amount of error. The Supreme Court said it flat out in *Sullivan*: the "erroneous statement is inevitable in free debate, and . . . it must be protected if the freedoms of expression are to have the breathing space that they need to survive." That legal scheme reflects a bedrock American belief: despite the screw-ups and failures and perceived or real bias of America's press, we are all better off with an independent press allowed to make mistakes than a Ministry of Truth in Washington.

And that was why I was not racing to the First Amendment barricades in the days following the election. Maybe others looked up and saw the press freedom sky falling, but I saw sunshine. U.S. law was in no danger of being changed. Ignore the campaign noise.

The guy wasn't even in office. As president, Trump would have little to say about either the Constitution or state law, the two drivers of press law in this country.

What I didn't quite get was that the anti-press fervor that had been stirred up by the Trump campaign was not really about rewriting the law of libel or letting rich guys with fancy legal briefs win their suits against news organizations. Something deeper and darker was taking shape.

Three days after the election, an editor had forwarded me an email from one of our Washington reporters. "Nothing to be done, but just letting you know," the editor wrote. Below it was the reporter's email: "Someone used my home address off that 8chan list to send me three pages anonymously of anti-Semitic material." Nobody comes into journalism thinking that one of the requirements of the job is to be ready to surrender one's personal safety and well-being, and the safety and well-being of one's family, at least not outside places like Kabul or Baghdad, and certainly not in America. On the one-week anniversary of the election, I was asked to convene a session for Times journalists to let people talk through their concerns about safety and what the company could do about it. "I'm not sure what I am supposed to say," I told Janet Elder, the editor in charge of newsroom administration. "It doesn't matter," she said. "Your presence will make people feel better." Perhaps, but this was not dashing off an in-your-face letter to Trump's attorney or telling reporters that their stories were legally sound. The session in the newsroom turned out to be a grim hour. The place was packed. I walked through the things we could do to respond to the threats, the security measures we could put in place, what people could do to make themselves less of a target in the vicious echo chamber that social media had become. It all sounded hollow. The questions kept coming, all of them understandable, few of them lending themselves to satisfying answers. What can The Times do when names and addresses get posted on right-wing web channels? How easy will it be for the government to get access to our emails? What has the company done to harden its physical security? Weren't we a most obvious target, easy to find in the middle of New York?

The First Amendment came up in the Q&A. An editor wanted to know what recourse there was when threatening messages popped up online. I started to explain how the law worked—that abstract threats were protected by the First Amendment, just the way our journalism was, and that the police couldn't do anything unless a threat communicated "imminent" harm—but I let it go quickly. Legal niceties about imminence and abstraction, which played so sensibly in law school classrooms, seemed disconnected and off target in that room.

Meanwhile, far beyond the walls of The Times's offices on Eighth Avenue, Trump's willingness to egg his supporters on at the expense of the press continued unabated. In his first major post-election rally, he jazzed up a crowd at U.S. Bank Arena in Cincinnati with another of his anti-press riffs. "The people back there are the extremely dishonest press. Very dishonest people. . . . I mean how dishonest." The boos and jeers showered down. Trump smiled. "I love this stuff. Should we go on with this a little bit longer?" he asked. The crowd roared.

Even before the Trump campaign rolled through America, threats were becoming part of the landscape in which our reporters worked. One day while packing for an office move, I came across a drawer where I had stored away hundreds of threatening cards and letters sent to reporters—held there in case someone acted upon one of the threats and the police needed evidence. They ranged across a spectrum, from the outraging to the bizarre to the absurd, most of them anonymous. In neat handwriting with perfect punctuation and capitalization: "I am coming to see you, Bitch. You are not going to enjoy the visit." Or the Hanukkah card emblazoned with glitter and "Shalom" across the front and inside: "You Stupid Bitch, I wish you and your loved ones nothing but pain and misery in this upcoming year." Another writer with a Melbourne, Florida, return address wanted to know, after denouncing *The Times*'s coverage, whether she should now expect an IRS audit. A postcard with two kitties in a Christmas scene on the front closed with the lines: "The NYT SUCKS. Except the crossword."

In the aftermath of the Trump victory, those of us inside The Times building, whether we were journalists or lawyers or the people running the business, were all trying to find our footing, to figure out how we were to proceed after a bruising campaign with a new political order about to descend. Not long after the election, The Times held a town hall meeting for employees. Someone asked the executive editor, Dean Baquet, how *The Times* intended to cover a president who had campaigned not just against the Democrats but the press as well, and *The Times* in particular. Dean laid it out: Whatever had happened in the campaign, news organizations ran a huge and untenable risk in making common cause with the political opposition. The reality, he said, was that the other party was someday going to be back in power, and at that point the press would just be a lapdog.

Something like that idea had been at the core of a memo to readers he and *Times* publisher Arthur Sulzberger Jr. had sent out the week after Trump's victory, in the midst of a public firestorm over *The Times*'s coverage of the campaign, with the paper being attacked from both the left (bitter about the hard coverage of Hillary over her email problem and feeling despondent) and the right (bitter about the hard coverage of Trump over, well, just about everything, but gloating). The memo said:

> After such an erratic and unpredictable election there are inevitable questions: Did Donald Trump's sheer unconventionality lead us and other news outlets to underestimate his support among American voters? What forces and strains in America drove this divisive election and outcome? Most important, how

will a president who remains a largely enigmatic figure actually govern when he takes office?

... We aim to rededicate ourselves to the fundamental mission of Times journalism. That is to report America and the world honestly, without fear or favor, striving always to understand and reflect all political perspectives and life experiences in the stories that we bring to you. It is also to hold power to account, impartially and unflinchingly. You can rely on The New York Times to bring the same fairness, the same level of scrutiny, the same independence to our coverage of the new president and his team.

Two days later, Trump would put his own spin on the note: "The @nytimes sent a letter to their subscribers apologizing for their BAD coverage of me. I wonder if it will change - doubt it?" Not exactly a great day for reading comprehension. To me, though, Arthur and Dean's statement had hit the right note. We weren't the opposing party. We shouldn't be pursuing an agenda of political resistance or political change. Our role was to go out and tell stories as fairly and fully as we possibly could. There were days when we didn't get there, but that wasn't the point. The point was that we knew what our role was and we would keep trying to get it right.

I thought that those of us who were lawyers for the press needed to follow in their footsteps. Play it straight and address real legal problems as they arose—not react viscerally to Trump and his election. We were so far removed from the fears that had shadowed the lawyers who came before us. That point was driven home for all of us early in the new administration when the story of the Pentagon Papers—well, at least one version of it—was told by Steven Spielberg in the movie *The Post*, the mere mention of which drives old-time Timesmen and Timeswomen into low-grade apoplexy. No need to revisit that brouhaha except to say this: it was *The New York Times* that first received the leaked government documents, a secret history of the Vietnam War showing that the government had lied to the American people, and it was The Times that bravely stood tall for the First Amendment in warding off the government's attempt to stop the publication. The Washington Post came late to all of it, arriving in the middle of the litigation after The Times had already risked everything.

Lawyers fare surprisingly badly in *The Post*, given that—not to put too fine a point on it—they won the case for the newspapers. The movie makes sport of the Post's own lawyers, particularly (and unfairly) Roger Clark. He is portrayed as an overpaid, humor-impaired fretter, ever ready to stand between the newspaper and the future of press freedom, lining up on the wrong side of history as he sweats the legal details, or sometimes just sweats.

That could have been me, I thought as I watched the movie. That could have been what being a newspaper lawyer was like, had the Supreme Court gone in some other direction in *Sullivan* and the Pentagon Papers case and all the others. I could have been that gloomy angel of overwrought caution, visiting the newsroom with dire warnings about the legal perils that were about to befall us, with angry threat letters from the lawyers for the rich and powerful clasped in my sweaty palms.

But beyond my bedrock belief in the resiliency of American press freedom there was one other thing driving my reluctance to sign up for the war. There was a fundamental question that had never really been answered: what exactly did Donald Trump believe about the First Amendment? It was a little bizarre. If you listened closely to Trump, he actually seemed to be in favor of the current law—even if he himself didn't know it. In February 2016, he had issued a First Amendment pronouncement: "I'm going to open up our libel laws so when they write purposely negative and horrible and false articles, we can sue them and win lots of money. We're going to open up those libel laws. So when *The New York Times* writes a hit piece, which is a total disgrace, or when *The Washington Post*, which is there for other reasons, writes a hit piece, we can sue them and win lots of money instead of having no chance of winning because they are totally protected."

Had a student in one of my law school classes written that as the answer to the question "What was the main holding of *Times v. Sullivan*?," I would have been flummoxed. The kid obviously knew the law—journalists are liable for defamation when they purposely write untrue statements about someone—aka act with reckless disregard of the truth. But the diction and syntax? Call it a B in this age of grade inflation. OK, maybe a B-minus.

Two days before Thanksgiving 2016, Trump would again back away from his "we need to change the law so I can sue you losers into the Stone Age" rant, this time in the most unlikely of places to find him: the home office of The New York Times Company. It had not been easy to get him there.

The Times wanted him to meet with editors and reporters, but had insisted that the session be on the record. His people finally agreed to that, although there would be a 15-minute private meeting with publisher Arthur Sulzberger Jr. beforehand. The morning of the scheduled sit-down, Arthur stopped me in the cafeteria. Trump wasn't coming, he said. As was Trump's wont, he had announced he would be a no-show via Twitter:

> I cancelled today's meeting with the failing @nytimes when the terms and conditions of the meeting were changed at the last moment. Not nice

A few minutes later, he posted an addendum:

> Perhaps a new meeting will be set up with the @nytimes. In the meantime they continue to cover me inaccurately and with a nasty tone!

It wasn't true. There had been no change in any "terms and conditions." Arthur had responded to Trump's tweet by contacting Hope Hicks, Trump's aide, and pointing out that the tweet was, to coin a phrase, a lie. A short time later, the meeting was back on. Trump met privately with Sulzberger in the Churchill Room on the 16th floor of The Times, and then Arthur escorted him across the hall to the boardroom, where *The Times* journalists waited. The boardroom is lined with decades of photographs of famous people who visited the paper. Arthur later told me that as they walked across the hall, he mentioned to Trump that the boardroom collection included a photograph of every American president since Teddy Roosevelt, and his would be there someday. Arthur urged Trump to take note of the Richard Nixon photograph. Nixon had written, "To the New York Times. Some people like it. Some people dislike it. But everyone reads it." Nixon was the last president to declare war on the press, Arthur said, and look how things turned out for him. The comment didn't seem to register.

After 75 minutes of questioning, Trump was finally queried about his commitment to the First Amendment. His answer was classic Trump: "Actually, somebody said to me on that, they said, 'You know, it's a great idea softening up those [libel] laws, but you may get sued a lot more.' I said, 'You know, you're right, I never thought about that.' I said, 'You know, I have to start thinking about that. So, I think you'll be OK.'"

He must have been feeling it. He closed the session by declaring, "The Times is a great, great American jewel. A world jewel." He then exited the building through the crowd of gawkers in the lobby. (He had been brought into the building via the basement—a mistake not to be repeated when he learned that a crowd had gathered around the main doors.)

So there it was. Trump said we were going to be OK.

Nobody I knew believed it.

Nobody thought we were going to be OK.

The clarion calls to action kept coming in.

I was invited to join a coalition of media lawyers meeting in New York. The invitation advised that we all had "to be ready to (wo)man the front lines and be prepared to protect the media's right and ability to cover the new Administration fully and fairly despite the likely steps President-Elect Trump will take to hinder such coverage."

Meanwhile, a friend from Boston wrote about a campaign he hoped to launch so people would be ready for the soon-to-be-unleashed assault on press freedom. He took to quoting Russian dissidents. His email built up to a long and good quote from Aleksandr Solzhenitsyn: "Woe to that nation whose literature is disturbed by the intervention of power. Because that is not just a violation against 'freedom of print,' it is the closing down of the heart of the nation, a slashing to pieces of its memory. The nation ceases to be mindful of itself, it is deprived of its spiritual unity, and despite a supposedly common language, compatriots suddenly cease to understand one another."

I told him I wasn't quite registering Solzhenitsyn-level pain just yet. I wondered whether we were getting ahead of ourselves. I held out the possibility that some balance would be restored, that the skirmishes between Trump and the press would ebb and flow but ultimately reach some sort of equilibrium, more Nixon than Obama, but within the range of acceptable. I continued to think that our highest and best use as people devoted to First Amendment values would be to try to remedy one tiny bit of the breach, to resurrect a left-right national coalition that would stand behind a free press—the old *I disapprove of what you say, but I will defend to the death your right to say it* thing. "I think we're making a mistake by painting our side as pro-freedom and the other side as anti-freedom," I wrote, going into full raving moderate mode. "The fact is that

Breitbart News is as committed to free speech as The New York Times. Maybe we should figure out how to tap into that."

I allowed in closing that there was some small possibility that I was being "dangerously naïve."

I passed on joining in his effort. I skipped the meeting of the media lawyers "(wo)manning the front lines." I wanted to wait and see.

I wasn't alone in thinking we should step back and take a deep breath. President Obama had gone to Peru in the weeks after the election and told a group of Latin American students, "I think it will be important for everybody around the world to not make immediate judgments, but give this new president-elect a chance." Dave Chappelle, the African American comedian, had closed out his monologue on *Saturday Night Live* hitting pretty much the same note: "I'm wishing Donald Trump luck. And I'm going to give him a chance, and we, the historically disenfranchised, demand that he give us one, too."

If "wait and see" was good enough for Barack and Dave, it was good enough for me.

A few weeks later, our wait was over. It was January 20, and here is what I saw: Sean Spicer on my television, looking like a junior college basketball coach at a postgame press conference trying to explain away his 21st loss in a row. Spicer let it fly: the crowd at the Trump inauguration was bigger than the one at the inauguration for Obama. "This was the largest audience ever to witness an inauguration. Period. Both in person and around the globe. These attempts to lessen the enthusiasm of the inaugural events are shameful and wrong." In the corner of the screen CNN was broadcasting pictures showing the crowd at Obama's inauguration and the crowd at Trump's inauguration. Nobody watching could have missed the obvious: the Trump inauguration crowd was much, much smaller. Not that it mattered to Spicer. His words were going one direction

and the truth was going the other, right there on national TV before millions of eyeballs.

It finally sank in. I finally saw where this was heading. Forget
1964. Forget *Times v. Sullivan*. The war over press freedom was not
going to be a fight about changing America's laws. It was going to
be a fight about the very nature of truth, about who could capture
the hearts and minds of the American people, about who got heard
and who got believed. It was going to be a daily referendum on
whether we as a country still believed that a free press counted for
something and, ultimately and inevitably, whether we were still
willing to stand up for press freedom. As for all those who threatened and harassed our newsroom, they were out there on the fringe,
but they were in their sickening way part of the very same fight: an
attempt to back the press into a lightless corner where it didn't really
matter what the First Amendment said.

I should have seen it coming. In a decade and a half at The Times,
I had had my moments with Trump and his lawyers. I knew how
they played the game.

3

Mystery Mail and
the Box in the Courthouse

Donald Trump: I was going to sue you. I was seriously going to sue you because of that one story. I have a good lawyer.

Tim O'Brien: The one in September?

DT: The one we were arguing about with your lawyer, who by the way, was very good. The guy . . .

TOB: David McCraw?

DT: Yes, he's a great lawyer. You know why? He's got a great way, a great bedside manner if he were a doctor.

—Donald Trump interview, Feb. 16, 2005

SEPTEMBER 23, 2016. It had been a bad day on La Jolla Cove. The waves broke hard and my kayak kept getting pushed back out toward the ocean. My son had long before made it back to shore by the time I managed to drag myself in through the swell. "Where have you been?" he asked, the 27-year-old libertarian, helpful as always. This was the short break I was taking in San Diego, a couple of days away from the unrelenting craziness of work and the over-heated presidential campaign. Election Day was still more than six weeks away. I was wet and tired and miserable. As we drove away from the beach, we stopped at a Starbucks so I could fish my iPhone out of the pile of dry clothes on the back seat of the rental car.

I clicked on an email from Sue Craig.

David,

Can you call me when you have a chance? I have what may be a partial copy of Trump's 1995 tax returns and Matt P wanted me to touch base with you on it.

Sue

Long ago I had learned not to be thrown off by the too-cool-for-school casualness with which reporters contacted their attorney. It is, in a way, a good thing, a testament to the freedom of the press in the United States, where so much is allowed that reporters often think of legal concerns as passing inconveniences, speed bumps on the road to reporting and photographing. No need to fret. When I was the newsroom lawyer at the New York Daily News in the days right after 9/11, a reporter called me to just sort of let me know that he and a photographer had been arrested trying to scale the security fence at one of New York City's reservoirs in Westchester County. They were trying to show how easy it would be for terrorists to poison the city's water supply—the old "if two out-of-shape journalists could do it, imagine what those buff jihadists could do" approach to reporting. He thought it might be helpful for me to talk to the local chief of police, who apparently failed to share the reporter's expansive views of the First Amendment and the importance of a free press in America. I have been called by reporters who managed to get to the home of a terrorism suspect before the authorities and wanted to know what I thought about going through the guy's garbage—"I mean, it's right there ready to be picked up by the sanitation department." Once, in 2016, in the middle of the immigration crisis in Europe, I received an alarming report that our photographer Tyler Hicks and two of our other journalists had been detained for entering a refugee camp in Greece without permission.

I called Tyler's cell phone. He answered. It was his fault, he said; he went somewhere he wasn't supposed to go—he is a photographer, after all—but everything was fine. The journalists were pretty sure they were about to be let go and given their equipment back. Besides which, I was interrupting. They were just sitting down to eat with the officers who were holding them. Tyler later texted his editor, David Furst: "Yeah man. They're giving back all our stuff. Just waiting for something from Athens. The guy who detained me wants to stay in touch. He was married to a woman from Connecticut and lived there for a while."

Somehow, Donald Trump's tax return seemed different, not the sort of thing you offhandedly mention in a two-sentence email. The game of hide-and-seek—will he or won't he release the returns?— had been front and center in the campaign for months. By late September, when Sue's email arrived, it had become apparent that no tax returns were going to be disclosed before the American people went to the polls in November. I called Sue.

She described how an envelope had shown up in her Times mailbox (with Trump Tower listed as the return address). Inside were what appeared to be some pages from Trump's 1995 state tax returns from New York, New Jersey, and Connecticut when he filed jointly with his then-wife Marla Maples. No note. No way to know who sent them. No way to know whether they were real. Sue and others were going to try to figure out discreetly whether they were authentic. I told her that we were legally free to possess them—a topic we would return to a few days later, and then again and again.

For all the uncertainties surrounding Sue's documents, I knew three things for sure when I hung up: The Times was not about to put the envelope aside. If there was any way for journalists to confirm that the documents were real, Sue and her colleagues were going to find it. I also knew that no one in the newsroom was going to barge ahead with a story that wasn't bulletproof. Both Sue and I realized the very real possibility that this was a setup—an elaborate ruse by someone to lure The Times into a mistake. With the Trump campaign syncopating every campaign appearance (at least it seemed that way) with anti-press riffs about dishonesty and bias and fake news, we would blow ourselves up if we got this wrong. A story this big, an error that large . . . it would turn us into everything that Trump falsely accused us of being: craven, inaccurate, untrustworthy, out to get him for getting him's sake.

And the third thing? I knew that, if we decided to go forward with a story, the Great Trump Lawyer Machine would kick into gear and come rumbling into my life once again. It is one of the subspecialties that one develops as a lawyer for The New York Times: the art of the deal(ing) with Donald Trump's lawyers.

I began my schooling in this obscure art in 2004 when The Times ran a piece by real estate writer Charles Bagli under the headline "Due Diligence on the Donald" about the "new hit reality show" The Apprentice. In its opening paragraphs, the story said:

> Over aerial views of Manhattan's glittering skyline, he intoned, "My name is Donald Trump and I'm the largest real estate developer in New York." The camera panned across Trump International Hotel and Tower at Columbus Circle, and he continued: "I own buildings all over the place, modeling agencies, the Miss Universe contest, jet liners, golf courses, casinos and private resorts like Mar-a-Lago."

So far so good. It was the second paragraph that cut home: "For those who follow the New York real estate market, the show provides something else: a hilarious look at Mr. Trump's blend of fact, image and sheer nerve." Charlie went on to slice and dice the real estate numbers and show that no matter how you counted, developers like Leonard Litwin, Stephen Ross, and the Elghanayan brothers were bigger in the residential real estate business, and the same story played out for commercial real estate development.

Trump's lawyers—from a small firm at 40 Wall Street, a building that happened to be owned by a certain real estate developer and reality TV star—raced to his defense, blasting the story as a "vindictive and personal attack," demanding a correction and threatening a lawsuit. Donald Trump was the largest real estate developer in New York. Period.

I am not the sort of lawyer who sees much purpose in arguing about the facts. The guy was either the largest real estate developer in New York or he wasn't. Maybe the lawyer could give me the list of properties and the numbers. We would look at them and decide whether a correction was warranted. The facts were the facts. In time, the list came in. I looked over the properties and suddenly felt compelled to point out to Trump's lawyer that—just to take one example—Palm Beach is not in New York. There ensued one of those "you have to be a lawyer to engage in this sort of thing; please shoot me now" discussions about whether the statement "the largest real estate developer in New York" means "the largest real estate developer who lives in New York" or "the largest real estate developer of properties in New York." Not that it mattered. Donald would not top either list. Corrections were demanded. Lawsuits were threatened. We did in fact publish a correction, just not the one that Trump and his lawyers wanted:

CORRECTION: February 8, 2004, Sunday. A picture caption on Jan. 25 with an article about "The Apprentice," the television series featuring Donald Trump, misidentified the location of the Trump Village residential complex where Mr. Trump was shown with his father, Fred C. Trump. It is in Brooklyn, not Queens.

It was sometimes hard for *The Times* to keep those outer boroughs straight.

So it went every time we dared to say something critical of Trump. (One of his lawyers once assured me that we were absolutely free to criticize Trump's hair. That was not a sensitive topic for his client, he advised.) Just a few months later, Trump's lawyers and I were at it again. *The Times Magazine* ran a piece, "Trumpologies," that stated flat out, "Like it or not, Donald Trump is now the No. 1 guy in the world's No. 1 city." What was not to love about a piece like that? Yes, there was the bit about Harvey Weinstein:

> One afternoon, as we were standing on the steps of the Trump International Hotel and Tower at Columbus Circle, he said, apropos of I don't know what: "Harvey Weinstein calls—he's a friend of mine; you know, he's the head of Miramax—and he says, 'Donald, you know you're the biggest star in Hollywood.' I say, 'What are you talking about?' He says, 'You're the No. 1 star; you're a superstar on the No. 1 show in television [No. 4, actually]. You saved NBC.' I never thought of it, because the rest of the time I'm negotiating with contractors. So I said: 'You know what? It's true.'"

But being a bud of Harvey Weinstein's would not seem problematic for at least another 13 years. And, yes, I had given the NYT Legal's seal of approval to the paragraph about the Trump hair, taking full advantage of the privilege that had been extended by Trump's lawyer: "Maybe his hair is as ridiculously concocted as some nouvelle-cuisine dessert, but what does he care? He's engaged to Melania Knauss, a Slovenian supermodel. (O.K., model.)" The rub for Trump's lawyers in the magazine story was the same as before: The piece dissected Trump's claims about how much he owned and found them at odds with the facts unless (as the writer suspected) "owns" means something different to Donald Trump than it does to the rest of the population. More meaningless lawyer back-and-forth ensued post-story with Trump's attorneys, as it routinely would over the next few years, usually before a story even ran. I developed a boilerplate letter to send—"Any article we publish will be done in accordance with our customary standards for fairness and accuracy." Nobody on Trump's side seemed to notice or care that I plagiarized myself when I wrote.

One run-in with the Great Trump Lawyer Machine from those days proved to be a harbinger. In 2005, Tim O'Brien published the book *TrumpNation*. Tim, then an editor at *The Times,* had spent hours with Trump, in his car, on his plane, taping interviews and researching the book. During one of those interviews, the conversation bizarrely turned to me and how Trump had almost sued The Times and Tim after Tim had done an earlier story questioning Trump's claims about his vast real estate holdings (some things never change). Trump admired the "bedside manner" I had deployed to pacify his lawyer and how I had stretched out the discussions endlessly (and pointlessly) for weeks by suggesting maybe somehow some way someday somewhere *The Times* could run a correction. My run-out-the-clock lawyer-to-lawyer kibitzing had gone on so long that Trump had forgotten what the story was about. Or in his words:

> So here's what happens. A week later, I'm thinking . . . I'm suing that motherfuckin' shit. Another week goes by and somebody says, "What are you saying? What do you want to do?" I said, "I don't know." What the fuck? I have a photographic memory. I have a great memory. I don't even remember what the fuck you said . . . in other words, and I'm the object of the story. So I say to myself, if I have this unbelievable memory and I had to think back to what he said . . . What the fuck?

TrumpNation, Tim's book, came out later in 2005, and there was no forgetting it in Trump's mind. The book, which *The Times* excerpted, is a rollicking account of Donald being The Donald, capturing the hyperbole, bluster, deceptions, and exaggeration of New York's No. 1 guy, right down to his taste in movies (Samuel L. Jackson should have won the Oscar for *Pulp Fiction*). As Tim described Trump, he was closer to Baby Huey, the overgrown and supercilious cartoon character, than former GE chairman and business mastermind Jack Welsh. "He's Baby Huey with a measure of P. T. Barnum tossed in," Tim once said. Actually, for all of its 280-plus pages and a cover that shows The Donald as a superhero striding through Manhattan, there was only one page in *Trump-Nation* that made Trump crazy, and it became the only passage he sued over. Tim suggested that, based on reports from confidential sources, Donald Trump was only worth $250 million, tops. He was not the billionaire he purported to be. Tim tracked how Trump's own estimate of his wealth ebbed and flowed almost day to day, $4 billion in one telling, a couple of billion in the next, and an eye-popping $9.5 billion in a glossy Mar-a-Lago brochure. One day Tim decided to ask Trump about the reports that he was not a for-real billionaire. Trump pooh-poohed the doubters as "guys who have 400-pound wives at home who are jealous of me."

When the book was published, Trump did what he rarely did: followed up on a threat of a libel suit and actually sued Tim and his book publisher. For reasons that were never clear, he did not sue The Times, even though that passage was dead center in the middle of our excerpt, which had run at the time of the book's launch. The litigation against Tim and his publisher jerked along for years before the New Jersey courts finally declared Trump the loser.

For The Times, Trump took a different tack. He fine-tuned the strategy that a decade later he would repeatedly use during the campaign. Why litigate when you can just lie? Cheaper, easier, and more likely to succeed if you are any good at it. Right after the excerpt ran, Trump took to his blog (writing as "Donald J. Trump, Chairman, Trump University").

The fact is The New York Times is going to hell. They published a major story about me on Sunday that they knew was wrong. On Sunday morning, right after the paper came out, my lawyer got a call from a lawyer at The New York Times asking if we wanted to correct the story. He didn't even wait until Monday, probably because he figured the lawsuits would be filed by then. The paper's editors knew the story was wrong, but they wanted to try and sell newspapers. . . . By the way, to the lawyer who called my lawyers on Sunday morning: Don't worry, we'll get back to you.

That would be me—the spineless lawyer who had that whimpering Sunday-morning phone call with his lawyer. There was some truth in what Trump had to say. I had called Marc Kasowitz, Trump's big-time lawyer. It was on a Sunday morning. I was in the Shreveport airport on my way home from a wedding. Marc was in his office preparing for a mega-trial he was handling for the government agency that had owned the World Trade Center. And, true, I was calling him about the Tim O'Brien story that Trump so hated. I had a good reason to call, just not the one that Trump made up. Kasowitz had called me the night before at 10:22. (Inexplicably, I was not in my office on a Saturday night.) I was returning his call. I heard Marc out and then I told him that if they wanted a correction, Donald's PR people should make their case to our editors. And if they wanted to sue, I couldn't stop them. I wished him well on his trial (I knew the lawyers he was working with). He thanked me. No correction followed. The Times was never sued. And, no, no one "got back" to me.

If I thought the Great Trump Lawyer Machine would shut down or at least dial it back once Trump went from businessman and TV star to Republican presidential candidate, I was sadly mistaken. The campaign had barely taken off when *Times* columnist Joe Nocera did the unthinkable: he quoted Tim O'Brien in a column accusing Trump of dealing in snake oil. The letter from Trump's in-house lawyer Alan Garten was like a defamation-law random word generator: "discredited," "false," "misleading," "blatant factual inaccuracies," "single unreliable source," "shoddy"—and that was just one paragraph. It concluded in Trump's signature style: "Mr. Trump has authorized our legal team to take all necessary and appropriate action against the New York Times, including, without limitation, commencing a multi-million dollar lawsuit." New day, same drill. I sent my standard response ("no correction is warranted"). We never heard anything more about Joe's column—without limitation.

In the weeks leading up to Sue's email about the tax returns, I had been trying to unlock some of the secrets of Trump's wealth and reports of his personal misconduct in a decidedly old-fashioned way: by suing. Buried in the bowels of the New York State court system were the sealed files of *Trump v. Trump* from the early 1990s, the divorce papers from his first marriage, to Ivana. Over the late spring and early summer of 2016, I had debated with our senior editors and reporters covering the campaign about whether it was worth going after the papers. New York law has set a high standard for keeping matrimonial papers sealed. We would have to show "special circumstances," a term that had usually meant that someone had a need for the papers in another judicial proceeding, say, a criminal case involving one of the divorcing spouses. It had never been applied to the desire by journalists to find out what was in a file, no matter how they might dress that up as the public interest. On the other hand, had there ever been a case like this—sealed court records about someone running for president of the United States? And had there ever been a candidate like Donald Trump? Dean Baquet, *The Times*'s executive editor, understood that bringing the motion would feed into a Trump narrative—The New York Times shamelessly intruding on privacy—but kept saying it just "wouldn't feel right to know that at some courthouse there was a box of documents about Trump and we didn't try to get them." Others were more reluctant to line up as direct adversaries in a court proceeding against Trump in the midst of a campaign in which many of his supporters already saw *The Times* as a tool of Hillary Clinton, especially if the chances of winning were so anemic. I suggested we might be able to manage the optics if we brought in another news organization to join our motion, so it wasn't just The New York Times versus Trump. Great idea, everyone agreed. Fox, somebody suggested? Brilliant, but—just guessing here—maybe a long shot. In the end, I convinced Gannett, the publisher of *USA Today*, to sign on with us.

The legal heartburn was not just that New York law was so unfavorable. It was also that our argument was going to be a little sordid. The facts were not pretty. I knew, of course, that I could put some high-tone public-interest gloss on my papers, add a few paragraphs about transparency and the public's right to know. I wrote our motion in the way lawyers often do: as if they have just arrived from Mars and assumed that everyone around them is pretty new to the planet, too. One of my opening paragraphs actually read as if I thought the judge might well have spent the past few years locked in the root cellar of his house and not heard tales of this Donald Trump fellow before:

> The defendant in this action, Donald J. Trump, is now the 2016 Republican nominee for the Office of President of the United States, and the sealed records address issues directly relevant to the presidential election. From the very first Republican presidential primary debate over a year ago, Mr. Trump's political adversaries have raised questions about his credibility, his treatment of women, his finances, and his famously litigious nature. The records now under seal in this proceeding may well shed important light on how Mr. Trump exhibited these currently debated aspects of his character and capabilities during an important period in his life. Unsealing them would assist the American public in making an informed judgment in the presidential race.

From that high-minded peak of public interest, the papers rolled out our argument—the voters' need for information, the special circumstances presented when one of the litigants was running for the nation's highest office, the long passage of time, the limited privacy interest of celebrities and public figures—until, with nowhere else to go, I finally had to get to the unpleasantness: "Disclosure here may also help to resolve an ongoing campaign controversy over the allegation purportedly made in this divorce action that Mr. Trump sexually assaulted Ms. Trump." A Trump biographer 25 years ago had reported that Ivana made the allegation in a deposition in the matrimonial action. Prior to the book's publication, Ivana largely confirmed that was so, but later gave an interview saying that the rape allegation was "obviously false."

The whole incident had raised its ugly head during the campaign, most notably in the reporting of the Daily Beast. Trump's lawyer, Michael Cohen, confirmed that Ivana had made the accusation at her deposition, but denied that any such rape had occurred: "By the very definition, you can't rape your spouse." The quotation sent lawyers scrambling to find out when New York had changed its criminal laws and made spousal rape a crime (1984). The Trump campaign responded to the story by unfurling a statement from Ivana saying the story "is totally without merit." Nothing is a bigger giveaway that lawyers are involved in writing a celebrity's public statement than the precious lawyerly phrase "without merit."

I had no qualms about seeking the documents. The guy was running for president. The documents should be public. Maybe they vindicated him; maybe they didn't. But people had a right to see them before they went to their neighborhood polling stations and colored in the bubbles for the candidates of their choice. But writing those paragraphs was one more reminder of how very, very different a campaign this had become. My young associate Tali Leinwand, a brand-new lawyer, turned herself into our in-house expert on all things related to the first Trump marriage. A copy of

Ivana Trump's *For Love Alone* became a permanent fixture on the corner of her desk. So much for Jefferson and Madison or the U.S. Constitution and *Times v. Sullivan*.

The judge was not moved by our arguments. On September 22, the day before Sue Craig's email about the tax returns, the order came down. "Were the court to make the confidential records available for journalistic, and thus public, scrutiny, it would impermissibly inject itself into the process by making the value judgment of what information is useful in determining the present candidate's, or any other candidate's, fitness for office." It didn't make a lot of sense. By keeping the records sealed, the judge was in fact making the very decision he claimed not to be: deciding that this information should not be available to the public to determine a candidate's fitness for office. That box of documents that Dean Baquet saw in his mind's eye sitting in the corner of a courthouse basement somewhere is still sitting there.

4

Tax Day

The New York Times risked legal trouble to publish Donald Trump's tax return

—*Washington Post* headline, Oct. 3, 2016

Donald Trump Would Have Trouble Winning a Suit Over the Times's Tax Article

—*New York Times* headline, Oct. 4, 2016

FIVE DAYS AFTER Sue Craig's email, I sat in a conference room on the third floor of the newsroom with four reporters. The table was piled high with files and folders of public documents about Trump's finances gathered over months. Sue was there, along with David Barstow, Russ Buettner, and Megan Twohey, all of whom had been working on stories about the labyrinths that were Trump's businesses. Someone handed me the three pages that had come in the mystery mailing: one page each from the 1995 returns that Trump and his then-wife Marla had filed in New Jersey, New York, and Connecticut.

For months, the questions about whether Trump would release his returns, and the possibility that someone might leak them, had been one of the minor chords of campaign coverage. For those who were aficionados of Trump Tax Return Theater, the show had actually started way back in 2011 when, during the height of his birtherism fever, he tied the release of his returns to the release of Barack Obama's birth certificate. "Maybe I'm going to do the tax returns when Obama does his birth certificate," he said on ABC during an interview with George Stephanopoulos. A year later, he offered some free advice to Mitt Romney: releasing tax returns is a "positive" because it shows "you've made a lot of money." Then in 2014, he assured a TV interviewer that if he ran for office, he would definitely release the returns: "If I decide to run for office, I'll produce my tax returns, absolutely. And I would love to do that." Then as Candidate Trump in January 2016, he let the world know that he and his campaign were working on getting the paperwork together for disclosure but that people needed to understand there were some difficulties because—as if people needed to be told—his tax return "is not, like, a normal tax return." But by the time February rolled around, his stock answer had changed: the problem was now the audit. The IRS, he said, was in the middle of an audit, and as soon as that was over, the tax returns would be shown to the American people. Before long, after all the equivocating, there was little doubt that Trump was going to become the first major-party candidate since 1972 to decline to release his returns. As the months dragged on, editorial writers, including those at *The Times*, called out Trump for failing to disclose them. His political opponents banged away at the issue. Interviewers repeatedly asked him about it. But nothing was being shown to the public—not until Sue Craig checked her office mailbox.

Two weeks earlier, Dean Baquet had been at Harvard making his own headlines about Trump's tax returns. He was doing a presentation with Bob Woodward of *The Washington Post* and Laura Poitras, the independent journalist behind the Edward Snowden disclosures. The panel was covered by CNN Money, which headlined its piece the next day with "N.Y. Times editor: 'I'd risk jail to publish Donald Trump's taxes.'" Poitras had ominously informed

Woodward and Baquet that their lawyers would probably warn them that they would face jail time if they published leaked tax returns. She pressed the point with them: "If the Post or the Times were to get Donald Trump's tax returns, would you publish them?" As CNN reported it, "Both said yes, that they'd argue with the attorneys to do so."

I lost it as I read the CNN story that morning. Did Dean really think I would tell him that he might have to go to jail if he published Donald Trump's tax return? We had been through much harder stories than that—the secret WikiLeaks cables, the Snowden disclosures, the hard and powerful reporting done by Jim Risen and Eric Lichtblau on government surveillance in the Bush era. I had never said no. No Times lawyer had. No Times lawyer was going to walk away from the legacy of the Pentagon Papers. I shot off an intemperate email (abandoning my Trump-endorsed bedside manner): "This was embarrassing to me (and, yes, I am hearing from people already this morning). Do you really think I'd advise you not publish something like this? Has that ever happened on any story, including Risen/Lichtblau, WikiLeaks, Snowden, or anything else?"

Dean came back with an email telling me to watch the video. He hadn't said it, or at least not like that. It had been a confusing interchange among Bob, Laura, and Dean, working from Laura's mistaken assumption that publishing the returns would be a crime. It was all hypothetical anyway. Nobody had the tax returns.

The image of the naysaying newspaper lawyer standing in the way of the crusading journalist is baked into newsroom culture and a favorite of the movies. There are exceptions, of course. In *Spotlight*, the Academy Award–winning story of the Boston Globe's breakthrough reporting on pedophile priests, the paper's outside counsel, Jon Albano, is shown going to court and winning critical documents for Robby Robinson's reporting team. But the more common thematic note was the one struck in *The Insider*, the 1999 movie about how CBS had pulled its punches after *60 Minutes* reporters proved that tobacco companies were hiding what they knew about the real risks of smoking. The film stars Al Pacino as CBS producer Lowell Bergman, who tracks down the story of Big Tobacco's duplicity after cultivating tobacco scientist Jeffrey Wigand as a source. In a pivotal scene in the movie, the *60 Minutes* team is told by the CBS lawyers that they can't go ahead with the broadcast they had planned. Legal threats from the tobacco industry had made it impossible. CBS's reporting gets passed to other journalists, the story gets published, and Bergman walks away from CBS.

It was one of those movies that stays with you if you are a lawyer for a news organization. It also represented the sum total of my knowledge of Lowell Bergman on the day he walked into my office at The Times in 2002. He was now working with David Barstow on an investigation into the dangerous working conditions at foundries owned by McWane, Inc., a mammoth industrial concern that produced pipes. I had been on the job for maybe two weeks. Lowell started asking me legal questions about filming in Alabama, where they could go with hidden cameras, when they had to turn off the sound recorder (because of eavesdropping laws), what legal protections we had for any footage they got. I wasn't really sure what the law of Alabama had to say about any of those things. I just knew that I didn't want to end up in any movie portrayed, CBS-style, as some corporate legal puke telling Lowell Bergman he couldn't do something. He had ended up with Al Pacino playing him. God knows what fifth-tier actor would end up playing the sweaty-palmed New York Times lawyer in the sequel.

Not that it was much of a stretch to say yes. As a legal department, we had long embraced the ethos that we were there to help get things in the paper, not keep them out. We were blessed with a management team that stood behind us and behind our journalists, that understood risk was the price of doing high-end journalism, and that knew that if our journalists weren't pushing boundaries with stories, we as a paper weren't doing our jobs. Four months into my tenure at the paper, William Safire sent a draft of his column to Legal. It began:

> Let me see if I can write today's column without getting sued. It has to do with my old pal Lee Kuan Yew, who prefers to be called "senior minister" rather than dictator of Singapore, and whose family members have been doing exceedingly well lately.
>
> In kowtowing to the Lee family, the Bloomberg News Service—the feisty, aggressive newcomer to coverage of global finance on cable and computers—has just demeaned itself and undermined the cause of a free online press.

The column came to my colleague George Freeman, who had been in Times Legal for two decades and had seen just about everything there was to see in newsroom legal risk. Just not something like this. Singapore had notorious libel laws. Its leaders thought nothing of using the laws to go after American publishers (as well as the beaten-down local press). George did what he had never done before: he called our publisher, Arthur Sulzberger Jr. He wanted Arthur to know that Safire was about to take us legally somewhere we had never gone before. Arthur came down to the legal department in The Times's old headquarters on 43rd Street. He stood in the hallway between my office and George's and read Safire's column. "Publish and be damned," he said at last. He turned to walk away and then stopped, saying, "I've never understood what that meant, but I always wanted to say it." The column went out. Singapore didn't respond.

I couldn't quite grasp why anyone was struggling with the idea of publishing a story about Trump's tax returns. Sure, there were lines that journalists should never cross—somebody buying the files from a corrupt IRS official, someone breaking into an IRS office and absconding with them in the night, someone aiding and abetting a theft—but nothing like that was ever going to happen at The Times. Maybe the nervousness was just an offshoot of the Trump Factor. His repeated threats of lawsuits, his imposition of a blacklist of reporters banned during the campaign, his unceasing denunciation of The Times and other news organizations—maybe it all came together to create a sense of foreboding that things were different with Trump, that the normal rules didn't apply. Still, our reporters had continued to look for a source for the returns. One day in the summer of 2016, Sue Craig had shown up in my office and said she had a long-shot possibility as a source—an unlikely candidate to help us, but you never know. Like some demented host on a journalism game show during the lightning round, she asked me to name every type of person I could think of who may have seen Trump's tax files. I went for it: his accountants, his lawyers, the finance team at the Trump Organization, the lawyers at the company, everyone's secretaries, ex-spouses, his children maybe, their spouses maybe, the guys from IT (they know everything if they want to), the dude running the copy machine, Harold from the mailroom, the office cleaning staff, I give up. Sue got up to leave. "I just wanted to see whether my source would be identifiable if I got the returns," she said. I couldn't tell if I had won the lightning round or not.

Back in the conference room on the third floor, I studied the documents. They looked authentic, but the reporters needed more than that. We talked about whether there were documents somewhere that could confirm the numbers listed on the returns. Russ Buettner showed me files he had obtained through public records requests from the New Jersey Casino Control Commission from the time period in question. The key passages that could have helped us authenticate the document had been redacted. One number stood out on the tax forms: $915,729,293, the amount of the loss that Trump was declaring. The reporters had noticed how funky it looked: the first two digits did not line up with the other seven. It was suspicious, the kind of thing someone would do to entrap us, add a few hundred million to the most important number on the forms. On the other hand, had someone really gone through the trouble of creating pages from a 1995 tax return, down to the addresses and Social Security numbers? And why would a dirty trickster bother to do three states when the trap could be set with just one of them? David Barstow wanted to know if there were other places I could think of where the numbers might be hiding in plain sight but buried in some public record. Everything I came up with—regulatory filings, court cases—had already been pursued by the reporters. No luck.

The next time I heard from the reporters was four days later, on a Saturday afternoon, when David sent me, without comment, a draft of the story they had put together. He had managed to crack the mystery of the $915,729,293. Since our Tuesday meeting, he had made his way to Florida, looking for the retired accountant who had done the tax preparation: Jack Mitnick. It took some coaxing, the reporters later recounted in a piece for *The Times* Insider column, but David finally got Mitnick to meet him in a bagel shop. Mitnick confirmed that the pages were real. And what about those suspicious miscast digits? The result of the software he was using at the time. It couldn't accommodate a number that was so . . . well, as Trump would say . . . huge, so an IBM Selectric typewriter was forced into service. Meanwhile, as David corralled the accountant, the reporters began talking to tax experts and did a deep dive into the 1995 tax code.

As the story draft was coming to me, David was contacting the Trump campaign:

Dear Mr. Trump,

We are writing to seek your comment for a story we are preparing to publish as soon as possible. We've obtained portions of one of your tax returns and those portions reveal

that you declared a nine-figure net operating loss that, according
to the tax experts we've retained, could have legally allowed
you to avoid paying federal income taxes for up to 18 years.

We ask that you or your team get in touch with us immediately.

Sincerely,
David Barstow

The initial response came from Hope Hicks of the Trump communication staff:

David,

Please provide us what you are referring to so we can
adequately respond. Additionally, we request that you do not
publish until we have had the opportunity to review what you
submit and we provide a response.

Best,
Hope

David responded: "Are you guys able to meet with me in NYC
right now?" Hope said that was not possible. She asked him to email
whatever he had. He did:

Hope,

We've obtained portions of Mr. Trump's 1995 tax returns. The
documents show that Mr. Trump declared a loss of $915,729,293
for that year. The documents also show, among other things,
that Mr. Trump filed jointly with Marla, claimed one dependent
child, reported $7,386,825 in taxable interest income, $3,427,092
in business income and $6,108 in wages, salaries and tips. But
the main focus of the story is on the NOL of $915 million and
how, according to the tax experts we've consulted, that could
allow him to avoid paying federal income taxes for up to
18 years.

We can give you the rest of the afternoon to decide how you
want to respond.

Please let me know,
David

That was all that Trump's legal team, led by Marc Kasowitz,
needed to gear up. One of Kasowitz's partners dashed off a one-page
letter to The Times.

"As you are no doubt aware, an individual taxpayer's income tax
returns are confidential and statutorily protected from public disclosure by state and federal law." He then pointed out with lawyerly
obviousness: "Mr. Trump has not authorized the disclosure of any
federal or state income tax returns to the New York Times." The release was "unauthorized, improper and illegal," and legal action
would be taken "if necessary."

Dean jumped in on his own (worried perhaps that The Times's
legal department would get as weak-kneed as Laura Poitras predicted it might at Harvard the month before), making the case
for the public interest in the information. Kasowitz replied: "I
demand that The New York Times promptly return to me any of
Mr. Trump's tax returns or copies thereof in its possession, and
refrain from any disclosure of those returns or any information
from them." We ignored him.

Meanwhile, Hope Hicks was back on her email, giving Barstow
what can only be described as one of the classic Trumpian responses:

David,

Please see the campaign's statement below. It is our strong
preference you use this in its entirety.

The only news here is that the more than 20-year-old alleged tax
document was illegally obtained, a further demonstration that
the New York Times, like establishment media in general, is an

extension of the Clinton Campaign, the Democratic Party and their global special interests.

What is happening now with the FBI and DOJ on Hillary Clinton's emails and illegal server, including her many lies and her lies to Congress are worse than what took place in the administration of Richard Nixon—and far more illegal.

Mr. Trump is a highly-skilled businessman who has a fiduciary responsibility to his business, his family and his employees to pay no more tax than legally required. That being said, Mr. Trump has paid hundreds of millions of dollars in property taxes, sales and excise taxes, real estate taxes, city taxes, state taxes, employee taxes and federal taxes, along with very substantial charitable contributions.

Mr. Trump knows the tax code far better than anyone who has ever run for President and he is the only one that knows how to fix it.

The incredible skills Mr. Trump has shown in building his business are the skills we need to rebuild this country. Hillary Clinton is a corrupt public official who violated federal law, Donald Trump is an extraordinarily successful private businessman who followed the law and created tens of thousands of jobs for Americans.

Best,
Hope

I was confident that we were right on the law, but I did worry about the way some judges get confused about the First Amendment. I was concerned that a soft-headed judge could be dredged up by the Trump lawyers and issue an injunction. We would ultimately win on that, but why get caught up in a legal drama? I recommended to Dean and his deputy Matt Purdy that we publish as soon as possible. The story appeared online that night under the byline of the four reporters:

Donald J. Trump declared a $916 million loss on his 1995 income tax returns, a tax deduction so substantial it could have allowed him to legally avoid paying any federal income taxes for up to 18 years, records obtained by The New York Times show.

That night, Barstow wrote to me saying he was outraged by the legal position being taken by Trump and his lawyers. I told him he should ignore the noise. "They labor under the mistaken belief that the Bill of Rights starts with the Second Amendment."

The Trump spinners descended on the Sunday talk shows the next morning. They were surprisingly silent on the legal issue of disclosing the tax returns. They also decided to give their incantation of "fake news" a rest. Good thing, since the only fake news to be found that morning was what they were saying. Rudy Giuliani, the Sunday-morning apologist in chief for the Trump campaign, praised Trump for being so smart about taxes and then recast himself as a journalism critic: "The New York Times writes this long story, and then somewhere around paragraph 18, they point out there was no wrongdoing." It wasn't exactly paragraph 18. It was more like . . . paragraph 1. That would be the paragraph that first mentions that what Trump was doing in 1995 he was doing "legally."

On Saturday night, as the story was about to be blasted onto the internet, I had shared with my boss, Times general counsel Ken Richieri, the correspondence from Trump's lawyers. "Just so you are in the loop. I am not worried about this one. The story is close to ready."

I was at the Yankees game the next afternoon. They were playing dismally against the Orioles. Baltimore catcher Matt Wieters had hit a home run in the second and then another in the sixth. My phone rang. It was Sue Craig. She wanted to know whether I had seen The Washington Post story. I explained to her about how the Yankees were sucking and Wieters and the two home runs, all of which meant I had no idea what *The Washington Post* was saying.

"The New York Times risked legal trouble to publish Donald Trump's tax return," read the headline. "Dean Baquet was not bluffing," the story began, and all of a sudden we were back at the Poitras-Woodward-Baquet gabfest at Harvard with the brave promises to take one for the team and go to jail to publish the returns. After citing various scary statutes that make it a crime to reveal tax returns (if you happen to work for the government), the article begrudgingly acknowledged that most experts thought that the First Amendment would provide a defense to The Times, but the point was buried, and the headline got punched up on Twitter and shared. Even *The Times*'s own reporters were pushing it out. (Another writer at *The Post* attempted something of a course correction later that day, posting an article headlined "Donald Trump, victimized by the First Amendment he abhors.")

Back at the office Monday I was repeatedly asked about whether we had broken the law. I understood that it was all a little counterintuitive for people who didn't spend their days immersed in the powerful—some would say "disturbing"—ways the First Amendment worked when government tried to criminalize true speech. But after decades of laying down the law in this area, the Supreme Court had left little in doubt. Forty-one years earlier, almost to the day, *The Virginian-Pilot* newspaper had published a story identifying a Virginia judge who was under investigation. A grand jury indicted *The Pilot*'s parent company, Landmark Communications, for violating Va. Code § 2.1-37.13, which made it a crime to divulge the identity of a judge facing disciplinary proceedings by a state ethics commission. Joseph W. Dunn Jr., the paper's managing editor, took the stand at trial. He testified that he considered the information of significant public interest and decided to publish it. He knew that Virginia law made it a crime for someone involved with the disciplinary proceeding to disclose the name, but he didn't understand that to apply to a newspaper reporter covering the story. The court saw it differently and found the newspaper guilty of a misdemeanor and set a fine of $500 plus the costs of the proceeding.

When the case finally arrived at the Supreme Court in 1978, the court was still in the midst of its decades-long push to give serious heft to the First Amendment. It acknowledged that Virginia had good reasons to keep judicial disciplinary procedures confidential as a way to assure fair adjudication of complaints and protect the reputation of judges who might not have done the terrible things they happened to be accused of. But, in the end, *The Pilot* was talking about a constitutional right to publish something true and in the public interest. It was the business of state officials to keep secrets, and those people directly involved in the proceeding could be punished for talking, but none of that extended to the press, which was in the business of publishing secrets. In the sort of deadly judicial language that always manages to make pedestrian what should be cloaked in grandeur, the court said, "We conclude that the publication Virginia seeks to punish under its statute lies near the core of the First Amendment, and the Commonwealth's interests advanced by the imposition of criminal sanctions are insufficient to justify the actual and potential encroachments on freedom of speech and of the press which follow therefrom."

If Sue's mystery mailer happened to be a government employee who pinched the forms and headed for the copy machine, that person was likely in trouble. No First Amendment right protected the source. For us, it was just the opposite. Whatever those scary statutes quoted in the foggy-brained article in *The Washington Post* might say, we were on the right side of the law. The decision in *Landmark Communications v. Virginia* would cut off at the knees any misguided attempt by prosecutors or Trump's own lawyers to punish The Times.

Over the next 20 years, the Supreme Court kept coming back and driving home again *Landmark*'s core principle: governments were free to pass laws making it a crime to reveal certain kinds of information—the names of juvenile offenders, the identities of rape victims, the wiretapped contents of a phone call—but none of those laws could get over the high wall that was the First Amendment and be used to penalize journalists when the information was in the public interest and the journalists had done nothing wrong to get it. That was true even if the reporters' sources had themselves engaged in lawbreaking to get the information. An anonymous delivery not unlike the one that graced Sue's mailbox had played a leading role the last time the Supreme Court took on the issue. In a 2000 case called *Bartnicki v. Vopper*, some civic-minded good citizen discovered that his cell phone was picking up private phone calls between the head of a teachers union in Pennsylvania and the union's top negotiator. Like all good negotiators, the two brainstormed about the right strategy that would be needed to persuade the school board to stop being so cheap with the teachers, one bit of which was dramatically captured on tape and then forever enshrined in the Supreme Court record: "We're gonna have to go to their, their homes. . . . To blow off their front porches, we'll have to do some work on some of those guys. (PAUSES). Really, uh, really and truthfully because this is, you know, this is bad news. (UNDECIPHERABLE)." Always nice to see the people charged with educating our children showing their creative problem-solving skills.

The good citizen—that would be the person committing a crime by illegally recording the calls, which may explain why he never chose to out himself—decided the right course of action was to drop the recording off anonymously in the mailbox of a man called Jack Yocum. Yocum sat as the titular head of a taxpayers group that was not so fond of the teachers union. He found the tapes too good to keep to himself. He handed them over to a radio station, which broadcast them, undoubtedly putting the local citizenry on high alert for porch bombings. The negotiator and the union head sued the radio host, but nothing had changed in the First Amendment since *Landmark*. Whoever recorded their porch-bombing conversations had broken the law, and the union reps were free to go after that person (good luck finding him), but that had zero to do with the radio station's First Amendment right to air the recordings. Absent some compelling government interest that has never been found in any of the Supreme Court cases, publishers and broadcasters remain free to publish even pilfered information.

It's easy to understand why that body of law could confuse people. The laws imposing confidentiality on our private phone calls and rape victims' names and juvenile court proceedings strike most people as right-minded, the kinds of laws that we should have. If the press is free to ignore those laws, even when their sources have broken them, it seems to defeat the whole purpose of trying to keep the information confidential in the first place. Shouldn't the press have to obey the law like everyone else (even if the distinction between who is the press and who is everyone else has faded)? The hard nut is realizing that the alternative—permitting governments to pass laws that would force the press to hide valuable and true information from its readers—would be worse. The First Amendment, as we have come to understand it over these last 60 years, is designed to prevent just that. Whether reporters are barred from reporting a story prior to publication or have to face penalties and lawsuits afterward, the impact is the same. The government is being given the power to decide what should be published. That is not how America is supposed to work, no matter how many letters Trump's lawyers write to The New York Times. The system is far from perfect. The government has enormous powers to root out and punish public employees who leak secrets, even when the leaked information is of indelible value to the public. (Edward Snowden is still sitting in Russia, avoiding prosecution, while all of us over here now know just how out of control the intelligence agencies had been, sucking up data about our private phone calls and emails.) And we are doomed to debate for a long time whether all those

Supreme Court rulings apply only to people who look like the journalists in *All the President's Men*, *Spotlight*, and *The Post* or whether the 19-year-old slacker sitting in his mom's basement in his underwear manning his Twitter account and eating Twinkies can partake of the First Amendment's protection when he receives leaked information, just the same as The New York Times. Talk all we want about those legal puzzles, there was absolutely no doubt in my mind that our Trump tax story was sound.

Some of our readers failed to share my certainty. There were those—this was to be expected—who had a hard time focusing in the midst of the campaign's furies. One wrote in the story's comments section: "The American Mass Media has gone totally berserk! They are lying. They are manufacturing stories. They are hiding bad things about Hillary and good things about Trump. This is incredibly dangerous for our freedom - when the entire national media has completely ejected Journalistic Integrity, Objectivity, and their duty to just report the facts. Are we being prepared for a coup?" But others cut to the chase: "Has any commentary addressed the fact that the New York Times just violated the law? Intentionally, wantonly viciously . . ." Others found common cause with that reader: "Please explain how the Times [and any other media outlet reporting same] is different from Gawker or their ilk? Private information—and admittedly illegally gained—being published and disseminated. Public filings certainly are such: public but private records are private are they not? Public interest you say? Well perhaps it would be in the public interest if some of the Media's personal info such as family, residence, or compensation were published; e.g. to better understand their respective bias's or perspective. Utterly ridiculous and a testament to the subjective application of laws."

On Monday evening, 48 hours after the story landed, Barstow caught me in the lobby of The Times. My emails to him and his editors may have assured them of the rightness of our decision, but out there in the larger world a lot of people hadn't gotten the memo. *The Post* story was still ricocheting around the internet, and other media outlets were giving fresh air to the faux debate over the legality of publishing the information.

Inexplicably, and rarely to be repeated, Fox News got the law right. Its on-air legal analyst declared that "[The Times] can't be sued and they can't be prosecuted. I understand the Trump campaign's frustrations, but the law is not on their side." It would have been too much to ask that Fox lead with that thought. No one gets rich at Fox by airing stories headlined "Times Well Within the Law by Publishing Trump Tax Returns." Fox chose instead to go with "'Someone Broke the Law' Sending Trump Tax Return to NY Times." It had no proof of that, naturally—the mystery mailer, depending on who he or she was, may have been under no duty to keep the returns secret—but we were not going to call over to Fox hoping to get a correction. Life is too short.

Barstow pressed me to write something for the paper setting people straight on the law. I was reluctant. I may have been sure about our legal position, but something about being the public voice on the issue struck me as askew. While it would have been foolish for Trump to sue, "being foolish" didn't necessarily rule out the possibility that Trump might sue. I was the lawyer throughout all of this, and I didn't relish having some piece I wrote being held up in litigation as a waiver of the attorney-client privilege or distorted by a Trump lawyer and attached as Exhibit A to a legal complaint. I also wondered whether people would believe it coming from the guy who was defending his own legal position. To me, I told Barstow, it sounded like a job for Adam Liptak, our Supreme Court reporter. Liptak was ideally positioned. Before he became a *Times* journalist, he had been a Times lawyer. When he departed Times Legal to start his career in the newsroom, it was his job that I filled. He knew these issues backward and forward. More important to me, I was completely certain he would agree with the legal position I had staked out.

When Adam called me the next day, he was not particularly thrilled to have been pulled into the story. Writing about well-settled law and Supreme Court decisions from 15 years ago is not exactly a reporter's dream assignment. His story popped up online later that day under the headline "Donald Trump Would Have Trouble Winning a Suit Over The Times's Tax Article." He stopped short of saying it was a complete no-brainer ("the First Amendment poses a very high barrier to any such litigation"), but he cited a First Amendment legal blog that had surveyed 11 experts, all of whom lined up, more or less, with my take. In the middle of the piece, Adam turned to Gabriel Schoenfeld, who had once called for the prosecution of The Times for publishing information about a secret surveillance program during the second Bush administration. "I strongly hope that Donald Trump sues The New York Times for publishing his tax returns," Schoenfeld said. "Any such lawsuit—which in all likelihood would be shot down by the courts on First Amendment grounds—is likely to help further unravel the candidacy of a man who is, among other disqualifying flaws, an enemy of a free press."

When Fox News and The New York Times agree on something, there is little left to be said that would be of interest to anyone. The Trump lawyers were never heard from again, and the discussion went back to where it should have been from the beginning: on the astonishing and strangely typed number $915,729,293 and whether the man who wanted to be the next president of the United States had managed to legally avoid paying taxes for two decades. Sue Craig continued to invite readers to send her any Trump tax returns they happened to have lying around. Someone got in touch with her in early October and said he knew how to get the returns, proposing they work together. It sounded like a setup. She passed. He disappeared. Meantime, in November, the departing commissioner of the IRS said the agency was planning to move President Trump's tax returns to a new safe from their previous locked filing cabinet.

The legal controversy was not completely over, as it turned out. In December, former Trump campaign manager Corey Lewandowski showed up at Harvard for a retrospective forum on the campaign. He recalled how Dean Baquet had told a Harvard audience just months earlier that even though it might be a crime to publish Trump's returns, he was willing to do it. Lewandowski now jumped into the fray offering his considered legal opinion: Baquet "should be in jail" for publishing the returns. The guy was obviously not watching enough Fox News.

5

Day of the Gaggle

I love the First Amendment; nobody loves it better than me. Nobody.
I mean, who uses it more than I do?

—Donald Trump, in speech to conservative activists,
Feb. 24, 2017

"phony and non-existent 'sources'" "Failing" "Wrong!" "Failing" "Bad
Reporting" "Another false story" "wrong so often" "the pipe organ
for the Democrat Party" "Failing" "has totally gone against the
Social Media Guidelines that they installed" "a virtual lobbyist"
"many of their biased reporters went Rogue!" "naive (or dumb)" "hates
the fact that I have developed a great relationship with World leaders
like Xi Jinping" "weak and ineffective!" "Failing" "failing" "Failing"
"Failing" "Fake News" "Collusion?" "anti-Trump" "Failing" "massive
unfunded liability" "non-existent sources" "failing" "Fake News" "totally inept!" "made every wrong prediction about me including my big
election win" "failing" "big losses" "Failing" "every story/opinion,
even if should be positive, is bad!" "Failing" "Failing" "sick agenda"
"don't even call to verify the facts of a story" "A Fake News Joke!"
"failing" "writes false story after false story about me" "failing"
"Fake News" "Fake News" "just got caught in a big lie" "has been calling me wrong for two years" "Failing" "failing" "has disgraced the
media world" "failing" "Gotten me wrong for two solid years" "their
coverage was so wrong" "Now worse!" "failing" "would do much better if they were honest!" "failing" "failing" "failing reputation" "has
become a joke" "Sad!" "failing" "the enemy of the American People!"
"failing" "FAKE NEWS" "Failing" "failing" "failing, does major
FAKE NEWS" "Now they are worse!" "was forced to apologize to
its subscribers for the poor reporting it did on my election win" "failing" "making up stories & sources!" "writes total fiction concerning
me" "failing" "have gotten it wrong for two years" "is still lost!"

"FAKE NEWS" "bad and inaccurate coverage of me" "DISHONEST" "got me wrong right from the beginning and still have not changed course, and never will" "dwindling subscribers and readers" "so false and angry" "FAKE NEWS!" "wrong about me from the very beginning" "failing"

—Words used by Donald Trump to describe The New York Times, according to a *Times* news article (first year of his presidency only)

BY THE TIME February 24 rolled around, it was pretty clear that Inauguration Day had not just been one bad and regrettable go-home-and-sleep-it-off moment in the life of Sean Spicer—some random screw-up caused by first-day jitters, an impossible boss, and the emotional drain of an inauguration. For a month, the battle inside the White House press room had raged on with no sign of an armistice. The president's bad-mouthing of the press spewed forth unchecked on Twitter. Any hopes had disappeared that Trump was going to become a different man once the word "president" was attached to the front of his name or that being in the White House and feeling history's hand would somehow magically transform Trump's staff into the keepers of democracy's best traditions. The administration's push-and-shove with the press was not about politics or reporters with bad manners, as much as the president and his supporters wanted to frame it that way. Reporters got in Sean Spicer's face. Reporters asked rude questions. Got it. There were some charm-school dropouts in the White House press corps. (There were also a few stunningly unqualified lapdogs who had no business being there.) But it's hard to be a check on power if you're not, at times and in some fashion, confrontational. And it's hard to have a democracy if there are no checks. The day-to-day interactions between the press and the new administration had begun to feel like a low-burn war, a war about truth and the independence of the press and, in the darker moments, the future of democracy. Little of it seemed to have much to do with the law or with lawyers, which was, in and of itself, telling of how much democracy was built not on rules and laws but on shared beliefs and values and the well-tested customs and habits of freedom. And then came February 24, when all the ugliness, when everything that had gone off course, was thoroughly and glaringly on display for the whole world to see. By day's end, Sean Spicer would be barring reporters from a press briefing, and journalists would start calling their lawyers for real.

My day had begun like too many days over the past decade, with an unhappy note about troubles abroad. It was five in the morning when I got a message from our local lawyer in Turkey.

> Dear David,
>
> I hope you are well. I would like to update you about the recent developments in Turkey. Safak Timur informed me last week and said that she was not allowed access to a reception at the presidential office despite the invitation on security reasons but without no further explanations . . .
>
> Kind regards,

Safak was one of the local journalists in Turkey who worked for The Times. I worried about her and the other locals. They labored under real hardships to try to tell the story of what was going on there. Turkey had been a more or less constant issue for The Times for nearly two years. Threats from the Erdogan government. Hateful media attacks on The Times and its reporters. The barring of a veteran *Times* reporter from even entering the country. Now our Turkish reporter was being locked out of a presidential press event. It was infuriating, outrageous, wrong. But it was Turkey. No surprises there. Turkey, once a model of an emergent democracy, was in an endless downward spiral, with a government intent on controlling the press through intimidation, arrest, denunciation, and every other tool in the autocrat's toolbox.

For a decade and a half, I had worked with reporters who found themselves in jams in hard places around the world as they tried to report freely on countries that rarely even feigned an interest in the truth or transparency. Threats, detentions, attempts at censorship—the world worked that way these days. But I did worry that something had changed abroad. Whether there was a Republican or Democratic administration in office, I had always known that we could count on the State Department to stand with us, sometimes openly, sometimes quietly, in protecting journalists. More than that, diplomats in the past had thought it was part of their mission to encourage a free press in the countries where they served. Now? Who could blame Erdogan if he thought a good way to curry favor with the American government in 2017 was to attack The New York Times? From everything I could see, he was probably right in his calculation.

But nothing was going to help us this day. Reporters being barred from a presidential event? Just another day in Turkey.

There was a second early morning email, this one from one of our journalists based overseas, who was sending me details about an upcoming trip: his flights, his cell phone numbers, his plan for staying in touch. It was a precaution. He was a Canadian with an Indian name and dark skin. He was about to take what was once a routine trip but was now fraught and unpredictable: he was coming to New York. He was going to let me know when (if?) he got through customs at JFK.

Meanwhile, at the White House, the president was up and tweeting:

> The FBI is totally unable to stop the national security "leakers"
> that have permeated our government for a long time. They can't

even find the leakers within the FBI itself. Classified information is being given to media that could have a devastating effect on U.S. FIND NOW.

It could not have come at a worse time. We were in the midst of doing a sensitive national security story, the kind of story we had done dozens of times before, and our reporters were talking to White House officials. It was standard operating procedure with a story like that to give senior government officials a chance to comment on what we intended to publish, and as much as officials hated the idea that we were about to publish classified information, they understood the value of engaging. Only now the rules seemed unclear, or maybe there were no rules. With all of that going on in the background, Trump's tweet was jarring.

The president was due to speak later that morning at the annual meeting of the Conservative Political Action Conference. The chances that he was going to forgo another anti-press rant were about zero. He had capped off the week before with the notorious and chilling tweet labeling news organizations "the enemy of the American people."

Nothing about that tweet afforded even a dash of hope that it was the product of a bad moment, a misfire in the presidential synapses. He had just arrived at Mar-a-Lago on a Friday afternoon. At 4:32 p.m., he posted the first version of the tweet:

> The FAKE NEWS media (failing @nytimes, @cnn, @nbcnews, and many more) is not my enemy, it is the enemy of the American people. SICK!

Moments later the tweet disappeared, only to be replaced in 16 minutes with a more permanent version, adding ABC and CBS:

The FAKE NEWS media (failing @nytimes, @NBCNews, @ABC, @CBS, @CNN) is not my enemy, it is the enemy of the American People!

Put aside for a moment that he was talking about the press. Accept that any president is entitled to express his displeasure with anyone, citizen or otherwise. That was not the point. The point was this: when had it become acceptable for a president to denounce an entire group of American citizens—any group, pick one—as traitors? I had resisted, in my raging moderate style, all those overheated comparisons to Nazi Germany that too many of my liberal friends offered up much too easily. Now I was no longer sure.

Most everyone I knew in the press tried to make light of it, dismiss it as just more Trump noise, loved by his base and dismissed or ignored by everyone else. The next morning I was emailing with a government lawyer who noted I had been at my computer at 5:30 on a Saturday morning and wanted to know why. "The enemy of the people never sleeps," I tapped out. The response came immediately: "Jesus. I am laughing at the absurdity of this." At some level, though, the smear stung. It was a hateful justification just waiting there for those in the alt-right who were already programmed to abuse reporters. It demonized and divided, the classic bully stratagem to create us versus them.

As the president was making his way to CPAC, I worked with Phil Corbett, our standards editor, to try to figure out how to fashion an editor's note for a story that the paper could no longer vouch for. The last thing we needed was a full-blown retraction of a story. It didn't really matter what the story was about. It fed into the presidential narrative that reporters made things up and could not and should not be trusted. The article had been done by a freelancer and was far removed from the paper's political coverage, but what did it matter? It was the wrong time to have to fall on a sword.

The piece was from December and was about fentanyl overdoses on Long Island. Questions had been raised about its accuracy by another newspaper. Mostly the story checked out, but editors at *The Times* had been unable to locate or confirm the existence of two people who were named and quoted. The writer continued to insist that the sources were real, but, as a long editor's note would soon explain, the editors "concluded that The Times cannot vouch for the accuracy of those sources, and that material has been removed from the online version of the article." It was the right thing to do. Our readers needed to know. None of that made the episode any less painful.

As if on cue, just as I was reviewing the note, the president went onstage at CPAC and was not a minute into his speech before it started again:

Sit down, everybody. Come on. (Applause.) You know, the dishonest media, they'll say he didn't get a standing ovation. You know why? No, you know why? Because everybody stood and nobody sat, so they will say he never got a standing ovation, right? (Applause.) They are the worst.

And I want you all to know that we are fighting the fake news. It's fake—phony, fake. (Applause.) A few days ago, I called the fake news "the enemy of the people"—and they are. They are the enemy of the people. Because they have no sources, they just make them up when there are none. I saw one story recently where they said nine people have confirmed. There are no nine people. I don't believe there was one or two people. Nine people. And I said, give me a break. Because I know the people. I know who they talked to. There were no nine people. But they say, nine people, and somebody reads it and they think, oh, nine people. They have nine sources. They make up sources.

They are very dishonest people. In fact, in covering my comments, the dishonest media did not explain that I called the fake news the enemy of the people—the fake news. They dropped off the word "fake." And all of the sudden, the story became, the media is the enemy. They take the word "fake" out, and now I'm saying, oh, no, this is no good. But that's the way they are. So I'm not against the media. I'm not against the press. I don't mind bad stories if I deserve them. And I tell you, I love good stories, but we won't—(laughter)—I don't get too many of them.

On and on it went. The president meandered to his declaration that he was a lover of the First Amendment ("Who uses it more than I do?") and some faint praise for a couple of reporters from Reuters who had just interviewed him. There was, as far as I could tell, no after-speech Q&A in which a razor-sharp CPAC member might ask how the president knew who the sources were even though the sources didn't exist and had been made up? Trump had doubled down on the "enemy of the American people" bit. I didn't need to follow the coverage in real time.

Emily Bazelon was doing a long magazine piece on how the Trump White House was angling to use the Department of Justice, or DOJ, to carry out its political agenda. Her editor, Ilena Silverman, asked me to look at a final proof of the story as it headed toward publication. It was titled "The Department of Justification," and it carefully laid out the case for the ways in which politics could reshape the DOJ. It was a stark reminder of the damage that can be done in a democracy when the institutions designed to be a brake on executive power are attacked, undermined, and compromised. On a day that had begun with the president doing a Twitter-scream at the DOJ about leakers—"FIND NOW"—it was a lesson worth remembering.

Only I was about to learn another lesson: the meaning of the term "gaggle." Word had started trickling up from D.C. in the afternoon that something had gone terribly wrong during a press briefing at the White House. Not much was very clear except (1) we knew that a *Times* correspondent and others had been barred by Sean Spicer from attending a press event and (2) it was outrageous.

A minor scrum had broken out when the White House press staff let the approved journalists move from the White House briefing room to Spicer's office for the briefing while the others were turned away at the door by a press aide. Soon the Secret Service was pulled into action to herd the unwelcome reporters out of the way.

The first details to reach me were hazy, and there were conflicting accounts of who got in and who got excluded and why. But whatever the answers to those questions were, I knew right away there was going to be another, harder question coming my way, one that would demand an answer in short order: was The New York Times prepared as an institution to sue the president of the United States over what Spicer had done? And once you started turning that question over in your mind, it was impossible not to entertain a second: what the hell would we do if we lost?

In the next day's paper, *The Times* would put the whole event into blunt context: "Hours after the [CPAC] speech, as if to demonstrate Mr. Trump's determination to punish reporters whose coverage he dislikes, Sean Spicer, the White House press secretary, barred journalists from The New York Times and several other news organizations from attending his daily briefing, a highly unusual breach of relations between the White House and its press corps."

That was not how the White House saw it, not surprisingly. The details get tedious, but here is what you need to know: There are gaggles and there are standard press briefings. The standard briefings were the ones in which Spicer fielded questions from the press, his head always looking as if it were on the verge of exploding as the questioning grew more contentious. America knew about those. Spicer's daily performance had become a staple of TV viewing for hundreds of thousands of Americans and, for those with better things to do in the afternoon, the briefings had become a rich comic vein for *Saturday Night Live*, with Melissa McCarthy cast as a gum-chewing "Spicey" outfitted with a motorized lectern on wheels.

Those were the standard briefings. Then there were gaggles, more informal and smaller gatherings of reporters, often with no cameras present. "Pool reporters," who are designated by the White House Correspondents Association, would cover the event and then share notes with those who had not been present.

In the aftermath of the showdown with reporters at the White House, Spicer and his team embraced a "Gaggle Defense." There had been no lockout of reporters, the White House announced. There was a gaggle, just a gaggle. The pool reporters represented the entire press corps, just like always. It was business as usual. "Claims that outlets were excluded are not factual," Stephanie Grisham, a White House press aide, told one reporter, sounding strangely restrained and diplomatic for someone whose boss would never reach for the tongue-twisting "not factual" when "fake news" would do the job just fine. She also sounded seriously untruthful (or, as she would put it, "not factual"). The reporters herded into the hallway and then moved along by the Secret Service were excluded, factually and in every other way.

The short story is this: The White House decided to do something of a super-gaggle. It would still include the designated pool reporters, but the Spicer team had invited a few of its favorite apple-polishing news outlets to come along. Only no one seemed to know who exactly was going to get an invitation to be part of the event. The Times asked about being included. The request was met with silence. At one point, the session was going to take place in the briefing room—suggesting that everyone with press credentials was welcome—but was then shifted to the cozier confines of Spicer's office.

By the time the appointed gaggle hour rolled around, a crowd of White House reporters, not sure whether they were invited and suspecting—rightfully—that something not good was brewing, had gathered in the briefing room. The White House press office began culling the crowd. The invitees—the designated pool reporters and a group of White House faves—were ushered toward Spic-er's office; the excluded were physically prohibited from attending. Those left behind began demanding to know what criteria were be-ing used to separate the favored from the unfavored. The press staff stonewalled them, suggesting they submit their questions by email. Some of the barred reporters understandably lingered nearby hop-ing that somebody would finally explain how it was the White House could decide to reward certain reporters with access to a news event while punishing others by prohibiting their attendance. The press office had the Secret Service move them along.

Largely because of the traditional pool arrangement, the gaggle had included some of the Twitter-slapped "fake news" outlets most scorned by the president. NBC was in. So were CBS and ABC. But the special invitees tilted heavily toward the president's go-to news sources: Breitbart, Fox, *The Washington Times*, and One America News Network. Pointedly not on the approved list were news organ-izations that had consistently done tough reporting on the new Trump administration: Buzzfeed, *The Guardian*, CNN, BBC, the New York *Daily News*, Politico—and *The New York Times*. Even some of those reporters who made the cut were incensed by the White House's crude attempt to divide and conquer. *The Wall Street Journal* and the McClatchy news organization had their reporters in the gaggle but announced they would not play Spicer's game again in the future. The reporters for *Time* and the Associated Press, who were among those to be let in, turned and walked away when they learned what was happening.

Confronted with the facts about the ugly turn of events, Spicer quickly lapsed into Inauguration Day Crowd Count Mode. "I think we've gone above and beyond when it comes to accessibility and openness," he said. Not that Spicer and the White House were hid-ing their motivation for excluding *The Times* and others: they didn't like what they read. "We're not just going to sit back and let false narratives, false stories, inaccurate facts get out there," he said in defending the briefing room blockade. Although the administration was barely a month old, people had quickly learned that terms like "false narratives, false stories, inaccurate facts" were just code words. Loosely translated back into real people's English, they meant, "We don't like the facts that you are reporting." Earlier that month the president had tweeted, "Any negative polls are fake news, just like the CNN, ABC, NBC polls in the election." As for the lovable bunch of conservative outlets allowed to join and turn a regular gaggle into a super-gaggle, that, Spicer said, was just his prerogative.

But was it? Did the law really allow the White House to favor some news organizations and punish others with exclusion?

Back in New York, as the story broke across the internet, it was raining lawyers. One of the things that makes being a lawyer for The New York Times either easier or harder than working elsewhere is that when there is a day like February 24, media lawyers all across America drop whatever they happen to be doing for their paying clients and start sending in free legal advice. It's a mixed blessing. Many just want to help. Some are hoping to land work as outside counsel. A few are showing off. Others fail miserably in trying to hide the fact that what they are really saying is that you don't know how to do your job. They do.

Before the afternoon was finished, I had received emails from lawyers in various cities citing cases they thought would be helpful and theories they thought might power a First Amendment case against the president. Some of the nation's top firms said they were ready to jump in. Others, like me, were just trying to figure out what had happened. "Declaration of war or shot across the bow?" read the subject line on the first email to come through. A friend from Iowa sent a case from 1971 in which the police chief of Davenport, Iowa, refused to provide any information to an alternative newspaper called *Challenge* while letting reporters from the mainstream papers and TV stations have access to the records. *Challenge* had only $10 in its bank account at the time, but its leadership knew something about the Constitution. The paper went to federal court and won a ruling that the city was violating *Challenge*'s constitutional rights. "An old one but a good one. Go get them," my friend wrote. He knew that I had once worked as a journalist in Davenport and would be a sucker for a strong decision filled with Iowa common sense.

Others admitted to having no particular expertise, but they thought the whole exercise in the White House press office stank all the same. "Of the many troubling things Donald Trump's White House has done since his coronation, I find this the most troubling," wrote a New York lawyer. "It would seem to me that choosing who will report the news is how dictators get their start. While I am neither a constitutional nor media lawyer, I am hopeful that the Times will take swift legal action to help declare this type of conduct unconstitutional."

Every lawyer in my position wants his or her Pentagon Papers moment. Jim Goodale, The Times's general counsel in 1971, had been convinced that the First Amendment allowed The Times to publish the classified documents that had been leaked to the newspaper, even after The Times's longtime outside counsel refused to take the case and told him that the paper was committing a crime. History had proved Jimmy right. To bring a case now challenging the president's exclusion of journalists—to draw a line on what a president could do to suppress voices he did not like—would have been an extraordinary legal undertaking, a bright, shining moment for press freedom.

If we won.

If we lost . . . it was hard to imagine a bigger misstep at that particular moment. Not only would we have lined up as a legal adversary to the White House, playing right into the Trump narrative, we would also be responsible for the courts' giving their legal blessing to Spicer's bad behavior, opening the door to even more abuse. Two of the most senior lawyers I knew in the media bar worried that one of the excluded media outlets from outside the mainstream would go rushing into court in anger, stumble on the law, and make everything worse for everybody.

My colleague Ian MacDougall and I were scrambling to figure out what the law actually said about excluding reporters from press events. As always, the text of the First Amendment itself offered no clue. "Congress shall make no law respecting an establishment of religion, or prohibiting the free exercise thereof; or abridging the freedom of speech, or of the press; or the right of the people peaceably to assemble, and to petition the Government for a redress of grievances." Decades of court decisions had breathed life into those words—and also turned the law into a minefield of complexities. One of those complexities stared us squarely in the eyes: elected officials don't lose their First Amendment rights, at least not all of them, when they step into office. They remain Americans free to speak, to criticize, and, yes, to tweet and to choose not to speak when the spirit moves them, just like the rest of us. They are not required to give access to everyone who claims to be a journalist— that would be just about everyone with a Facebook account or a Twitter feed—no matter how much the wannabe journalist wants to ask the president or Sean Spicer a few questions. No law says every citizen, or even every journalist, is entitled to a White House press pass.

Court decisions had broadly protected the right to speak and to publish under the First Amendment. But the legal landscape changes dramatically, and the going gets substantially harder for the press, when the question is whether there is an affirmative right to obtain information or a right to capture the news in a particular way. Television has been around for decades, the Supreme Court has been reshaping the contours of American life year after year, and no one has seen a broadcast of a single argument. It is not because CNN, NBC, and all the others don't want to be there with their cameras. As for the particular legal dilemma that faced us that afternoon—the exclusion of reporters from press events—the decisions from prior cases were a crazy quilt with no particular pattern.

Ten years earlier, Robert Ehrlich, the governor of Maryland, had engaged in a particularly egregious act of political hackdom: ordering all state employees to stop talking to two reporters for *The Sun* of Baltimore. His edict left little room for doubt:

> Effective immediately, no one in the Executive Department or Agencies is to speak with [*The Sun* reporter] David Nitkin or [*The Sun* columnist] Michael Olesker until further notice. Do not return calls or comply with any requests. The Governor's Press Office feels that currently both are failing to objectively report on any issue dealing with the Ehrlich-Steele Administration. Please relay this information to your respective department heads.

When Nitkin tried to get information from state officials, he was told that "the ban is still in effect" or "I can't talk to you." He was barred from one press briefing and not invited to a second. The Sun sued. The case finally made its way to the Fourth Circuit Court of Appeals, which acknowledged that a government violates the law when it responds to a reporter's "constitutionally protected activity with conduct or speech that would chill or adversely affect his protected activity." But it was all downhill for The Sun after that. The court looked at how reporting got done on the ground and how journalists and government officials interacted in real life. "Government officials frequently and without liability evaluate reporters and reward them with advantages of access. Government officials regularly subject all reporters to some form of differential treatment based on whether they approve of the reporters' expression," the court wrote.

That, the court said, was not punishment or retaliation but just the way of the world when it came to covering government. The judges fretted that if they ruled in favor of The Sun, every interaction between government employees and reporters angling to beat their competitors would become a matter of constitutional rights. The Sun's case was not helped by the fact that neither writer claimed that the governor's directive had chilled their speech or that *The Sun* was able through other reporters to carry out the work of covering the statehouse. As for Ehrlich's written directive, the court embraced the First Amendment—the First Amendment rights of Governor Ehrlich, that is. His "pique, criticism, and explanation" for the ban was just the governor doing what the First Amendment allowed him to do. In other words, a case that was meant to vindicate the First Amendment rights of reporters blew up in the media's face like a box of Acme dynamite in a Road Runner cartoon. The Sun had made First Amendment law with a decision that affirmed the First Amendment rights of thug politicians to punish reporters they don't like much. Not exactly the outcome I would be looking for in *The New York Times Company v. Donald J. Trump*.

Lawyers at other media organizations were not ready to be deterred by the Sun decision. I knew that Buzzfeed and other of the newer media companies were particularly jazzed about finding some way to take on Spicer's ban in court. No wonder. Trump had singled out Buzzfeed for a special heap of abuse after it published the famous "dossier" compiled by the British spy Christopher Steele outlining links between the Trump campaign and the Russian government. Buzzfeed's reporter had been among those banned from the gaggle.

If you could get beyond the Baltimore case, there were other decisions that gave some hope. Those cases had been decided by judges who read the First Amendment very differently than the judges who decided The Sun's appeal. In Louisiana in the 1980s, a federal judge had torpedoed the rationale that Spicer would embrace 30 years later: that a public official was free to bar reporters whom he found to be inaccurate. The Louisiana case involved Harry Lee, the longtime sheriff of Jefferson Parish who had earlier gained some well-deserved national attention by ordering his deputies to randomly stop black men in white neighborhoods. The order was later rescinded, but Lee said he never figured out why the media had criticized him for what he thought of as just "good police practice."

By 1987, the focus of his attention was *The Times-Picayune*, the New Orleans daily. Unhappy with the coverage his department was getting in the paper, Lee shut out *Times-Picayune* reporters, banning them from press conferences, forcing them to make written requests for information, and generally doing what he could to impede their work. He was not a person known for his subtlety. When a *Times-Picayune* reporter sought the sheriff's comment for a story, Lee told an underling to tell the reporter, "Sheriff says screw press. Has no comment under any circumstances." The underling duly noted in his log that he had "called [the reporter] back and relayed the non-message."

When the paper sued in federal court, Lee explained that he felt he was entitled to ban the reporters because they had factual errors in their work. The court wasn't buying it. Before a reporter could be banned, the judge said, the sheriff would need to demonstrate that the ban served "a compelling governmental issue." Promoting accuracy or objectivity did not meet that test—especially "when the governmental official enforcing the discrimination is himself the subject of the news reporting which he purportedly wishes to purify of inaccuracy." And just in case the sheriff wasn't fully grasping the point, the judge added: "This is the essence of censorship forbidden by the First Amendment and so abhorred by the founding fathers."

At least one other federal case, out of Hawaii, had come to the same conclusion, but the lawyers who were eager to battle Trump in court kept pointing to a decision that was nearly 40 years old, *Sherrill v. Knight*. Bob Sherrill was a veteran Washington correspondent who was denied a White House press pass even though he had press credentials to cover the House and Senate. It turned out that the Secret Service had recommended that Sherrill not be allowed into the White House press room because of an unfortunate incident—these things used to happen in journalism—in which he had assaulted the press secretary to the governor of Florida. Sherrill filed a lawsuit over his exclusion from the White House, and an appeals court in D.C. found that Sherrill could not be denied the pass unless he was given due process. That meant the White House needed to have a written policy setting forth the reasons a pass could be denied, and a reporter in Sherrill's shoes had to have a chance to challenge the denial, presumably a chance that didn't involve fisticuffs.

At first blush, the ruling seemed to be the legal hook we were looking for. It was about the access granted to those carrying press passes. Everyone in the press room that day, whether going to the gaggle or being barred from it, had press credentials, but the practical effect of Spicer's invitation system was that some press passes carried more privileges than others, or, to line it up with the decision in Sherrill's case, some pass-holders were arbitrarily denied privileges given to some of their colleagues. That all sounded good unless you happened to keep reading the decision in *Sherrill*. As the court went on, you could almost hear the air going out of our potential argument: "Nor is the discretion of the President to grant interviews or briefings with selected journalists challenged. It would certainly be unreasonable to suggest that because the President allows interviews with some bona fide journalists, he must give this opportunity to all."

Other complications could not be ignored. Some of the facts behind Spicer's stunt would undercut our arguments. Pool reporters were allowed in. By long tradition they were required to work as the reporters for all the news organizations that were not present. And no one with a press pass was being banned from the regular press briefings that Spicer continued to have. We also knew that any suit against the Trump administration would be met with one of Trump's favorite battering rams: what about Obama? In fact,

Obama had declined to let Fox News anchor Chris Wallace partici-
pate in a round of Sunday talk show interviews that Obama did in
2009. "We simply decided to stop abiding by the fiction, which is
aided and abetted by the mainstream press, that Fox is a traditional
news organization," Dan Pfeiffer, the deputy White House communications director, said at the time. The Obama White House tried
a similar tack when the networks were invited to interview Ken
Feinberg, who was overseeing executive pay for those companies
bailed out by the federal government during the 2009 financial
crisis. When other news organizations found out that Fox was to
be excluded, they threatened a boycott. The Obama team relented.

Yet one fact was not in dispute from the Day of the Gaggle: the
White House and Spicer had acted terribly. Maybe it was not illegal,
but between Trump's tweeting and Spicer's office blockade, they
were tearing at the fabric of democracy. We shouldn't be emulat-
ing Turkey. The First Amendment was written into the Constitution not to assure the rights of the lapdog press to flatter the people
in power but to protect the voices of those who were intent on challenging the sitting government, fairly or unfairly, accurately or in-
accurately, politely or stridently. Even presidents with hateful
relationships with the press seemed to get that, until now. The law
was an imperfect vehicle for forcing a president to respect the norms
and values that democracy depended upon. The First Amendment
can be stretched just so far. At some point, democracy assumes
that people in power will honor democratic norms and values
without being forced to do so by laws and lawsuits. Sometimes democracy assumes wrong.

The day after the gaggle, a lawyer for some of the other news
organizations wanted to know whether The Times would be willing to sign on for some sort of joint legal effort. I balked. "I thought
the NYT response [from executive editor Dean Baquet] yesterday—
undertaken with no input from Legal—was right: a strong statement about policy and norms from our executive editor," I wrote.

"I may be wrong but I think the media won that round. The Trump administration embarrassed itself and this is likely to go down as a ham-handed one-off (as happened when Obama tried to exclude Fox from the TV interview in 2009). If it continues, then there will be something for lawyers to do."

Baquet had struck just the right note on February 24, a day otherwise devoted largely to everything that was going wrong for people who cared about a free and independent press. "Nothing like this has ever happened at the White House in our long history of covering multiple administrations of different parties," he said in a statement. "We strongly protest the exclusion of The New York Times and the other news organizations. Free media access to a transparent government is obviously of crucial national interest."

Floyd Abrams, the lawyer who has made the single greatest contribution to press freedom in our lifetimes, also laid out the case neatly: "Unhappiness with and criticism of the press by American presidents has been the norm, not the exception," Floyd told *The Times*. "But daily denigration of the press as the enemy of the American people and statements that the use of confidential sources by journalists 'shouldn't be allowed' is both novel and dangerous."

Nobody filed a lawsuit. The gaggle blockade proved to be a one-off. The correspondents went back to their daily pitched battle with Spicer, trying to claw out a few truths from a White House whose instincts ran in a different direction. *Saturday Night Live* continued to have great material to work with.

In the midst of the uproar over Spicer and Trump on February 24, another email had come in, barely noticed in the hurly-burly of the craziness in D.C. The ACLU was offering to train reporters from various news organizations about what they should do if they are stopped at U.S. customs as they come back into the country and government agents want to seize or inspect their laptops and cell phones. Was The Times interested?

How could we not be?

6

Us vs. Us

> Wow. The @nytimes is losing thousands of subscribers because of their very poor and highly inaccurate coverage of the "Trump phenomena."
>
> —Donald Trump, Nov. 13, 2016
> (*The Times* circulation was in fact increasing at four times its usual rate)

> I'd be a pretty good reporter...
>
> —Donald Trump, Feb. 16, 2017

IN FEBRUARY 2017, barely a month after Inauguration Day, Stanley Dearman died. *The New York Times* ran an obituary but, outside of Mississippi and in a few places that care deeply about journalism, his name was unlikely to have triggered much of a memory. Stanley Dearman had spent 34 years of his life as the editor of *The Neshoba Democrat*, a tiny newspaper in Philadelphia, Mississippi.

In 1964, three civil rights workers, Andrew Goodman, James Chaney, and Michael Schwerner, two white, one black, were found murdered near Philadelphia. They had been arrested on June 21 by the local police, released, and then disappeared. Their burned-out car was located a short time later, and then in August the three bodies were uncovered, buried in an earthen dam. Dearman's predecessor as editor of *The Neshoba Democrat* had referred to the three as "agitators" and "so-called civil rights workers." Federal authorities convicted seven men of conspiracy charges in the deaths—none of them served more than six years—but years passed, and no one was ever prosecuted for murder.

As the years drifted into decades, many readers of *The Democrat* were happy to let that dark chapter pass into obscurity. Not Stanley Dearman. "I can say without exaggeration that in 40 years, not a single day has gone by that I don't think about those boys," he told *The New York Times* in a 2004 interview. "It's just something you can't wash off. People may not want to talk about it, but it will never go away. The thing won't let us forget."

Dearman had used his editorial page to keep prodding Mississippi officials to do something to bring the killers to justice. In his searing 2000 editorial "It's Time for an Accounting," he wrote:

> There are those in this community who will say that it's been too long. The trouble with that position is that they were saying it after five years, after 10 years, after 15 years. If it involved a member of their family or a friend, they would never say it's been too long. And if they claim that right for themselves, how can they in good conscience deny it to anyone else?

Dearman went on:

> None of this would be an issue if a group of self-appointed saviors of the status quo had not taken it upon themselves to murder three unarmed young men who were arrested on a trumped up traffic charge and held in jail like caged animals until night fell and they could be intercepted by the Ku Klux Klan, a group whose bravery increases in direct proportion to their numbers and how long the sun has set.

His paper kept the case alive, and four decades after the crime, prosecutors finally brought a murder case against Edgar Ray Killen, a 79-year-old sawmill operator. He was convicted.

Jerry Mitchell of the *Clarion-Ledger* in Jackson, Mississippi, one of the country's best investigative journalists, understood what Dearman had been up against. "He called on his community to prosecute the very killers who shared the sidewalks he did in downtown Philadelphia. People in town told him to leave it alone. They told him to forget it, but the truth is, Stanley Dearman never forgot," Mitchell wrote in a tribute after Dearman had died.

Stanley Dearman was worth thinking about in February 2017. His story was not just about standing up to people in power but about standing up to his readers. It takes a particular kind of courage for newspapers to take on the powerful, to keep hewing to the truth despite the threats and the beratings and the daily frustration of trying to get over the huge walls of secrecy that every government manages to build around the information that the American people need to know most. But standing up to readers can be even harder at times. (I often make a similar point to editors when some newsmaker calls and points out an error. The easy part is dealing with the angry caller; the hard part is confronting a dug-in reporter.)

The newspaper industry over the past two decades has been devastated by fundamental changes in how companies advertise and where readers go to find news. Between 2000 (when I first went in-house at a newspaper) and 2015, print newspaper advertising revenue fell from $67 billion to less than $20 billion, shedding all the gains of the previous 50 years, according to the American Enterprise Institute. Over a decade, more than 100,000 jobs in magazines and newspapers had disappeared, *The Atlantic* reported.

In 2011, The Times had defied the experts who said that a paywall that required readers to pay for content would never work. "Information wants to be free," would-be visionaries would write back then, meaning . . . well, who knows what they meant? All we knew was that the paywall had worked financially. At the start of the century, 26 percent of The Times's revenue came from circulation. Fifteen years later, circulation was accounting for 60 percent of revenue, and the percentage was growing as Google and Facebook ate up the advertising market. And while everyone from Silicon Valley entrepreneurs to college professors to guys on the street would be happy to tell you that print was dead, the truth was it had remained alive at *The New York Times*, thanks largely to subscriber loyalty. In 2016, nearly 70 percent of The Times's revenue still came from the print edition's subscriptions and advertising.

By the time of Trump's election there was no doubt about the politics of our core readership: it skewed left, and, in any measure of its opposition to Trump, it went off the charts. In the aftermath of Election Day, the numbers were growing in ways that were hard to imagine. Trump was just flat wrong about the "failing *New York Times*," as he liked to call the paper. Shortly after Election Day, he lobbed a tweet about how *The Times* was "losing thousands of subscribers" because of its coverage of his campaign. It was so inaccurate that The Times's senior management decided to do what it had not done before: go mano a mano, or at least tweet to tweet, with a sitting president. There on the @RealDonaldTrump Twitter account was the paper's response:

> fact: surge in new subscriptions, print & digital, with trends, stops & starts, 4 X better than normal.

It was an undeniable Trump Bump. In the first quarter of 2017, *The Times* had a net gain of more than 300,000 digital subscribers, the biggest jump in any quarter since it had implemented the online paywall in 2011. The paper had grown to more than three million subscribers, online and in print. As our CEO Mark Thompson pointed out, every time the president criticized The Times, he drove up our subscription numbers. Americans concerned about what Trump might do next were looking to The Times to be the watchdog that the First Amendment envisioned, and they were willing to put their money down to support the paper. Even before the rise of Trump, a Pew Foundation study in 2014 showed that about two-thirds of *Times* readers identified as left of center (compared with 38 percent of all web respondents). Trump's election, along with the polarization of the country in both its politics and its choice of media, only reinforced that trend.

The Times had long prided itself on being an honest broker on the news side of its operation. The editorial page might swing left, but the news columns were to be on the other side of a very high wall, playing it straight with the facts, no matter who might be lifted up or skewered by the reporting. During the 2016 election, Dean Baquet was quoted in the public editor's column: "We have to be really careful that people feel like they can see themselves in The New York Times. I want us to be perceived as fair and honest to the world, not just a segment of it." It could be a challenge. Early in 2017, a friend who was a Trump-hating conservative and a careful reader of *The Times* told me he had grown increasingly unhappy with our coverage. He pointed to a story we had just done about Trump's new policy of embracing the autocratic Egyptian government and tamping down American criticism of that country's deplorable record on human rights, which had been a cornerstone of Obama's policy. After reporting out the White House policy announcement, the story then gave prominent coverage to both a human rights activist in the U.S. and a former Obama official, who each condemned the Trump approach. Many respectable experts actually think the new approach makes sense for America, my friend pointed out. He wasn't suggesting anyone had to agree with them, but why did no one at The New York Times think to include their views in the piece? Wouldn't it make a difference to know that Trump's view had some traction beyond the Trump foreign policy team (whose dysfunction and misdirection we had chronicled often)? They were good questions.

As the lawyer for The Times, I get to be an agnostic on most issues of fairness and bias. My job is to give our journalists my best judgment on what the law allows us to do, not to opine on whether a story could have been fairer or told more dispassionately, or have incorporated different voices. The calculation is pretty simple: when I am vetting stories before publication, I want journalists to take my legal opinions seriously. (OK, I actually want them to embrace my legal opinions as wise and prudent and the absolute embodiment of the law, but I'm a realist.) When I start serving up opinions on how journalism should be done, editors should be free to ignore me. They're the journalists. They get to make that call. I have seen too many press lawyers get ignored because they could not resist appointing themselves as uber-editors. Lawyers who get ignored end up in a very unhappy place, and so do their clients.

Of course, the line between fair and legal is often translucent. At its fundamental level, the law of libel addresses false statements that harm reputation. A story can be wildly unfair and still true and not harm the reputation of the subject of the story. But in many libel cases, the issue is not whether the story is true or false, but whether a factual error was made with reckless disregard of the truth or as a result of careless reporting that failed to live up to professional standards. Defending a fair story—a story that gives people who are criticized a chance to respond, that avoids insinuating language, and that isn't flavored by the personal judgments of the reporter—is always a lighter lift for lawyers.

For much of the campaign, it was often hard to find anyone outside The Times who thought the paper was being fair. My conservative friends thought the coverage of Trump was a daily takedown of the candidate, dismissing him as a sure loser and loose cannon (perhaps an unhinged cannon) who deserved to go down. (They were strangely silent when a controversy erupted over whether *The*

Times had misled the public on the eve of the election with a story that suggested the FBI had cleared the Trump campaign of charges of collusion with Russia.) The Clinton supporters railed about "false equivalency," the deeply held belief that journalists were so caught up in trying to look fair that a negative story about Trump would be matched with a negative story about Clinton, even though in their minds Trump's missteps were felonies and mortal sins while Clinton's failures were the equivalent of alternate-side parking violations. Liz Spayd, *The Times*'s public editor, waded knee-deep into the controversy at her own peril in September 2016, the height of campaign frenzy. She blasted away at those who seemed to think that Trump should get tougher coverage because, well, he was Trump and doing all kinds of Trump things all the time, or that The Times investigation into the Clinton Foundation—which didn't turn up much news—was just a lame attempt to have fake balance. To her, The Times should neither be counting stories in the pursuit of balance—one for him, one for her, one for him, one for her—nor making the judgment that one candidate deserved to have harsher coverage than the other. Liz came out for going after both candidates aggressively and letting readers decide how much weight to give to any story. Readers hated Liz's column with a passion. I happened to agree with her, and told her so, which probably didn't matter much in the scheme of things when online commenters by the dozens were treating her like a Trump shill.

The criticism of the political coverage from both sides was tinged with a certain disregard for readers' intelligence, or at least their complexity as human beings. Powerful news organizations undoubtedly shape public opinion, but it's complicated. We all bring our own filters to what we read, and we form our own opinions about what we read based on—pick as many as you want—our existing biases, our station in life, how critically we read a particular story, what we're hearing from those around us, and what we're reading elsewhere in a media environment that is saturated with alternative news sources. Maybe people expect nothing more than that both candidates will be covered fully. Maybe people see the difference between the parking ticket and the mass murder.

None of that proves (or disproves) whether there was bias one way or the other. And I don't buy the facile answer that if both sides are criticizing you, you must be doing something right. The exact opposite is just as likely true: you are doing a truly terrible job all around and hiding that fact from absolutely nobody.

But here is what I do know. I did the prepublication review, and was often involved in post-mortems, of the most controversial reporting that the paper did during the campaign: The stories about Trump's issues with women and about the claims of groping. The articles about whether Hillary Clinton had been an enabler for her husband's sexual misconduct, attacking women who dared to complain publicly. The whole saga of the Clinton emails and the investigation that followed. The Trump tax returns. The campaign-altering disclosures that came after the Democrats' emails were hacked. The ties between the Clinton Foundation and dubious foreign governments. Trump's breathtaking disregard for the truth. None of those stories struck me as cheap shots, taken out of anti-Trump fervor or a desire to "get" Hillary and even the score. Not once did I feel that the story was a hack job motivated by a personal agenda or an editor's agenda or some agenda of the newspaper. (I would not be able to say the same thing if I were the lawyer for Fox News.) When I do a legal read of an article in advance of publication, I am all about the villains—the doctor who botched the surgery, the insurance company that shafted its customers, the professor who hit on the student, the greedy industrialist who ground up workers to make a fortune. I try to see the story through their eyes, to look for the counternarrative that could be built from the same set of facts. It's a counterintuitive reading. I spent the 2016 campaign in the tank for Clinton and Trump, whoever happened to be the piñata on any given day, making certain, or at least as cer-

tain as you get in an uncertain world, that our stories were as close
to right as they could be. But whether it is Clinton or Trump or just
some poor shlub who wanders into the unforgiving spotlight of a
Times story, I routinely go back to the editor or the reporter and
ask the questions that the subjects of our stories would ask. There's
no magic here. More often than not, at least at The Times, the best
journalists have already asked themselves those same questions
somewhere along the road from the first interview to the last edit.

Late in the campaign, I was on a panel at NYU Law School with
Jack Goldsmith, the Harvard law professor and former Justice
Department official in the Bush administration. Amy Davidson of
The New Yorker and Jameel Jaffer, formerly of the ACLU, were also
there. Of the four of us, only Amy was convinced that Trump was
going to win. Jack offered, based on his own time in government,
that no president has as much power as you would think to move
Washington in a certain direction. Deeply rooted institutions, off-
setting sources of power, the permanent government that is made
up of long-term civil service employees—they all hem in a new president. I weighed in with the idea that it wasn't really clear which
of the two candidates was going to have a more open administration.
Trump had been abusive to the press on the campaign trail, worse
than that actually, but he came to the phone when our reporters
called, and his campaign staff appeared to be genetically unable to
stop leaking. Megan Twohey, who had been one of our lead reporters on gender issues during the 2016 campaign, spoke to my law
school class in the fall and talked about what it was like to seek comment from the campaigns. She had walked both sides of the street,
writing about Trump's problem with women and Clinton's role in
turning back the accusers of her husband. Trump himself returned
her call late at night when she was already at home (and, yes, after
the expected charm offensive, he proceeded to denounce her and
The Times). Clinton ducked her calls for comment and had a high-
level campaign official try to get editors to pull back on the story.

I had never understood why so many Clinton supporters saw the email scandal as trivial and overblown. Maybe you had to be sitting where I sat to understand what it said about her and the administration she would be putting in place if elected. Elected officials use private email accounts for official business for only one reason: to keep the public from getting at the emails—as is the public's legal right—under the Freedom of Information laws. It was a tired dodge. I had seen variations of it with officials in New York City and the governors' offices in both New Jersey and New York. Not exactly the giants of public service whom one would choose to emulate if one were running for president, although, in fairness, none of them had been crafty enough to have a private server (they tended toward the random Gmail or Yahoo! account). FBI director James Comey would ultimately make a hash of the election with his public announcements about the investigations, but that had nothing to do with the reason the emails were there in the first place—to deny the public its rights and be free to govern in greater secrecy. As I made my case at NYU, I could feel the unhappy stirring of the audience. The Clinton email story was a trigger, especially coming from someone from The Times.

We had no one to blame but ourselves. On July 23, 2015, *Times* reporters Mike Schmidt and Matt Apuzzo had landed a bombshell front-page story: two inspectors general, who act as internal governmental watchdogs, had asked the Justice Department to launch a criminal investigation into whether Clinton had "mishandled sensitive government information on a private email account she used as secretary of state."

A tsunami of protest from the Clinton campaign followed, and before it was over *The Times* had published two corrections and an editor's note, saying that the matter had not been a referral for a criminal investigation but a lower-level "security referral." *The Times*'s public editor, Margaret Sullivan, blasted The Times for running with the story. The Clinton campaign piled on with a letter to The Times from Jennifer Palmieri, the Clinton communications director: "I feel obliged to put into context just how egregious an error this story was," wrote Palmieri. She could not understand why The Times "rushed to put an erroneous story on the front page charging that a major candidate for President of the United States was the target of a criminal referral to federal law enforcement."

I knew Mike and Matt. They were among the best reporters I'd encountered, resourceful, connected, dogged (sometimes literally: Matt once was so excited about a story he sent me an email with the subject line "Woof, Woof"). I knew that a source had flip-flopped on them after publication and pulled back an earlier statement. What none of us could know then was why. Political pressure? Change of heart? Just plain error? It didn't matter. The criticism was scathing, both in public and inside The Times building. You can't get a story like that wrong.

It was only later that the truth finally came out: They hadn't been wrong. They had been right.

As Erik Wemple of *The Washington Post* put it two years later when the full story finally got out, "Now we know that the New York Times was understating matters." Two weeks before the Schmidt and Apuzzo story ran, the FBI had opened a criminal investigation. It was code-named "Midyear," and its focus was Mrs. Clinton's handling of classified information. Two dozen investigators were assigned to the inquiry.

That all came later. At NYU I was, to the large swath of the audience, just another talking head serving up a false equivalency between Trump and Clinton. I don't think I was wrong about Clinton—she had a hostility to openness that doesn't befit a public officeholder, whether in Albany or Washington. But on what a Trump presidency would be like, yes, Jack Goldsmith and I had a very bad day predicting the future.

Like much criticism of journalism, the charge that the convention of journalistic objectivity led to mindless and misleading coverage is not baseless, but it became more an easy cliché than a real critique in 2016. It's a well-rubbed stone. We talked about it in journalism school forty years ago. Somebody announces that the earth is flat, reporters quote him deadpan, and then they get an expert to say that, no, the earth appears to be round. The reader is left to sort out the truth. That was certainly the fashion in 1950s journalism, when the pursuit of objectivity could devolve into stenography. It played a role in fueling the rise of the demagogue senator Joe McCarthy, whose wild proclamations about the number of communists employed inside the U.S. government were reported without much pushback from the press, at least in the beginning. Trump's wild-eyed claims—there's too many to pick from: that Muslims were dancing in the street in New Jersey on 9/11, that Obama was born in Kenya, that Trump's own inauguration crowd was the largest ever (period), that he won the popular vote, that millions of ineligible voters went to the polls in 2016—were not blindly reported out as statements with the proper attribution "Trump said" at the end of the sentence. Nobody in America who was consuming the news even casually (except perhaps those Fox viewers hunkered down in front of their flatscreens) failed to learn—from the news media—that those claims were false. The strange idea that journalists should just ignore his most fanciful pronouncements was otherworldly in its own way. Journalists, when they are doing their best work, are reflecting what is going on in the real world. And if someone running for president of the United States starts spouting off like your crazy Uncle Al after the fourth drink on Thanksgiving afternoon, reporters do a disservice to their readers by ignoring the prattle. He is not your crazy Uncle Al; he wants to be president of the United States.

The harder question is how to report it out and where to put it in the report of the day. In the midst of the dust-up over the size of the crowd on Inauguration Day, a *Times* reader expressed her exasperation. She wanted to know what would happen if Trump said he had been to the moon and whether reporters would spend the next four years tracking down the serial numbers of spacecraft in the hopes of definitively proving him wrong (while back here on Earth an administration was quietly changing everything). As the campaign wore on and then later, when Trump took office, the debate over the L-word—lying—blossomed. Readers demanded that we call a lie a lie. The Times had never been there before— "wrong," "misrepresented," "misstated" . . . those were the words of choice in covering presidential candidates and presidents, even when they were, yes, lying. *The Times* editors finally decided the old rules could no longer hold when there was no doubt that the mis-statement was knowing and willful. The L-word made its way into our coverage with two stories in September 2016, both about Trump's decision to stop suggesting that Obama was not born in the United States. *Times* editors saw it as a word that should be used sparingly, and Dean Baquet said it was not a Trump-only rule but something that would apply to future coverage when called for.

After the inauguration, with Trump in the White House, *The Times* rolled out the "definitive list," an ever-growing, day by day, ledger of the untruths of the president. The then-editor of *The Wall Street Journal*, Gerard Baker, was not impressed. In an interview with Katie Couric, he said:

> What I think is not really important. I think the president prob-ably lies a lot, right? I think the president makes things up at times. I think I've got a fair amount of reasons for believing that.
>
> The difference is not what I think or what I might express [as] an opinion or even given reasonable grounds to believe, but what my reporters can report as facts. And if you're going to report as a fact that something is a lie, you have to know that it's not only an untruth, not only a falsehood, you have to be able to impute two things in the mind of the speaker: one, knowledge that it is actually untrue; and two, a deliberate intent to deceive.

An astute reader of *The Times* had gotten to the point much more quickly. She wrote in to urge us to stop saying Trump was lying. Didn't we know the difference between a delusion and a lie?

Whenever one of the periodic updates to the list of lies was going to be published, an editor from the opinion section would send me the latest version to read. All of Trump's tub-thumping threats of suing people made many journalists wary, even though the possibility of a lawsuit by Trump over a story alleging he was a habitual liar was roughly the same as the likelihood he would someday prove that his inauguration crowd was the largest ever. For one thing, truth is always a defense, even when, or maybe especially when, a newspaper is calling a public official truth-impaired. But I was never in love with the list. Trump's wacky theories, off-target predictions, and misleading explanations were treated as the equivalent of out-and-out lies. As one anti-Trump New Yorker wrote to me, "I thought the article the other day that included as one of Trump's exaggerations/falsehoods in his Davos speech basically accurate economic statistics on the grounds that in the first year of his term, a President has not yet begun to influence the economy was beyond lame. The guy tells lies (actual lies) on a daily basis, and there's just no point in NYT making hairsplitting distinctions that it has never applied to other politicians (and with good reason, since they all take credit for shit they didn't do)."

The decision to call Trump a liar was part of a larger reckoning at the paper about how to cover a politician who was like no one before him. After the election, senior management held a town hall–style meeting for employees. The questions told the story. One person from the newsroom who said she had grown up in the Midwest thought we had failed to grasp what was going on in the country. We had missed out on comprehending how many people who were not racists or bigots but felt left out and disrespected by the coastal elites were attracted to Trump's promise of shaking up the government. You can sneer at Trump, but you can't sneer at his followers, an editor at a rival news organization told me one night as he critiqued our coverage. During the last month of the campaign, I saw my stepsister in Illinois. Her husband had lost his job at a local factory. It had cut the hourly wages twice and then told the workers they had to take a third cut or see the factory shut down. At some point, when wages are cut nearly in half, the job just isn't worth it anymore. The workers refused, and the plant closed. The Democrats weren't to blame for that, and Trump didn't really have a solution, but something had gone terribly wrong, and who would blame the workers for wanting to punch the establishment in the face?

There were others at the town hall meeting who thought the paper had "normalized" Trump, failed to help readers understand how far outside the American mainstream he was on race and immigration and the place of women and common decency. (Had anyone imagined, say, four years ago, that a presidential candidate could refer to his opponents as Liddle Marco and Lyin' Ted in a nationally televised debate . . . and win?) I had been suspected of something akin to normalizing. After my letter to Trump's lawyer went viral, I had done a piece for *The Times* Insider section talking about how the letter had come to be written. I mentioned that the point of writing the letter was to defend the newspaper's coverage of the two women who claimed to have been groped and to lay out how the law protected our story. Then I said the unthinkable, at least in the minds of some people, about the reaction I had received from readers:

Lots of people took the opportunity to vent about Donald Trump. Not surprising, but not really my point. I grew up in a small farming town in Illinois. Both my father and my mother were World War II veterans who served in Europe. Unlike many of my Manhattan friends, I get why Mr. Trump appeals to good people like the ones I grew up with.

Months later, an old friend still remembered it and cornered me at a reception. What had I meant by that, by the reference to "good people"? I wasn't trying to be mysterious. They were people who volunteered at the local hospital or fire department, had kids who joined the military, went to funerals of people they didn't know that well because it seemed like the right thing to do. It was not a profound point. No medals needed to be handed out. They just shouldn't be painted with a broad brush as haters and racists. That answer didn't seem to please.

It was impossible not to get whipsawed in covering Trump. The coverage felt adversarial to conservatives. It was an easy argument for them to make. Part of the problem was the very nature of an internet news site. The print paper has an architecture that signals readers where they are going and what they will see when they get there. The editorial page and the op-eds are cabined in the back of the first section. When news analysis appears in the news pages, it is labeled and set off typographically. The news is over here, opinion is over there, and the latter does not color the former. That architecture breaks down on a newspaper's home page. Our op-ed columns and contributors are overwhelmingly anti-Trump, every day. It is hard to think of an op-ed piece from the campaign days that had anything to say on Trump's behalf, other than the occasional backhanded "he may actually be right about something—for once" sort of offering. On the home page all of the negative-opinion pieces, with blazing anti-Trump headlines, sat cheek to jowl with our news coverage of Trump, which was often, and necessarily, critical. That kind of coverage was unavoidable for a candidate who encouraged violence at rallies, made preposterous claims, insulted his opponents, and got caught on tape bragging about groping women. But the overall impression many days, with op-eds next to news coverage, was of a full-on slapdown of the Trump candidacy. And then there was that gauge we printed showing how unlikely a Trump victory would be as Election Day approached.

The perception of Times prejudice became, in its way, a legal issue. We were in a long-running legal fight with a libertarian professor named Walter Block. He had been a bit player in a story we
had done in 2014 about Rand Paul and the libertarian heritage
Rand had taken on from his father, retired congressman Ron Paul.
Block had been mentioned in passing and quoted as saying that
while he opposed slavery because it was involuntary, he thought it
was otherwise "not so bad." Block did not deny the quotation—he
had said it on his blog on multiple occasions. But he thought the
story had not conveyed his point in context: that the problem with
slavery was not the conditions under which slaves lived but the
immorality of the forced economic relationship between master
and slave. He sued for libel.

When Block's lawyers filed a brief in the first week of 2017, they
jumped on the notion that The Times had gone partisan: "The idea
being, in its role as social engineer, the NYTimes' agenda super-
sedes the central tenets which have *always* defined real journalism." They pivoted off a column that *The Times*'s media columnist
Jim Rutenberg had written in August, "Trump Is Testing the Norms
of Objectivity in Journalism." It began:

If you're a working journalist and you believe that Donald J.
Trump is a demagogue playing to the nation's worst racist and
nationalistic tendencies, that he cozies up to anti-American dictators and that he would be dangerous with control of the United
States nuclear codes, how the heck are you supposed to cover him?

Because if you believe all of those things, you have to throw
out the textbook American journalism has been using for the better part of the past half-century, if not longer, and approach it in
a way you've never approached anything in your career. If you
view a Trump presidency as something that's potentially dangerous, then your reporting is going to reflect that. You would
move closer than you've ever been to being oppositional. That's

uncomfortable and uncharted territory for every mainstream, nonopinion journalist I've ever known, and by normal standards, untenable.

But the question that everyone is grappling with is: Do normal standards apply? And if they don't, what should take their place?

Jim ultimately answered the question in his column: journalists had a duty

to ferret out what the candidates will be like in the most powerful office in the world. It may not always seem fair to Mr. Trump or his supporters. But journalism shouldn't measure itself against any one campaign's definition of fairness. It is journalism's job to be true to the readers and viewers, and true to the facts, in a way that will stand up to history's judgment. To do anything less would be untenable.

That point was made provocatively—that is what a column is supposed to do—but in the end Jim was saying something pretty unexceptional: that reporters needed to give readers a meaningful account of Trump and his campaign. Block's lawyers didn't see it that way: "In short, [Rutenberg] implored his colleagues to join him on the dark side and allow their partisanship to pervade their reporting, which no longer need be objective/truthful."

It was just one brief, in one case, but it was concerning, and not just because Block would ultimately prevail on an appeal, sending the case back to the district court. *The Times* had regularly been viewed by courts, whether the judges said it out loud or not, as something of the gold standard for journalism: trusted, straight, impartial. It helps in tough cases. Call it the benefit of the doubt. Every lawyer wants it, or needs it, in litigation. It can be a difference maker. I could see that, in the hands of plaintiffs' lawyers, our Trump coverage could feed a very different narrative: that of a news organization that was waging jihad against conservatives. Before the spring of 2017 was over, we would be sued for libel by a group of companies owned by the coal baron Bob Murray, an enthusiastic Trump supporter and bringer of libel suits, and Sarah Palin, the former vice presidential candidate. They both, in differing degrees, pushed the story line of a liberal newspaper that couldn't play it straight.

Many journalists are biased—just not in the way that most people think about it. The easy rap is that most reporters lean liberal (true), and that dictates how they cover a conservative like Trump (false). Journalists are brought up to see their role in the world as shedding light on wrongdoing and holding the powerful accountable. They believe, all other things being equal, that the little guy is getting screwed, economically, politically, and in every other way. The reportorial default is to think that most regulations are good, the rich and connected don't need more money or more power, and most social policies in the long run hurt the poor, the sick, and the disadvantaged, whose individual stories are profound and worth telling. A president who comes into office promising to cut regulations, give tax breaks to rich guys, and round up immigrants is a president walking full blast into the most basic prejudices of the profession. Bad coverage of a particular politician is rarely driven by personal animosity, although undoubtedly at times that does happen. The real explanation for most unflattering coverage is that beat reporters stand close enough to the politicians they cover to grow deeply skeptical of all of them. It is not a left or right thing. Based on nothing more scientific than my own conversations around the newsroom, Trump may actually have been better liked than Andrew Cuomo and Bill de Blasio, both liberals and both also combative in their dealings with journalists (made worse by the fact that neither of them was as entertaining or strangely likable as the president—they weren't even in the same league). The first time most politicians will get the fawning coverage they think they deserve will be the day after they die, when their legacy and contributions will finally be duly noted in their obituaries.

Jimmy Carter would say in 2017 that no president he knew had been treated to as much negative press coverage as Trump. "I think they feel free to claim that Trump is mentally deranged and everything else without hesitation," Carter said. Carter, it is worth recalling, never felt the need during the entire course of his presidency to publicly declare that he was a "stable genius." He didn't try to guide the ship of state with cable TV as his North Star. He never had the chance to fire an FBI director who was investigating his inner circle or proclaim the right to pardon aides and allies who were suspected of colluding with a hostile foreign power. The news is about—let's get basic—what is new. This was new. No president before Trump has tried managing by chaos. As Peter Baker reported in *The Times* when the administration was barely 13 months old, "Mr. Trump is on his second press secretary, his second national security adviser and his third deputy national security adviser. Five different people have been named communications director or served in the job in an acting capacity. The president has parted ways with his chief strategist, health secretary, several deputy chiefs of staff and his original private legal team. He is on his second chief of staff." The supply of White House aides ready to dish on each other and the president as anonymous sources is apparently bottomless, not surprising in an office where the exit door is never far from view, and nothing helps a career along like a well-placed shot at a rival.

Was the press prone to doing critical stories? Were they giving short shrift to the accomplishments of the administration? Yes and yes. That is how journalism works. Reporters aren't meant to be the royal scribes of a monarchy or portraitists removing the wrinkles and the warts. That is true for every presidency, but Trump was a hell of a story, and his administration seemed incapable of managing its own message. His White House was an all-you-can-eat buffet of news stories, open 24/7, with gigantic serving platters. No reporter was going to push back from the table, walk away, and instead do a story about, say, the daring new irrigation initiative that the Department of Agriculture was unveiling. Yes, it sometimes felt as if Jimmy Carter might have a point, that the press at times stretched too far in hopes of finding the negative. In the first minutes of the Trump administration, a journalist reported that Trump had removed the bust of Martin Luther King from the Oval Office. He was wrong. The bust was still there. He just hadn't seen it. He posted a correction. It was fair to ask why, on that impossibly rich day for news, a reporter was focused on whether Trump had removed the MLK bust. But if Americans want to worry about whether the press is doing its job, their time is probably better spent wondering not whether the president is getting a fair shake but whether major changes are taking place and going unreported as federal agencies dramatically change course, regulations are stripped down, agency information is quietly pulled from public websites, and regulated industries are being set free.

The Times itself was not spared the divisiveness that was fracturing the country. In early 2018, Dean Baquet and CEO Mark Thompson took the unusual step of reminding Times employees in writing that they needed to work a little harder at being civil. Some Times staffers had been enraged by the editorial department's decision to give space to conservative commentators and to mark the first anniversary of Trump's inauguration with submissions from Trump voters. Then in February a new hire for the editorial board was forced to quit before she even started when social media users discovered tweets mentioning her friendship with a neo-Nazi and using gay and racial slurs. The memo to employees from Baquet and Thompson was delicately worded. It said the right things about free speech in the workplace, but it chided employees who failed to meet the company's "expectation of respect and courtesy toward one another." It was a worthwhile message, and on target, but it was chasing a problem that wasn't easily solved by politely reasoned memos.

Living in the Time of Twitter further complicated the lives of our editors who were concerned that the paper was seen as biased. Twitter had become a perpetual open mic night for the world, and some reporters got in line to audition. Some smartly curated all that was happening in the world, others took it as a soapbox, and the line between the two was not always clear. In November, shortly after the election, a small brouhaha erupted after *Times* journalists tweeted about the president-elect's daughter hawking her jewelry online and how Trump's cabinet selection process resembled the beauty pageants he used to operate. A third tweet posted an *Atlantic* article that suggested the electoral college could reject Trump. Liz Spayd, the public editor, was pilloried for going on a Fox News program, calling the tweets "outrageous," and saying that consequences should be visited upon the tweeters. Spayd took a public beating for overreacting and failing to grasp that social media was now part of life's fabric for reporters, although some of the criticism, to be fair, seemed to be rooted in her having committed Mortal Sin No. 1—going on a Fox TV show.

The truth was that the house was divided inside The Times building. Lots of editors didn't like the idea of reporters airing their sarcasm about the Trump White House or venting low-burn outrage about whatever had just happened in D.C. And it wasn't just reporters. After a Times businessperson stationed in Europe tweeted, "Last week was my first time back in the states since Trump was inaugurated and I thought that America, as I knew it, had died," editors came to me asking what could be done. It was complicated. A company devoted to free expression hates to play Twitter nanny shushing its own employees. Social media was hugely important to our brand, a way to push out our stories to a bigger audience and introduce our reporters to readers. There was also the reality that leaders at The Times were reluctant to put any policy in writing, not only because it was hard to set out social media rules but also because the document would more or less instantly be launched onto the internet by someone. It didn't make management easy, and any misstatement was bound to become the outrage of the day on-line in journalism and political circles. We also weren't keen to call public attention to the errant tweets. So editors mainly watched the internet and made private entreaties to newsroom employees who seemed to cross a line on social media. Glenn Thrush, the newest of *The Times* reporters covering the White House, was a particular flash point for critics. Glenn had become a journalism celebrity thanks to his ever-present hat and *Saturday Night Live*'s spoof of his daily battles with Sean Spicer. He had joined The Times from Politico after the election and done exceptional old-fashioned reporting on the White House, but he wasn't shy about airing his views on Twitter (*"Would you keep working for a boss who consistently refuses to distance himself from virulent racists, antisemites and white supremacists?"*). In September 2017, Thrush closed down his Twitter account after realizing, he said, just how much time he was spending wading through tweets and responding. He conceded his bosses were not unhappy about the decision.

A month later The Times unveiled—in writing—its newsroom social media policy, which had been in the works for months. The editors no longer thought the whisper-in-the-ear approach with individual Twitter miscreants was working. The authors of the memo had come up with a strategy to win over the hearts and minds of the staff: they quoted high-profile journalists from around the newsroom talking about how an unthinking tweet by anyone identified with *The Times* could make their lives harder by undermining the paper's credibility with sources and readers. The nub of the new policy was stated up front: "If our journalists are perceived as biased or engage in editorializing on social media, that can undercut the credibility of the entire newsroom. We've always made clear that newsroom employees should avoid posting anything on social media that damages our reputation for neutrality and fairness." The policy ended with a series of questions people should ask themselves before they posted: "Would someone who reads your post have grounds for believing that you are biased on a particular issue?" "If readers see your post and notice that you're a Times journalist, would that affect their view of The Times's news coverage as fair and impartial?" "If someone were to look at your entire social media feed, including links and retweets, would they have doubts about your ability to cover news events in a fair and impartial way?"

The policy seemed to go down smoothly enough in the newsroom. Across town at the right-drifting *New York Post*, they were not so impressed. The headline for a column about the policy's rollout read "The Times' New Policy to Hide Reporters' Bias."

In the first year of the new administration, I kept coming back to Stanley Dearman's lesson about the difference between serving readers and catering to them. Over the past half-decade, the paper has committed itself to reader-centered journalism: opening up more stories to comments, creating a Reader Center to encourage dialogue between *Times* journalists and the reading public, and exploring new content to address the real-world needs and desires of our readers. For years, the paper had almost prided itself on its distance from its readers, as if knowing who they were and what they wanted would somehow taint the purity of the journalism. The shift in attitude was like opening a window after a long winter. Journalism should be done as if people mattered. But in a polarized America there was a risk, too—the risk that we would set our compass by what people wanted rather than giving them the journalism they needed. The appetite for tough Trump stories among our audiences seemed insatiable. There were times, though, when we needed to tell other kinds of stories if we hoped to reflect the world as it was, and the pushback from readers could be ferocious.

In late November 2016, Scott Shane of The Times's Washington bureau, one of the best and most conscientious journalists in the country, did a profile of Steve Bannon, at that time Trump's go-to aide. Scott's piece was a well-reported piece of journalism done by the book, a profile of a newsmaker with no ambition beyond letting readers know who this Bannon character was. As Scott put it:

> To understand what to expect from the Trump administration means in part to fathom the driven, contradictory character of Mr. Bannon, whom the president-elect has named senior counselor and chief White House strategist. Rarely has there been so incendiary a figure at the side of a president-elect, thrilling Mr. Trump's more extreme supporters while unnerving ethnic and religious minorities and many other Americans.
>
> How did this son of Richmond, Va., who attended Harvard Business School, spent years at Goldman Sachs and became wealthy working at the intersection of entertainment and finance, come to view the political and financial elites as his archenemy? Why does a man who calls himself a "hard-nosed capitalist" rail against "globalists" of "the party of Davos" and attack the Republican establishment with special glee?

As a reader watching Bannon make his way from the loony fringe of the right to the center of Washington power, I had wondered those same things. A day earlier, *The Boston Globe* had done an insightful profile of Bannon from his days at Harvard Business School. His classmates remembered him as a charismatic navy veteran, older, with a different life arc than many of his peers: "He, like they, was gunning for a top Wall Street job, and wanted to make a lot of money in a hurry. And yet, as classmates recall, something set him apart early on. Brash even by Harvard standards, intellectually dominant but also easy company. What most can't find in their recollections is the harshly divisive Steve Bannon they read about today."

Our Bannon piece set readers' hair on fire. Part of it was the headline describing Bannon as "combative" and a "populist" when many readers thought "racist," "white supremacist," or "xenophobe" might have done the trick. Reporters don't write their own headlines (editors have that job), and the word "populist" had become one of those terms that had slipped its anchor and drifted off into a sea of ambiguity. Bernie Sanders? Donald Trump? Neither? Both? Meaning what exactly? But the profile itself was attacked for serving up a balanced portrayal of Bannon rather than denouncing him. "I think what was particularly disappointing is that a lot of young, educated people saw a 4,500-word story and said 'You didn't use the right label,' instead of reading the story and drawing their own conclusions," Scott said in the aftermath for a column by the public editor. If people wanted to see Bannon as—choose your favorite term—a racist, white supremacist, or xenophobe, the facts for getting there were to be found in the story. But if readers preferred to see Bannon as an enigmatic figure with a résumé that should have led him anywhere but where he ended up, the story gave that narrative, too. It was discouraging that so many people apparently believed that the time-honored journalistic act of telling a story straight had become a problem and that The Times needed instead to be in the business of taking sides and coaching readers on what to think.

Almost exactly a year later, the same fight was waged anew when reporter Richard Fausset did a story headlined "A Voice of Hate in America's Heartland." That voice belonged to Tony Hovater, a 25-year-old newlywed who had become a white nationalist. "He is the Nazi sympathizer next door, polite and low-key at a time the old boundaries of accepted political activity can seem alarmingly in flux," Richard wrote. "Most Americans would be disgusted and baffled by his casually approving remarks about Hitler, disdain for democracy and belief that the races are better off separate. But his tattoos are innocuous pop-culture references: a slice of cherry pie adorns one arm, an homage to the TV show 'Twin Peaks.' He says he prefers to spread the gospel of white nationalism with satire. He is a big 'Seinfeld' fan." Hovater came across not as a monster but just another aimless guy from the Midwest with a fondness for Applebee's and a wedding registry at Target—only one with abhorrent racist and anti-Semitic views that he couldn't shut up about. To me, that was pretty much the point. Hannah Arendt had written about the "banality of evil" in her legendary book *Eichmann in Jerusalem*, suggesting that the truly frightening thing about Adolf Eichmann, the Nazi war criminal, was just how ordinary he appeared to be, how easy it was for people not that different from us to become, in the wrong circumstances, evil incarnate. As he wrote the piece, Richard struggled to find an explanation for Hovater, but it never came. "Sometimes a soul, and its shape, remain obscure to both writer and reader," Richard wrote later. "I beat myself up about all of this for a while, until I decided that the unfilled hole would have to serve as both feature and defect."

Lots of readers didn't see it that way at all. They responded with unbridled anger, and they refused to give The Times a pass. It is always hard to know whether the people who take the time to go on Twitter or lob dispatches at The Times via email represent a small motivated core or speak for a larger group of readers, but those who wrote saw Richard's piece as a "long, glowing profile" of a Nazi, a shameful effort by The Times to normalize the worst elements in American society. Back at The Times, the response stung. Before it was all over, *The Times*'s national editor, Marc Lacey, had apologized in a fashion: "We regret the degree to which the piece offended so many readers. We recognize that people can disagree on how best to tell a disagreeable story. What we think is indisputable, though, is the need to shed more light, not less, on the most extreme corners of American life and the people who inhabit them."

Those civil words masked the darker response we were seeing. The story appeared on a Saturday night, and on Monday I was alerted by our security staff that Antifa, the hard and often violent edge of the left, was going to "doxx" Richard—publish his address and contact information so people could target him for harassment or worse. Dealing with threats against journalists had become a sadly routine part of my work life, but each time a new one surfaced a feeling of discouragement about what the country had become would come over me again. I understood that the threats were not reflective of the nation writ large, but they now came too often, with too much hatred and viciousness. Most of it was just passing noise on the internet, but it was impossible to forget that it only takes one person. Witness the shooting of a Republican congressman and others at a ballfield in Virginia, or the "Pizzagate" incident in which a North Carolina man fired a gun inside a Washington pizza parlor after right-wing websites fabricated accounts of a child porn ring linked to Democrats operating there. I checked in by phone with Richard. I told him I thought his story did exactly what journalism was supposed to do: reveal the reality that exists out there, even when it goes up against what we think the world is or ought to be. The response had been brutal but he was philosophical. We both knew that, in the politics of 2017, it would only be a minute before something else suddenly happened, shocking the senses, exploding people's brains, and sending the national conversation hurtling toward the next great outrage.

Journalism was hard in a polarized country where people felt the failure to take sides was in and of itself a surrender. I knew that The Times didn't get it right all the time, that words could both mask and antagonize, and the discussion of what to call things—alt-right or white nationalist, lie or misstatement—kept cycling through the newsroom. Still, I remained a believer in a particular vision of journalism. I believed that there was a place for journalism that told stories without partiality, that followed the facts wherever they led, even if our readers (or our president) didn't want to be taken there. We needed to tell the truths that we found, no matter how imperfectly we did that, day after day. The alt-right had become the masters of trying to shut down and silence all the voices they found disagreeable. It was not a model I thought we should emulate. The great risk we faced came not in giving them voice but in taking their worst instincts and making them our own.

7

The Leaks Police

Leaking, and even illegal classified leaking, has been a big problem in Washington for years. Failing @nytimes (and others) must apologize!

—President Donald Trump, Feb. 16, 2017

Boy, I love reading those WikiLeaks!

—Candidate Donald Trump, Nov. 4, 2016

ON JUNE 5, 2017, the news website The Intercept published a major story about Russian interference with the U.S. elections. "Top-Secret NSA Report Details Russian Hacking Effort Days Before 2016 Election," the headline read. The article was built from a "highly classified" report from the National Security Agency that had been provided anonymously to Intercept reporters. It detailed a Russian cyberattack on an election software supplier and attempts by the Russians to compromise the email accounts of more than 100 local election officials on the eve of the 2016 election. The article was significant, but unmentioned in it was a second developing story in the background: the source for the piece, an NSA contractor with the unlikely name Reality Winner, had been arrested two days earlier in Georgia, accused of leaking the classified document about the Russian effort. Any doubts about whether the

Trump administration was going to get serious about leaks disappeared on that Saturday afternoon when armed agents arrested Winner as she returned home from the grocery store.

Journalists would ferociously debate whether The Intercept reporters were responsible for Winner's apprehension. The Intercept denied it, but, according to the government, the reporters had shared a photo of the original document with an NSA contractor as they sought to authenticate the report. Creases visible in the paper suggested that the reporters had received a hard copy, and that led investigators to a small group of people who had access to the paper document. One of them was Winner. But the finger-pointing was a distraction from the real takeaway: reporters were now on notice that their sources were in the crosshairs of the Jeff Sessions DOJ.

The president himself had his own dizzying past with leaked and hacked documents. During the campaign, Candidate Trump had been loving the emails that WikiLeaks had obtained from the Democratic National Committee and party bigwig John Podesta. "This WikiLeaks stuff is unbelievable," he said in October at a Florida rally. "It tells you, the inner heart, you gotta read it." But by February 2017, he was President Trump, anti-leaks jihadist blasting away at The Times for publishing stories based on leaks coming from a White House where competing factions seemed to spend as much time whispering to reporters as talking to each other. In fairness, his warm embrace of WikiLeaks was more about hacked documents stolen by outsiders from servers than documents leaked to reporters by government employees. But whatever the case, his anti-leak tweets were the first shot fired in a war on leaks. Before long, Sessions was dispatched to warn federal employees that they would be in serious legal trouble if they didn't stop talking to journalists without authorization, and the Justice Department announced that it intended to make it easier to subpoena journalists during leak investigations as prosecutors ramped up their efforts to track down the people inside government who dared to disclose the truth about what was really going on in the new administration.

And then there was the sliming part of the campaign.

In July 2017, Trump tweeted: "The Failing New York Times foiled U.S. attempt to kill the single most wanted terrorist, Al-Baghdadi. Their sick agenda over National Security." The president had watched a Fox News report that was presidential red meat: an account of remarks made by General Tony Thomas at the Aspen Security Forum. Thomas blamed a 2015 leak to The Times for disrupting a U.S. operation aimed at capturing the head of ISIS, Abu Bakr al-Baghdadi. The nub of Thomas's complaint was that U.S. forces had captured the wife of a senior ISIS leader during a raid that killed her husband and that she had given U.S. troops a "treasure trove of information" about Baghdadi's location. That lead "was leaked in a prominent national newspaper about a week later, and that lead went dead," Thomas told the crowd at Aspen.

The only problem with Thomas's account was that it was wrong. The leader's wife was captured on May 16, 2015. Her capture was publicly reported that day—by the Pentagon. *The Times* later reported that the raid had harvested important intelligence data about ISIS. Only it was not a week later, as Thomas said at Aspen, but more than three weeks later. Unless the U.S. military was sitting around doing nothing for three weeks, and Baghdadi had somehow missed the very public news of the wife's capture and the death of his top aide (before reading *The Times* that morning), *The Times*'s reporting had nothing to do with the failure of U.S. forces to capture the ISIS leader. That, of course, would not have been much of a story for Fox News or the president.

Leaking is a hard topic for lawyers. Whether we grow up to be tax lawyers or defenders of killers, help tenants avenge the misdeeds of their landlords, or shepherd the blissless through divorce court, we are baptized in the rule of law. We may try to twist legal precedents, urge courts to look at laws in nutty ways, and see exceptions where none could possibly exist, but at base we believe in rules and rationality and orderliness. We seek tidiness in a messy world.

Leaking, whether you call it that or dress it up as whistleblowing, is about just the opposite: going outside the lines, breaking the rules, and sometimes breaking the law.

Which is why it is so important.

When the rule of law is threatened or compromised—and let's face it: it is only as good as those charged with keeping it and honoring it—there is precious little to save democracy's day other than transparency: shining the harsh light of truth on the people in power trying to subvert legality, corrupt lawful process, or undermine justice. The executive branch gets to decide who the investigators are, who gets investigated, who gets charged with a crime, and, in the end, who gets pardoned. It is a stunning amount of power. And it becomes a scary stunning amount when it is coupled with the ability to decide who gets silenced and how much truth makes its way to the American public. That is so even when the ultimate executive holding that power isn't also standing dead center in the middle of an investigation.

Is every leak alike—a case of some beatified public servant saving the rule of law with a strategic phone call to a reporter in the nick of time? If only. Leakers are like other people: complicated. There are leaks done for petty motives or to avenge bad boss behavior. Some are the product of a misguided and obscure worldview, or done for no better reason than to stir the pot of politics. But every leak crackdown is alike: it works as a deterrent and threatens the future leaks that democracy depends on.

No president, Republican or Democrat, is ever going to embrace what Sessions calls the "culture of leaking." Liberals didn't like to dwell on it, but the fact was that the Obama administration had broken new ground in its pursuit of leakers, being more aggressive than any prior administration in prosecuting government workers accused of unauthorized disclosures. Leaking is the kind of topic that does not lend itself to simple answers (unless you are an attorney general with an agenda or a president with a Twitter account). You have to begin with two truths that run headlong into each other. You start here: a government needs to be able to keep some secrets. Real national security requires it, and even in the more prosaic corners of government, it is hard to manage in a fishbowl and get anything good done if every private memo and conversation is destined to be in a newspaper or on the internet. And then you go to the other side: Leaks are a powerful force for truth, and whether a government cracks down on leakers directly or bullies the press to find out who a reporter's sources are, the result is the same—the public more often than not pays the price. When people are allowed to know only what the government wants them to know, they become little more than sheep in a fog. If you are a lawyer in leak-world, you inevitably find yourself advocating for something that could best be described as a modicum of unlawfulness, which is not a concept they teach you in law school. There should be laws against some types of leaking; they just shouldn't be enforced very often. And the whole conundrum is made more complicated by this: the law does not allow leakers a public interest defense even if they can show that they acted for a higher purpose—a yawning gap in the law that is a disservice to democracy.

Over the Obama years, The Times had watched with anger and disbelief as the Justice Department initiated a series of leak investigations seeking the sources for stories we had published. Most went nowhere. But in the final months of the Obama administration we had come face-to-face with all the complexities of leak investigations and the uncertain rules of source-reporter relationships. In October 2016, retired general James E. Cartwright stood before a federal court and pleaded guilty to lying to the FBI agents who were looking for the sources of classified information used by David Sanger of The Times in his reporting on the most sophisticated cyber-operation ever conducted by one state against another: the joint U.S.–Israel attack on Iran's nuclear program. It was a stunning and sad reversal of fortune for Cartwright, the former vice chairman of the Joint Chiefs of Staff, once called "Obama's favorite general." On the day of the plea, Cartwright's attorneys at Skadden Arps had called me to give me the heads-up. I had been talking off and on to Cartwright's legal team for more than three years. I started working the phones, first making sure we had someone ready to cover the court appearance, filling in whatever background I could for the Washington bureau, and then looping Sanger in before letting our corporate PR staff know that we were about to get hit by a wave of press calls.

We never want to be in that position: news makers rather than news reporters. We rarely want to be pressed into talking about our reporting, especially when it's highly sensitive national security reporting. Still, the prosecution of Cartwright was outrageous. After years of investigation, there was no proof that any harm had been done by *The Times*'s reporting. (The computer code used in the cyberattack had leaked out in 2010 because of an error by the U.S. or the Israelis, revealing to Iran why its nuclear facilities were failing.) Prosecutors could not show that Cartwright had violated the Espionage Act. They were left to charge him only with lying to the FBI after he failed to keep his story straight when he talked to the investigators. We decided to take the opportunity to issue a political statement, to make the case for freedom of the press:

> In researching his book *Confront and Conceal* and his stories for The New York Times, David Sanger relied on multiple sources in Washington, Europe, the Middle East, and elsewhere. Most of them spoke on the condition of anonymity. As in the past, neither The Times nor Mr. Sanger will discuss whether a particular person was a source or the sourcing of particular information that was published, beyond what has been disclosed in our stories and in the book.

Reporting like this serves a vital public interest: explaining how the United States is using a powerful new technology against its adversaries and the concern that it raises about how similar weapons can be used against the U.S. We will continue to pursue that reporting vigorously.

We are disappointed that the Justice Department has gone forward with the leak investigation that led to today's guilty plea by Gen. Cartwright. These investigations send a chilling message to all government employees that they should not speak to reporters. The inevitable result is that the American public is deprived of information that it needs to know.

Shortly after the plea, I received another call from Cartwright's lawyers. The judge had set sentencing for January, just before Inauguration Day. They wanted to know whether The Times and Sanger would be willing to put in a statement in support of Cartwright. The prosecutors were looking to give their guy up to six months of prison time, but reserved the right to ask the court for more. Could we help Cartwright out?

I had expected the question, and still I was unprepared for it. The relationship between a confidential source like Cartwright and a reporter is complicated. When reporters agree to keep a source's identity secret, it is a big deal. They are willing to go to jail to protect that secret. But, beyond that, what is owed? It is one of journalism's operating principles that reporters are independent from their sources. They don't pay sources. The journalist and the source are not partners. Reporters avoid taking sides even when the people they have used as sources end up as parties in litigation. Readers expected that sort of professional distance. Readers want us to be honest brokers of the news, not mouthpieces for the people who spoke to us. But Cartwright's case struck me as different. He was not some rogue insider recklessly spilling secrets for political or personal gain. While he was one of many sources in David's reporting on the cyberattack code-named "Olympic Games," they had met late in the process after David knew much about the program. The White House had encouraged David to meet with Cartwright to get fuller grounding on the topic of cyber-weapons.

Still, The Times had never stepped up so publicly in support of a source.

At the end of the afternoon on Election Day, as the newsroom buzzed outside Dean Baquet's office, David and I met with the paper's senior editors to make the case for writing a letter to the sentencing judge. There were risks, I said. The biggest was that the letter could open the door for David to be a witness at the sentencing hearing, where he could be asked about his reporting and his other sources. It seemed unlikely, but over the years we had burned through hundreds of thousands of dollars in legal fees trying to keep our reporters off the witness stand when they received subpoenas. To now voluntarily jump into a criminal case was not in our DNA. The optics of it weren't great either. Any letter we wrote was certain to get coverage, much of it likely to be negative. Times critics would see us as having thrown our support behind a lying general who had betrayed his oath. Over at Fox, they wouldn't overlook the fact that Cartwright was an Obama favorite. Closer to home, some journalism purists were going to say a line gets crossed when journalists decide to link arms with a source in a court proceeding.

Was there a way to avoid all of that and still write a letter that might do Cartwright some good? It was Election Day, and the editors in the room had more pressing things to do than debate the esoterica of a letter, even one that was going to be ridiculously hard to write and take The Times to a place that it had never gone before. They were happy to leave it to David and me to figure all that out.

Writing a letter to Donald Trump's lawyers was one thing; this was another. This one was not going to be from the "let it rip" school of writing. This one was going to require us to keep our eyes on the ultra-thin line between saying something helpful and crossing over into advocacy about what the judge should do in sentencing, all the while avoiding, if we could, putting a target on David's back. It was not hard to picture some eager-beaver federal prosecutors telling the judge they needed to explore through testimony whatever facts we put before the court.

My draft was bare bones, a tight four paragraphs, 11 sentences all in. No need to give the prosecutors anything more than we had to. The letter said that we believed Cartwright had acted in good faith with no intention to harm the country. I forwarded it to Sanger with the message "edit away."

He did.

His version, when it arrived in my inbox a couple of days later, was no "less is more" letter. It was, instead, an attempt to make the judge understand how a certain type of national security journalism got done. Sometimes confidential sources expose misconduct or raise red flags, taking a calculated risk in doing so—think Edward Snowden—but much reporting on national security and law enforcement was like David's. It was not cloak-and-dagger spy stuff, with government secrets triple-locked in a cabinet and then purloined by the source, who nervously passes them to a journalist under the cover of darkness. David had done deep reporting on the country's cyber-warfare capacity, talking first to experts to parse the leaked computer code and find out who had written it. He then used sources in the U.S., Europe, and Israel to learn how the code, known as "Stuxnet," had been written. There is a certain give-and-take to that kind of reporting, even as the reporter and the sources inevitably end up talking about classified matters, with the reporter trying to get the fullest story possible and the government trying to make the case for those facts that really need to be secret.

David's letter explained that his interview with Cartwright had not been extraordinary. At one point, after David laid out to the administration what he planned to publish, the White House had authorized the deputy director of the CIA to meet with David and discuss his reporting and the risks of certain disclosures. And it was also a senior White House official who encouraged David to meet with Cartwright, one of the country's most knowledgeable experts on cyber-warfare. "This is a standard, if little-understood, practice in the course of reporting on sensitive national security affairs," David wrote. "Far from harming U.S. interests, his interview contributed to my efforts to provide the public with a comprehensive account of a critical new element of the American use of force, while trying to avoid harming future operations."

As much as the government postures about how every secret absolutely has to stay secret or the world will go to hell in a handbasket, the reality on the ground is starkly different. For one thing, the government is not particularly good at keeping secrets. At the time that Sanger and Cartwright were talking, more than 790,000 people in government had top-secret security clearance, according to the prosecutors. Overclassification was the government's contagion of choice. In 2016, a House committee reported that the government had spent more than $100 billion over a 10-year period on classification activities. The net result of the bill being handed to taxpayers? An estimated 50 to 90 percent of classified material was not properly labeled. A little-heard-from (thankfully) federal agency called the Information Security Oversight Office issued a report disclosing that there were 92 million decisions made to classify information in 2011 alone. The truth is that the drunken, profligate use of classification was undermining secrecy and making the nation less secure. That was hardly a big or new revelation. Supreme Court Justice Potter Stewart had made the point four decades earlier in the Pentagon Papers case:

> I should suppose that moral, political, and practical considerations would dictate that a very first principle of that wisdom would be an insistence upon avoiding secrecy for its own sake.

For when everything is classified, then nothing is classified, and the system becomes one to be disregarded by the cynical or the careless, and to be manipulated by those intent on self-protection or self-promotion. I should suppose, in short, that the hallmark of a truly effective internal security system would be the maximum possible disclosure, recognizing that secrecy can best be preserved only when credibility is truly maintained.

That message never got through to the Executive Branch.

If you want to understand how topsy-turvy the system of secrecy is, consider this: the intelligence and law enforcement agencies actually authorize the leaking of classified information to reporters at times. There is even a name for the practice: "save the secret." If a reporter is already in possession of classified information, an agency will reveal further information, either to convince the reporter of the risk of publication or to give context to whatever was going to be published. It is all a little inverted—"to save secrets we have to disclose secrets"—but much about governmental secrecy is like that, part real, part illusion, overlooked when it serves the government's purposes, rarely talked about honestly, at least publicly. In 2018, in a brief filed in a case called *Johnson v. CIA*, the CIA baldly argued that certain information remained classified even though the agency had officially provided it to three journalists to use as part of an effort to "protect intelligence sources and methods." Never mind that the information was no longer secret, the court bought the CIA's argument that the information had never been formally declassified and was therefore still classified.

As a lawyer, I wasn't crazy about David's letter. It might be read as an open door for prosecutors interested in finding out the details of his reporting. But it was hard to fault it for the larger point it was making about justice: Cartwright was no leaker, not even a whistleblower. In his compelling account of the recent history of cyber-combat, *The Perfect Weapon: War, Sabotage and Fear in the*

Cyber Age, Sanger would later note that by the time he went to see Cartwright about the Olympic Games, he had already written two chapters about it. "My goal in seeing Cartwright was twofold: to check that I had the history and implications right, and to get an independent view of whether any details I was reporting could jeopardize national security," Sanger wrote. It was, Sanger said in *The Perfect Weapon,* a mystery why the investigators decided to point a finger at Cartwright when so many others had already talked to him about the program before he made his way to the retired general. No one else was ever prosecuted. There was no indication that national security had been harmed by anything in the book or our newspaper stories. Yet, in the final days of the Obama administration, here was a distinguished military officer facing jail time.

We submitted the letter. When the prosecution filed its brief, the government revealed that it had rethought things and now believed Cartwright should get two years in prison, not six months. Sentencing was postponed to the early days of the Trump administration. On January 17, David wrote to me. There were 72 hours to go in the Obama presidency. Was a pardon still a possibility? I knew Cartwright's lawyers had made the request of the White House, but I had heard nothing more. Then, a few hours later, the announcement came: Obama had decided to issue the pardon. Our reporters were later told by sources at the White House that The Times's letter had made a difference. It highlighted Cartwright's role in persuading The Times to withhold some particularly sensitive details. By doing so, it had cut through the prosecution's meanspirited account of Cartwright's actions and put David's interview with Cartwright into context.

Cartwright's pardon was the coda to a perplexing eight years of dealing with leak investigations in the Obama administration. Many reporters and press organizations denounced Obama as an enemy of the free press because his administration had been unusually aggressive in going after leakers. (None of them apparently saw what lay ahead with the next administration. As one former member of the Obama cabinet said to me in year two of the Trump administration, "Miss us yet?") It was not that simple to pigeonhole the Obama record. Some parts of it were deeply troubling. Under Obama, the administration had prosecuted nine government employees or contractors suspected of disclosing classified information to media outlets, according to data compiled by Gabe Rottman of the Reporters Committee for Freedom of the Press. That compared to three in the prior 40 years.

For much of the past half-century, a balance had been struck. Both sides lived in an imperfect world of discretion (a better and dressed-up lawyer term for that "modicum of unlawfulness"). News organizations tried to make informed decisions about what to publish, weighing the risks to the nation and the benefits to the public, and the government held back from tracking down and prosecuting leakers except in the rarest of cases. So the reality on the ground was that if you were an employee toiling away in the government bureaucracy and felt the need to make *The New York Times* aware of some particularly bad move by your agency or boss, you could feel relatively sure that you would not have FBI agents at your door some night. And if you were the president or other high-ranking government official, you could be pretty certain that *The Times* was not going to publish something that jeopardized lives or endangered the nation's security. And for all the outbursts of hysteria about leaks that came from the government side from time to time, few people outside government seriously doubted that the real problem for America was not the unauthorized revelation but an excess of secrecy.

Obama decided that there needed to be less discretion and more prosecution. Maybe the change was driven by the fear and realization that the purveyors of news were no longer just *The New York Times* and *The Washington Post* and the major TV networks but also rogue organizations like WikiLeaks that did not necessarily share traditional journalism's ethical standards. WikiLeaks and even some established news organizations saw those of us in the mainstream as huge sellouts, timid, holding back when the government raised national security concerns, no matter how vague or amorphous. Snowden had specifically chosen to provide his leaked data to news organizations that were not going to engage in conversations with the government before publication—in other words, not *The New York Times*.

Whatever the thinking of the Obama administration, leakers were pursued. The number of prosecutions—the nine cases—may seem tiny in light of all the reporting on classified national security matters that is done week after week by *The Times*, *The Washington Post*, and other major news organizations, much of it fueled by leaks of classified information, but the numbers don't tell the real story. The real story is that those sorts of prosecutions send a one-word message to thousands of others inside government who might be thinking about talking to reporters: Don't.

For once, the Trump administration showed itself eager to emulate the Obama administration. By August 2018, the Department of Justice had brought charges in four national security leak cases involving the media, including the Reality Winner case. (By then, she had pleaded guilty and received a five-year sentence.) The other cases involved a Senate aide, a former FBI agent, and a onetime CIA employee.

There was another side to the Obama approach, though, and most of us in the media were hesitant to say much about it. The Department of Justice had largely refrained from serving subpoenas on reporters intended to force them to identify sources. Two of the major leak prosecutions started under Obama had involved *The Times*: the Cartwright case and the prosecution of John Kiriakou, a former CIA agent who also pleaded guilty. In neither case did government investigators ever contact me or anyone else at *The Times*. The same was true for other investigations that did not lead to prosecutions. There was no showdown with The Times over a reporter's refusal to reveal a source as there had been in 2005 when *Times* reporter Judith Miller went to jail for 12 weeks. The government had grown much better at tracking down leakers without having to come after journalists to provide evidence. The targets' emails, cell phone records, credit card receipts—they became the building blocks for prosecutions. The FBI broke the Cartwright case by subpoenaing his Gmail records from Google and confronting him with contradictions in his earlier statements to agents.

No one in my business could complain about being left alone. Subpoena cases are bruising for news organizations. Federal law provides very little protection to journalists who refuse to name names when subpoenaed. And reporters are the most obvious witnesses to have knowledge of who leaked information. If they refuse to testify, they are not charged with a crime but are held in contempt, allowing the court to send them to jail as a way to pressure them to change their minds. So we end up litigating those cases with little more than an airy hope that something will go right for us as the proceedings grind on, dragging our feet whenever and however we can. Maybe the prosecutors will drop the case. Maybe sources will decide on their own to acknowledge their role. Maybe a plea deal will get struck. Still, even when the prosecutors left our journalists alone, journalists and their lawyers could never feel good about the prosecutions. They inflicted costs on people who helped us, and every one of the investigations made it less likely that some government worker in the future, confronted with wrongdoing or incompetence or misguided policies, was going to be brave enough to talk to a journalist.

While the feds largely let reporters be, there was one huge and disturbing exception: Jim Risen, a *Times* reporter who had written a book that laid out the absolute bungling of U.S. intelligence agents as they schemed to undermine Iran's nuclear program. Jim had originally been subpoenaed under the Bush administration, but Jim refused to cooperate, the case lingered, and Obama came into office. The Department of Justice was able to bring an indictment against Jeffrey Sterling, a former CIA agent, charging him with espionage for purportedly leaking information about the failed Iranian operation. The government did not stand down with the arrival of Obama's team at Justice. They continued to press Risen for his source for the chapter in his book. He continued to say no. After years of proceedings, the case went to the Fourth Circuit Court of Appeals. The court's decision could not have been worse for the news media. With one dissenting vote, the court held that reporters had no right to refuse criminal subpoenas unless the government was acting in bad faith. Risen had not met that standard, the court ruled.

Risen still refused to testify. The prosecutors finally gave up on him, put together their case, and convicted Sterling without Risen's testimony. It seemed like particularly bad legal theater. For years, the DOJ had been saying that Risen's testimony was necessary to get a conviction, and that was simply untrue. The prosecutors had made Risen's life miserable, forcing him to live under the continuous threat of going to jail to protect a source. Along the way, they managed to get an appeals court to issue a decision that undermined the public's right to know. And only at that point, after doing damage, did they walk away from the subpoena. It had all been unnecessary.

Two other ugly incidents also scarred the Obama legacy. In 2013, the DOJ disclosed that it had seized reporters' records in two leak investigations. In the first, FBI agents had secretly obtained the phone company records of reporters for the Associated Press. In the second, FBI agents had obtained the emails and phone records of a Fox News reporter. In the affidavit filed by the FBI to obtain a court order for the email search, an agent had characterized the Fox reporter as engaging in criminal activity by seeking classified information from his government source—in other words, the most routine act of journalism, asking a source for information, was being treated as a crime. The press screamed—in fact, screamed loudly enough for the president to hear. Nothing cuts through the Washington political fog like having both Fox News and the legacy news media jumping up and down in an unhappy frenzy together.

A few weeks after the AP and Fox disclosures, I joined a group of representatives from major news organizations for a meeting in Washington with Eric Holder, the attorney general. The president had directed him to work with the news organizations to come up with policies that would balance the press interests in protecting sources and the needs of law enforcement. Decades earlier, the DOJ had set down "news media guidelines" that prosecutors were to follow before serving a subpoena on a reporter, whether the government was looking for a leaker or simply trying to use reporters as witnesses for other criminal proceedings. The guidelines, which made subpoenas on reporters a last resort to be used only when other investigative means had failed, worked, by and large, although, as the AP and Fox discovered, the rules had gaps.

In truth, federal subpoenas were uncommon for The Times. In the decade-plus since the Miller case, no *Times* journalist had received a federal subpoena seeking a source. (Risen's subpoena had arisen from his book, not from his reporting for *The Times*.) More typical were subpoenas that sought better copies of photos or videos we had already published. A few years ago, *Times* reporter Walt Bogdanich had done an investigative story on how civil servants claimed to be disabled at retirement to feather their own nests. We posted videos online showing some of the retirees out enjoying a long day of free golf (one of the perks of being a disabled retiree at public courses on Long Island). The federal prosecutors subpoenaed us for better-quality copies of what we had put on our website, all the better to convict the retiree/scamsters with. We had no legal objection to giving them what we had already voluntarily made public. The defense lawyers, however, for reasons that were never clear, decided to seek all the outtakes—apparently believing they would help their case by having even more footage of happy-go-lucky golf outings by their fake-disabled clients. Before the judge, the prosecutors could not contain themselves, making like ACLU lawyers on the topic of press freedom as they joined our objection to turning over outtakes and let the court know just how wounded the First Amendment would be if we were compelled to turn over unaired footage of fake-disabled people playing golf. It was quite a performance. And it worked. I was not going to complain about the whiff of hypocrisy.

After the Fox-AP incidents, the DOJ came up with stronger guidelines, and it also started holding regular meetings with representatives of the press to discuss the issues of leaks and protection of sources. With the arrival of Jeff Sessions, safe to say, the DOJ was decidedly less enthusiastic about sitting down with the media to discuss how to minimize press subpoenas. As if to accentuate the obvious, the Department of Justice served its first subpoena on a reporter three weeks into the Trump presidency, demanding that a radio reporter in Oregon testify about his interview with one of the ranchers involved in the armed takeover at the Malheur National Wildlife Refuge. It was no leak investigation. It was instead a bare-knuckled attempt to commandeer reporters into being agents of the prosecution, helping make the case against a newsmaker who was interviewed. A judge ultimately quashed the subpoena, but the message was sent to the press—and to those who might now want to think twice about agreeing to interviews.

Soon enough, Sessions had gone public with his intentions to change the department's subpoena guidelines. The details were sketchy, the direction was not: he intended to roll back the protections. Picking up on one of his boss's favorite themes, he was gleeful to point out that the department had tripled the number of active leak investigations. Sessions would later tell Congress 27 leak investigations were in progress, although it seemed unlikely that all or even most of them involved leaks to the media. Sessions drew the line on giving reporters a pass in his new leak-investigations-on-steroids program. "We must balance the press' role with protecting our national security and the lives of those who serve in the intelligence community, the armed forces, and all law-abiding Americans," he said. It was all about a "culture of leaking" in his mind—that would be the culture that was threatening to provide a few truths to all those law-abiding Americans. "When few investigations take place, criminal leaks may occur more often, and a culture of leaking can take hold. So today, I have this message for our friends in the intelligence community. The Department of Justice is open for business, and I have this warning for would-be leakers: Don't do it."

Surprisingly absent—or maybe it wasn't so surprising—was any acknowledgment that most of the high-profile leaking in the early days of the Trump presidency posed no threat to national security but instead involved the investigation into the ties between the Trump campaign and the Russians or the foreign policy missteps of the new administration. Going forward, critical reporting was going to be done under a cloud. Even though the DOJ did not move ahead with its plan to weaken the rules limiting subpoenas on news organizations, the possibilities of a crackdown on leaks and subpoenas for reporters could never be far from our minds.

The zeal of President Trump to use the DOJ to pursue government insiders who went to the press was dramatically underscored in September 2018 when *The Times* published an op-ed from a senior government official who signed the piece "Anonymous." The article laid out how there was a "resistance" inside the administration, a group of officials quietly working to deter the president from taking actions that undermined U.S. interests or the rule of law.

Shortly before the op-ed was published, James Dao, the editor of the op-ed section, called me out of the blue. He let me in on the secret that we had received the piece, and he wanted to know whether I saw any legal problems. I was sure the article was going to be provocative but nothing struck me as a legal concern. Our news columns had been filled with insider accounts, as had a series of books about the Trump White House, all detailing the chaos and backstabbing inside. Interesting to now have someone do it firsthand through our opinion pages, but nothing groundbreaking. Jim and I talked again the next day, and we were confident that we had taken the necessary steps to make sure the official's identity was protected. As Jim would later write in a piece for *The Times*, the op-ed had come about when an intermediary for Anonymous had reached out to the paper to see if there was an interest in publishing it.

"Should I tell you who it is?" Jim asked at one point in our first call. I didn't want to know. Well, as a reader and a citizen and a generally curious person, I really, really wanted to know. But as a lawyer I prefer to work on a need-to-know basis when it comes to confidential sources. Typically, it is enough for me to know in general terms the source's position and how the source could be in a place to witness what we were about to report, but I think we're better off limiting who inside The Times knows the identity to an absolute minimum. It reduces the risk of inadvertent disclosures and gives sources greater confidence that their identities will be protected. Still, there are times when I come to learn the identities. Reporters volunteer the name to me sometimes, or I need to know because it helps me assess whether we should be concerned about a libel claim and our ability to defend against a future lawsuit. It doesn't always go the way you would think. Once, as the editors and I were working through an unusually hard-hitting story about the illegal activities of a businessman, I expressed grave doubts whether any unnamed source could confirm the details we were about to put in the paper. He's one of the sources, I was told, the businessman himself.

Dao would later say he was surprised by the overwhelming reaction to the piece by Anonymous. So was I. Caught up in a flurry of other business, I had pretty much forgotten that the op-ed was in the works until a friend's email popped up on that Wednesday afternoon with the subject line "Wow. What an Op-Ed." I clicked over to the home page to read the piece for the first time. Within 24 hours, 10 million other readers had done the same thing. When Dao agreed to take questions about the op-ed for a *Times* feature, more than 23,000 people queried him.

Trump went ballistic, blasting The Times and the writer and calling the piece an act of treason. Before the week was out he had asked the Justice Department to find out who Anonymous was. It seemed beyond preposterous. No classified information was even hinted at in the op-ed. Nothing illegal was remotely suggested. An official disagreed with the president and chose to use *The Times* to make the criticism public. It happened every day in every administration. The context was dramatic—an unsigned op-ed—but it was business as usual in a democracy.

Still, this was a new era in Washington, and the president had been hammering away at Attorney General Sessions for months for failing to do the White House's bidding. Our top editors and executives wanted to know in real time whether the law would protect the paper's right to keep the identity secret. I was pinned down with an emergency overseas, so my two young colleagues, Al-Amyn Sumar (in his first week on the job) and Christina Koningisor (on her last day), dropped everything to crank out a memo over the course of 90 minutes laying out various legal theories. They did a brilliant job. Of course, no one could answer the question of whether the government was going to care about the law and abide by it.

In the midst of that morning, Dao showed up in Legal. We retreated to a conference room. He had come to tell me that he wanted me to hold on to papers from the publication of the piece. He held up an unsealed envelope. With the story of Anonymous exploding around me, the temptation was enormous, but I hesitated. I knew my own rules, and I knew myself. I asked him to seal the envelope. I sat saying nothing as he licked the flap, sealed it, and signed it before he handed the envelope over to me.

Leak investigations can take strange turns. From time to time, I would be contacted by attorneys looking for our reporters to do something to help quietly clear their client who was caught up in a leak investigation. They made it sound simple: tell prosecutors that their client had not been a source. But it wasn't that simple. For one thing, we knew that by telling the prosecutors that any particular person was not the source, we were increasing the likelihood that a case could be made against someone else. Only so many suspects are targeted in any investigation. It also made our reporter look like a willing witness for further questions from investigators.

More awkward was when the attorneys showed up on behalf of a client who had assured the lawyers that it was all a misunderstanding—he was no leaker. I once had a long, difficult meeting with attorneys for the target of an investigation who wanted our reporter to confirm that no classified information had passed during the reporter's interview with the guy now caught in the investigators' crosshairs. The reporter couldn't do that. It would have been a lie. I tried to figure out why the lawyers were even asking. It may have been that at a time when overclassification is rampant, the source didn't realize what was secret or what was not as he spoke to the journalist. Or maybe he just didn't recall the interview clearly. The reporter had been taking notes; he hadn't. Or maybe he wasn't being honest with his attorneys and thought we would help him out. Who knows? In another case, a source who was under investigation came forward looking for us to help show that his interview had been authorized by his agency as part of a "save the secret" session. The reporter had every reason to believe that the interview was no leak but an authorized disclosure designed to get certain information about governmental surveillance out to the public. I worked with the source's lawyer through the awkward business of trying to get language into a letter that would help his client but not open our reporter up to being a witness if the prosecutors wanted to question him. We finally got to language that worked for both of us. I never learned whether the letter made a difference.

As sure as I was that leaks, in the end, made America stronger, there was a troubling new development that made the whole topic more complicated. Once upon time, unauthorized disclosures meant a guy like Daniel Ellsberg, a government contractor concerned about the lies being told to the American people by their government, standing at a copy machine making copies of the Pentagon Papers. Now there was hacking—which shared little in common with the leak of information by someone inside the walls of government but tended to get rolled into the same conversation. Hostile foreign governments launched cyberattacks to steal email accounts and then released them through intermediaries, knowing the press would not be able to resist publishing. The North Koreans hacked Sony in 2014, unhappy about a silly movie that Sony was making about that funniest of topics: North Korea. The spoof had the CIA hiring two reporters to assassinate Kim Jong-un after an interview. The stolen emails showed the insidious games played by Hollywood insiders but little more. Sony's outside lawyers wrote letters threatening lawsuits against any publisher who used the emails. Even they must have known it was an empty threat. U.S. law allowed news organizations to publish the emails if they chose, just as we were legally free to publish the pages from Trump's tax returns. Still, being a tool of the North Korean security apparatus felt wrong. Our editors resolved that we shouldn't break any stories. If accounts based on emails became public elsewhere, nothing was to be gained by standing down, and we could follow up with our own stories, but we didn't want to lead the parade for Kim Jong-un.

Then came the hacks of the Democrats' email systems during the 2016 election by the Russians. WikiLeaks ended up with a set of the documents and pushed them out. The hacking wasn't all that different from that of Sony. A foreign power hostile to the United States was attacking nongovernmental systems. However uneasy that made editors feel, the documents were too important to ignore. They shed light on the biggest story of the year, the presidential election. Besides, the press is not a monolith. There is no collective decision-making. If there were, maybe more judicious use of the documents would have been made. But competition drove publishers, and voters undoubtedly learned valuable information. Yet anyone thinking beyond the next big story couldn't help but wonder whether hacker-aided journalism was doing damage to America.

But that issue was not getting much air time. The narrative about the harm from leaks had been hijacked by Trump and General Thomas with their implausible tale of how *The Times* had published secrets that allowed the leader of ISIS to escape. Thomas had given his account of that at a forum in Aspen. For the general, it soon became a "people who live in glass houses" moment. During his appearance at the forum, he was also asked about a *Washington Post* story that was based on confidential sources and reported that President Trump had decided to cease CIA funding of the rebels fighting against the Syrian government, a move that would surely please the Russians as Syria's allies. Thomas rushed in with an insider account. "From at least what I know about that program and the decision to end it, [it was] absolutely not a sop to the Russians," he said. "It was I think based on an assessment of the nature of the program, what we're trying to accomplish, the viability of it going forward, and it was a tough, tough decision."

It was not just a tough, tough decision by the president. It was a top-secret tough, tough decision. No one in the government was authorized to talk publicly about the funding or its cessation. Maybe Jeff Sessions should have opened one more leak investigation, declared the Aspen Institute a crime scene, and put up yellow tape around the meeting hall.

8

The Don of Defamation

Really dumb @CheriJacobus. Begged my people for a job. Turned her down twice and she went hostile. Major loser, zero credibility!

—Donald Trump tweet, Feb. 5, 2016
(Tweet that prompted Cheri Jacobus to sue for libel)

The president is very pleased with this decision. He believes that justice was served.

—Trump lawyer Lawrence Rosen, Dec. 12, 2017
(after Cheri Jacobus lost an appeal of her libel case)

THE TIMES'S FIRST libel suit of the Trump era showed up in May 2017. For months, people in the media and in legal circles had been anxiously predicting that libel suits would once again be the litigation weapon of choice for well-heeled conservatives hoping to inflict pain on the liberal media they despised. And why not? Trump's toxic incantation of "fake news," his own long history of threatening libel suits, the weakened financial state of legacy media—these were ripe conditions for politically tinted libel suits. And the first one to come could not have been more infused with the flavor of Trump. The plaintiffs were six coal companies that had one thing in common: they were all owned by Bob Murray, the coal baron whose enthusiasm for a president who loved, loved, loved coal mining knew no bounds.

The Murray suit was pinned to an editorial that *The Times* wrote about Murray and other big-dollar contributors to the president's inauguration. The Murray suit, filed in coal-friendly West Virginia, was a throwback to old-time libel lawsuits when the rich and powerful summoned their lawyers at the first sign of unfavorable press. *The Times* editorial, published in April, had raised questions about the rich people who financed the inaugural events and whether they expected some help from the new administration on the back end with federal regulations they would like to see stricken from the books—among them, those annoying regulations about health, safety, and the environment for coal mining. One paragraph dealt with Bob Murray. It mentioned that Murray Energy is a "serial violator of federal health and safety rules" and then noted that Bob himself had "falsely insisted that the 2007 collapse of his Crandall Canyon mine, which killed six workers, was due to an earthquake."

The Murray companies did not deny that they had racked up their share of federal health and safety violations, but they were unhappy with the label "serial violator," which they said made it sound as if they were the worst companies in the industry when in fact their dreadful record was just like the dreadful record of every other coal company—sort of the "we're all serial violators here" defense. Crandall Canyon was more complicated. At least two major investigations had concluded that the mine collapse was not caused by any earthquake—the federal government determined that the disaster was caused by unauthorized mining practices—although, yes, there was seismic activity in the area that tragic day. Even Murray's lawyers stopped short of saying that it was an actual earthquake, instead opting to say that the mine collapse was caused by "something that is commonly understood as an earthquake." As The Times's feisty West Virginia lawyers Holly Planinsic and Bob Fitzsimmons pointed out to the court, "something that is commonly understood as an earthquake" is by definition not really an earthquake. Lest there was any doubt about the larger context of the suit, Murray's complaint reprised that The Times had endorsed Hillary Clinton and broadly suggested that may have been the source of the problem with the editorial. A company press representative apparently concerned that the connection was too subtle issued a statement: "The New York Times, of course, supported Hillary Clinton, who famously declared her agenda to 'put a lot of coal miners and coal companies out of business.' Murray Energy instituted this suit, in part, in [an] attempt to ensure that such an agenda is not furthered by The New York Times' false and defamatory statements."

Shortly after our editorial ran, HBO's brilliant comedian John Oliver decided to do a tribute to Bob Murray, or, as Oliver called him, "a geriatric Dr. Evil." Oliver marched through the Murray companies' woeful record on safety and health and reprised an incident in which Murray miners, offended by the paltry bonus checks they received, returned them to the company with "Eat shit, Bob" and "Kiss my ass, Bob" scrawled on them. Oliver's big finish came when a giant squirrel named Mr. Nutterbutter appeared. (Inside joke: there were rumors that Murray had decided to start his company after a squirrel advised him to do so.) The squirrel then announced, "Hey, Bob, just wanted to say, if you plan on suing, I do not have a billion dollars. But I do have a check for three acorns and eighteen cents. It's made out to, 'Eat shit, Bob!' Memo line: 'Kiss my ass!'"

Murray was not pleased. Which was how we came to have HBO as a travel companion on our voyage through the West Virginia judicial system, each of us facing separate Bob Murray defamation suits. The Times moved to dismiss the case—we were confident that our statements about Murray happened to be true—and HBO did the same. It was then that Jamie Lynn Crofts showed up. Jamie Lynn Crofts is the legal director of the American Civil Liberties Union in West Virginia. She wanted to know whether she could file an amicus brief in our case and HBO's to help make the point that Murray's libel lawsuits should be dismissed. Briefs have a long and distinguished place in American legal history. They are, at their apex, dispassionate explications of complex legal principles, filled with careful citations to binding legal precedents and finely crafted logical arguments. Safe to say that there had never been a brief quite like the one that Jamie Lynn Crofts and the ACLU wanted to file. One of the headings proclaimed: "Anyone Can Legally Say, Eat Shit, Bob!" Elsewhere it opined that it was "apt that one of Plaintiffs' objections to the show is about a human-sized squirrel named Mr. Nutterbutter, because this case is nuts." It went on to lay out a fundamental principle of American libel law: "You Can't Sue People for Being Mean to You, Bob."

It was a great brief. It was unmistakably right about the First Amendment. Defamation suits can't be based on insults or opinions or hurt feelings. Plaintiffs must instead prove that there is a factual error that harmed their reputation. More than that, the ACLU brief said all those delicious things that lawyers usually wish they could say about the people who sue their clients—and then, lawyers being lawyers, don't say. Of course, sometimes The New York Times can't help but be The New York Times. Which is why I got on the phone to tell Jamie Lynn Crofts that we would appreciate it if she did not file her brief in our case. It was hilarious, it was irreverent, it was laced with obscenities. In other words, it was everything *The Times* was not. We worried that it would be a distraction in our case, which after all was based on two passing factual sentences in a decidedly unfunny and sober-minded editorial. John Oliver's bit was fantastic, but we didn't want the courts to see our editorial as one piece in some broader no-holds-barred takedown of Bob Murray. The ACLU filed its brief only in the HBO case. We went it alone.

Upon reflection, that may not have been the smartest legal calculation of my life. Maybe Jamie Lynn's brief had nothing to do with it, but the sad reality is that in the HBO case the judge dismissed Murray's lawsuit while the judge in our case decided that the case should proceed to further fact-finding on whether our two statements were true. The unmistakable message: the First Amendment protected Mr. Nutterbutter saying "Kiss my ass" and "Eat shit, Bob"—those were clearly not statements of fact—but was not so certain about our calling Murray's business a "serial violator." That actually makes sense in the law of libel, no matter how screwy it may sound to the world at large, or how unhappy it made me.

Even before Trump's drum-banging about the need to make it easier to sue, libel had become an unavoidable topic of news coverage, public conversation, fretting, and, now and then, confusion. For years, libel had been largely off the radar, with few high-profile suits being brought. Then *Rolling Stone* magazine had been sued for a botched 2014 article telling the story of a University of Virginia undergraduate who said she was raped at a fraternity party. Following publication, huge holes were found in the tale provided by the undergraduate—identified only as Jackie in the story—and *Rolling Stone* found itself on the wrong end of a libel suit brought by a university dean mentioned in the article (a jury in 2017 awarded her $3 million, an amount later reduced by settlement), the fraternity (the magazine settled for $1.65 million), and three members of the frat (the case was settled confidentially). ABC, which had reported extensively on what the network called "pink slime"—an unappetizing meat product sold to school cafeterias and restaurants— was sued by a meatpacking company that claimed the ABC stories made the product sound unsafe. In midtrial in 2017, ABC settled. The full amount was not disclosed, but public filings by ABC show that it was more than $177 million, and maybe a lot more, an amount never before seen in American libel litigation. Buzzfeed, the cheeky online news outlet, became a magnet for libel litigation when it published the infamous "dossier"—the compilation of research done by a former British spy about the connections between the Trump campaign and the Russians, including the over-the-top allegation that the Russians had a tape of Trump frolicking with prostitutes in a Russian hotel. At a January 2017 press conference, just after the publishing of the dossier, the president-elect deemed Buzzfeed "a failing pile of garbage." Buzzfeed responded by selling "Failing Pile of Garbage" T-shirts. Less funny for Buzzfeed was the libel suit that followed, not from Trump but from a Russian businessman named Aleksej Gubarev, who was mentioned in the dossier. A Russian bank followed with its own suit against Buzzfeed over another section from the dossier. Then came a libel suit from a particularly unlikely source, Trump's personal lawyer, Michael Cohen, another person cited in the dossier. The wheels soon fell off that case when Cohen sank into his own deep well of legal problems, finally hitting bottom with a guilty plea to eight crimes. Buzzfeed aggressively fought back against all the suits.

Inevitably, the conversations about the resurgence of libel claims swept in the lawsuit brought by professional wrestler Hulk Hogan (real name: Terry Bollea) against the scandalmongering website Gawker, although it wasn't a libel suit. It was an invasion-of-privacy case, born of Gawker's decision to play some highlights of a video showing Hogan having sex with his best friend's wife, shot in the woman's bedroom. Hogan said he was emotionally ruined when the video was aired, despite his frequent bragging on radio shows (including one hosted by the best friend whose wife was in the video) about his sexual prowess. Gawker said the video was newsworthy. A jury in St. Petersburg, Florida, said Gawker should pay Hogan $140 million. The verdict forced Gawker out of business and into bankruptcy. Hogan settled for $31 million. But one of the more shocking parts of the whole sad saga was the disclosure after trial that Hogan's lawsuit had been financed by a Silicon Valley billionaire, Peter Thiel, whose animosity toward Gawker came, at least in part, from a 2007 story on a Gawker website headlined "Peter Thiel Is Totally Gay, People." Convinced that his personal life was nobody's business and Gawker was an online menace, he began secretly funding the legal fees of people with lawsuits against Gawker.

The idea that billionaires were using their riches to attack media companies they did not like was unsettling. It was easy to conjure up dark visions of America's plutocrats—tired of spending their mountains of cash on seaside mansions, impossibly large yachts, and third or fourth wives—turning their impatient attention to breaking the backs of America's media companies with punishing litigation. Only the picture was not that simple or clear. For one thing, litigation financing was usually not illegal and in fact had been viewed as a protected First Amendment activity by none other than the U.S. Supreme Court at the height of the civil rights movement. In the early 1960s, Virginia had passed a law aimed at preventing the NAACP from financing civil rights suits brought by individuals victimized by discrimination. The court struck down the law as unconstitutional, finding that the funding of litigation was a protected form of speech. The funding of frivolous suits, designed not to rectify a wrong but instead to inflict hurt on a defendant, was a different matter, but the line between a long-shot lawsuit and a frivolous one is often undetectable, at least in the eyes of many judges. And supporters of Hogan and Thiel pointed out, accurately, that most media companies carried insurance to cover their fees in libel and privacy cases. They saw litigation funding for plaintiffs as a leveling of the playing field. Of course, there was one difference worth thinking about: publishers were required in most courts to disclose right away whether they had insurance policies to cover the case. That seemed very different from the shadowy world of private litigation financing, where typically no one other than the plaintiff—not the judge, not the defendant, not the public—knew whose bankroll was behind the case. It lent itself to a system in which marginal cases would be kept alive for political reasons, reasonable settlement offers would be rejected, and litigation strategies aimed at running up the other side's costs rather than getting at the truth (or even just winning) would be the norm.

It was hard to know what to make of the Gawker verdict itself, though. The case was an outlier in many ways. The testimony of Gawker's witnesses had been deplorable. The case was tried in St. Petersburg, Florida, Hogan's home turf, where he was a hero. Had Gawker been properly insured and able to go forward with the litigation, the case would likely have been won on appeal. Privacy cases are rarely brought and almost never won. Publishers are able to prevail, even when a disclosure is salacious and offensive and tasteless (that would be any video showing Hulk Hogan having sex with anyone under any circumstances), if the publishers are able to establish that their publication was "newsworthy" or in the "public interest." Courts are reluctant to second-guess editors' decisions about what constitutes news and what the public needs to know. Right after the Gawker verdict, *The Times* published a piece quoting media lawyers as saying the verdict in the case was wrong and regrettable but predicting it did not mark the start of a trend—that is, this is no big deal. Gawker's general counsel and I engaged in a polite back-and-forth one night at a bar association meeting about whether that was so. Later, a couple of lawyers for tabloid news sites confided in me that the real problem was that Gawker "didn't know how to do sex tapes." As this was not an area of legal expertise I had spent much time on during my career at The New York Times, I admitted to a certain curiosity about how "to do sex tapes." The playbook, it turned out, was this: A website should first say in a story on day one that Mr. Celebrity was having an affair with Ms. Other Guy's Wife but not go to the videotape. Then when Mr. Celebrity denounced the report as scurrilous fiction and claimed nothing was going on, the website could then unleash the video evidence on day two, which was of course now extremely "newsworthy" and totally in the "public interest" to put to rest the raging and consequential controversy over whether Mr. Celebrity was an adulterer or not.

For those who believed that libel suits were going to be weaponized by conservatives, the theory ran like this: Put aside the idea that American libel law is set up to protect the publishers and make

it difficult for libel plaintiffs to win. Not only was the president filling the federal bench with conservative judges, his "fake news" message seemed to be resonating with some portion of the public. Jury
pools were going to be drawn from the same population that was
being tracked by pollsters. If 45 percent of the people thought that
the press willfully told lies about the Trump administration, no one
should be surprised if juries doubted evidence showing that an error made by journalists was a good-faith mistake and not part of a
plot to get somebody. Jurors who thought they were sitting in judgment of the enemy of the American people were not likely to give
journalists the benefit of the doubt. All of that made the idea of suing seem less like a hopeless long shot and a lot more like a viable
alternative for people who were unhappy with the media, or unhappy with their coverage in the media, or just unhappy.

In the four years prior to Inauguration Day, only four libel suits
had been filed against The Times (if you didn't count the occasional
loony tunes filings by pro se litigants). We had been seeing the downward trend for years. We liked to think that the drop-off in suits
was the result of our policy of not paying money to plaintiffs to
settle libel suits against the newspaper in the United States.
(The Times Company had paid on fairly rare occasions to settle
cases for its other publications and in lawsuits brought abroad.)
The no-pay model had been a Times policy dating back to the
1920s. In 1922, Adolph Ochs, the publisher of The Times and
great-great-grandfather of the current publisher, wrote in a letter:

> I would never settle a libel suit to save a little money. If we have
> damaged a person, we are prepared to pay all he can get the final
> court to award, and we accept the decision as part of the exigen-
> cies of our business. I am aware that in some cases this may cost
> us more than necessary, but in the long run I think it is a wise
> policy.

The truth was that no one knew what was driving down the numbers. Nothing dramatic had changed in the law or the nature of the legal system over the preceding decade. Maybe plaintiffs' lawyers were just catching up with how hard it was to win a libel suit (The Times Company had not lost a U.S. libel case over a *New York Times* article in decades) and how much work was involved. A lawyer's time was better spent on a decent car crash or a good slip-and-fall. Even libel suits from abroad had tapered off. The internet in the late 1990s and early 2000s pushed us into foreign countries, and then into foreign courts, and at one point in 2009 we had eight cases pending abroad, including in countries like China and Iraq and Indonesia, whose legal systems ranged from incomprehensible to unfair and permanently broken. Then those foreign suits disappeared, too. Over a stretch from 2009 to 2017, we had only one foreign libel suit, brought in Russia by one of Putin's cronies. Perhaps it goes without saying: we did not win.

Then in May 2017, just months after Trump took office, Murray's suit against The Times landed. Three days later, an Ohio State University professor sued us over a story about a controversy that had broken out over the accuracy of his cancer research. While not political, the complaint plunged headfirst into the fight between the Trump administration and the news media. After dozens of pages claiming the story was false, the complaint veered and made sneering reference to the ad campaign that The Times had launched in response to Trump's attacks. "The Times was in the midst of a massive marketing campaign, rolled out in January of 2017, positioning itself as a warrior for truth, with such taglines as: Truth. It Is Hard to Find." Then, barely five weeks later, another libel suit was lodged, this one by Sarah Palin, the conservative icon and former Republican vice presidential candidate. The suit arose from a less-than-clear editorial hastily written about gun control following the shooting attack on congressional Republicans at a baseball field in

Virginia. Palin claimed that the editorial blamed her political advertising for prompting Jared Loughner to shoot Congresswoman Gabrielle Giffords in 2011 during an appearance at a shopping center in Tucson, Arizona. Papers served by Palin's lawyers made clear that they wanted to use the case to investigate not just the writing of the editorial but whether there was a wide-ranging bias against Palin and other conservatives throughout The Times.

To have three libel suits in seven weeks to start 2017 felt ominous in the midst of the president's regular carpet-bombing of the press on Twitter, the discouraging poll numbers on trust in the media, and the administration's frightening embrace of the notion that there were "alternative facts." A couple of years earlier, I had worked on a pro bono project in Montenegro with a newspaper that was in open warfare with a government devoted to silencing the independent media. The government's tactics were familiar anywhere autocratic regimes flourish—random violence against journalists, government financing of favored news outlets, the demonizing of independent journalists by top officials in the government, questioning their loyalty and patriotism. Libel lawsuits were an essential tool of oppression, too. I asked the editors at the Montenegro newspaper about the current status of libel suits brought against the paper. They pulled out a huge spreadsheet filled with some 25 cases. In the spring of 2017, back in America, I wondered whether that was the new normal we were heading toward.

Whether you thought that the press was under siege from runaway libel suits or whether you were in the "it's too soon to say" camp, the problem in spotting any trend was the same. It was the problem of small numbers. Not many libel cases are ever filed. If a paper has two libel cases one year and four the next, the urge to say that libel suits have shockingly doubled in just one year's time was strong—and media lawyers were nothing if not alarmist—but maybe upon honest reflection we were talking about a strange fluke rather than the end of a free press as we know it.

Before Murray and Palin, as the number of Times libel suits declined over the previous two decades, cases brought by the rich and powerful had been the rarest of exceptions for us. Their lawyers wrote letters by the pound. The threat letter was pretty much a cottage industry among Beverly Hills law firms with Hollywood clients who seemed to faint at the utterance of an unkind word in a review. But the lawyers on the other side knew what we knew: Unless something had gone seriously wrong inside The Times, the law gave them little shot of winning. They would have to prove not just that the story was false and defamatory but that The Times had acted with actual malice—meaning, for all intents and purposes, that we knew the story was wrong and published it anyway. Good luck with that. We always worried more about the lawsuit brought by the minor players who wandered through the bottom halves of stories. They tended to be private individuals, and therefore the law made it easier for them to win—and at times coverage of them was a little thin or lacking in context. They sometimes sued not because something was actually wrong but because of what you might think of as the "Google effect." They were mentioned in stories about real villains, and they now faced a life sentence of being permanently associated on the internet with those bad guys. Every time someone did a Google search for their names, no matter how innocent their own behavior had been or how remote their connection to the real subjects of the piece was, up would pop the article.

When I came to The Times in 2002, the "little guy" lawsuit was a staple of my work, thanks to the company's ownership of a group of smaller newspapers and broadcast stations in local markets. They generated the kinds of lawsuits that spoke to close-to-the-ground local journalism: the TV report that ran the security-camera picture of a woman using a stolen ATM card, only it was the wrong woman (we blamed the police for giving us the wrong video); the lawyer-turned-fringe-congressional-candidate who was called a "dope" and a "birther" in online reader comments (he claimed he never said that Obama was born abroad, only that he just wasn't sure); the family that made low-rent commercial videos of young women in bikinis fighting but were described as "pornographers" in the paper (not exactly a film genre that has captured America's imagination). One of our papers managed, incredibly, to be sued over a picture of a small child on Santa's lap. The picture was taken at a community party for needy children, only the kid in the photo wasn't actually needy, nor was her mother, with whom she lived. The girl had been brought to the charity party by her divorced and lamebrained father who wangled his way in for some no-cost entertainment for the kid on dad's weekend.

But now it was Sarah Palin and Bob Murray. The Palin case, like Murray's, had its roots in an editorial. On the morning of June 14, a gunman opened fire on Republican congressmen as they practiced at a Virginia ball diamond for a charity baseball game. That evening, *The Times* went online with an editorial condemning the violent rhetoric that had infected politics and pushing for stricter gun control laws. The editorial included two paragraphs about Palin:

> Was this attack evidence of how vicious American politics has become? Probably. In 2011, when Jared Lee Loughner opened fire in a supermarket parking lot, grievously wounding Representative Gabby Giffords and killing six people, including a 9-year-old girl, the link to political incitement was clear. Before the shooting, Sarah Palin's political action committee circulated a map of targeted electoral districts that put Ms. Giffords and 19 other Democrats under stylized crosshairs.
>
> Conservative and right-wing media were quick on Wednesday to demand forceful condemnation of hate speech and crimes by anti-Trump liberals. They're right. Though there's no sign of incitement as direct as in the Giffords attack, liberals should of course hold themselves to the same standard of decency that they ask of the right.

Social media lit up minutes after the piece went live. There was no proof that Loughner had ever seen the Palin campaign ad, which showed Giffords's congressional district in crosshairs. The sentence referring to "incitement as direct as in the Giffords attack" became a lightning rod. Editors at *The Times* quickly concluded that they needed to fix the piece. The next morning *The Times* published a correction and revised the language of the editorial. Thirteen days after the editorial came out, Palin filed a libel suit claiming that her reputation had been sullied and that she had been financially damaged by *The Times*'s piece.

Whatever the merits of the case, the fact that Sarah Palin, a darling of the Trump movement, was suing The New York Times, that bastion of all things liberal, was too rich of a story line for anyone to ignore, on the right or on the left. The right saw their champion giving The Times its long-overdue comeuppance. Palin had just been photographed wandering the halls of the White House with Kid Rock, mocking a portrait of Hillary Clinton. On the other end of the political spectrum, it was taken as further evidence that Trump's cronies were intent on lashing and silencing The Times with burdensome lawsuits, envisioning a world in which Fox News was ascendant, one more step on the path to the complete Foxification of America.

The judge, Jed Rakoff of the Southern District of New York, had other ideas. He dismissed the case, finding that Palin could not credibly allege that The Times had acted with reckless disregard of the truth in making the error, the standard that Palin needed to meet as a public figure. As Rakoff saw it, the notion that *The Times* had intentionally published a falsehood about Palin made little sense, not when the correction came so quickly, when *The Times* in a news article—on the very same day—reported that there was no evidence linking the shooter Loughner to the Palin political ad, when no reasonable person could have thought that a misstatement about Palin in a paper as closely read and critiqued as *The Times* would slide by unnoticed. It looked to the court more like an honest mistake, and Palin would need to show more than that if she hoped to win her case.

Palin appealed and in 2018 the case continues to wend its way through the federal court system. Meanwhile, the Murray suit was settled without payment.

As it turned out, after getting those first three libel cases, the old calm returned, at least for the time being. Over the rest of the year, only one more libel suit was filed, more or less par for the course, a case brought by a Florida professor with strong objections to a story we had done two years earlier about his involvement in the controversy over genetically modified food.

Trend or no trend, Trump himself was still in the defamation lawsuit game in 2017. Just not in the way you would expect. Over the course of his life as a real estate tycoon, gambling magnate, and reality TV star, he couldn't seem to stop himself from threatening to sue people for defamation—it was like some sort of strange tic— and, on rare occasions, he actually followed through. But in January, with his inauguration just a few days away, a New York state court was weighing in on a decidedly different type of Trump libel case—one in which he was the defendant, accused of having been the defamer rather than the defamed. Trump won, but the decision in his favor was much more than just another court victory. He and his lawyers had become legal trailblazers of sorts, arguing that nobody but a pea-brain would come to Twitter expecting to find . . . well, the truth. Yes, Donald Trump had become a First Amendment pioneer.

The court case had its roots in a dust-up between then candidate Trump and Cheri Jacobus, a Republican strategist who doubled as a CNN talking head during the presidential campaign. She regularly used her CNN gig to say things about Trump in 2015 and 2016 that ranged from unkind to unflattering and back again. What happened next is not surprising. What happened next is that

Donald Trump pulled out his cell phone and gave Cheri a Twitter beating. He pronounced her "really dumb" and a "major loser" and suggested she was honked off because she had "begged" his campaign for a job and been turned down. She declared that the tweet was untrue, damaged her emotionally, and scarred her reputation—all of which is to say she sued Donald Trump for libel.

She soon ran headlong into Trump's "Hey, It's Just Twitter" defense. To be the subject of a legitimate libel suit, the offending statement has to be a statement of fact that is inaccurate. Statements of clear opinion, hyperbole, name-calling, loose and colorful language, rank speculation, insults—they may sting, they may inflict emotional distress and hurt the person's standing in the community, but they are not libelous if reasonable readers would not take them to be factual statements. To be libelous a statement has to be false, and there is no such thing as a false opinion (dumb, misguided, crass, uninformed, yes, but never false).

In moving to dismiss the case, Trump's lawyers framed the anti-Jacobus tweet as a textbook example of opinionating, protected by the First Amendment. The judge agreed. Taking her star turn as a literary critic well schooled in the genre known as Trumpian Tweets, she showed a deep appreciation for the author's style: "His tweets about his critics, necessarily restricted to 140 characters or less, are rife with vague and simplistic insults such as 'loser' or 'total loser' or 'totally biased loser,' 'dummy' or 'dope' or 'dumb,' 'zero/no credibility,' 'crazy' or 'wacko,' and 'disaster,' all deflecting serious consideration." And then she cast a critical eye on Twitter itself. She doubted whether people anywhere should be saying that they saw something on Twitter and believed it to be factual. "Indeed, to some, truth itself has been lost in the cacophony of online and Twitter verbiage to such a degree that it seems to roll off the consciousness like water off a duck's back." If no reasonable person could expect to find anything approximating facts in the cesspool of hate, lies, and insults that Twitter had become, it was pretty much a libel-free zone, a place where anyone could say just about anything about anyone without fear of a libel suit. The judge conceded that Trump's motive was "to belittle and demean" Jacobus—not nice, and thoroughly unbecoming, but, more to the point, not the stuff of a libel claim. If there was no statement that could be reasonably read to convey facts, there could be no falsity, and that meant there was no libel case.

When the decision was handed down, Jacobus's lawyer declared it "a sad day for freedom of speech, a sad day for the First Amendment, and a sad day for democracy." In other words, he got it completely backward. It was actually a pretty good day for the first two, and the judge was hardly to blame for the third. Every day tends to be a sad day for democracy on Twitter. But the blame is properly placed in large measure on Twitter itself, which stands like a man on the edge of his lakefront property, hands firmly in his pockets, shrugging, as his lake fills with raw sewage, dead fish floating to the surface. The disappointment of Jacobus's lawyer was understandable (a lawyer who doesn't hate losing is a lawyer not worth hiring), and he did have his finger on a problem. Somebody should do something about Twitter to make it what it could be and should be—a voice for common people to speak out in astonishing numbers on the issues that divide and unite a country—but trying to get judges to limit free speech and dictate which opinions are permitted to be heard and which are silenced is not the way to get there.

There was other news on the libel front, as well. A few days before Trump's inauguration, word arrived that Alexis "Magic Alex" Mardas had died. Some people remembered Magic Alex as a friend of John Lennon's, a member of the Beatles' posse in the 1960s, the former TV repairman who epically failed at designing the recording studio for Apple Records. He was the inventor of the "Nothing Box," a small plastic box with randomly blinking lights that Lennon would stare at for hours while on LSD. Mardas purportedly told the Beatles that he was working on a sonic force field that Ringo could use in place of baffles, wallpaper that would transmit sound, and paints that could make things invisible or be turned different colors with a switch. He later denied having said such things. In British design circles, though, his fame lives on in the term the "Mardas Gap," which is the "distance between the idea of something and its manifestation." I knew Magic Alex only as a guy who sued The New York Times for defamation in 2008.

The tale of Magic Alex's unhappiness with The Times started with the death of Maharishi Mahesh Yogi in 2008. The maharishi had been the Beatles' spiritual guru 40 years earlier, and in 1967 John, Paul, Ringo, and George had traveled to the maharishi's ashram in Rishikesh, India, along with a collection of hangers-on, including Magic Alex. Things did not go well, and the Beatles abruptly ended the pilgrimage and broke with the holy man. There had been rumors of sexual improprieties involving the maharishi and female followers. When the maharishi died in 2008, The Times marked his passing with an essay tracking his influence on the Beatles' music. It included this passage:

> In the years since Lennon's death, in 1980, Harrison and Mr. Mc-
> Cartney reconsidered the accusations against the maharishi.
> Mr. McCartney has noted that the rumors of sexual impropriety
> were raised by Alexis Mardas, a supposed inventor and charlatan
> who had become a Beatles insider. "Magic Alex," as he was known,
> had agendas of his own, and may have fabricated (or at least ex-
> aggerated) the story. (Mr. Mardas has never commented on the
> incident.) During the 1990s both Harrison and Mr. McCartney
> were suitably convinced of the maharishi's innocence that they
> reconciled with him and offered apologies.

In the days after the story was published, Mardas not only "commented on the incident" but sued The Times, first in England and then in Greece, where he lived on an island in retirement. He took exception with the account of the rumormongering and bridled in particular at the description of himself as a "charlatan," a word that apparently is particularly unflattering in both British English and Greek. Mardas protested he was no "supposed inventor" but in fact the holder of scores of patents. (One of his most famous productions was a model of armored car that was sold to various royal families, but which blew up on at least one occasion when tested under live fire by the royal purchaser's security staff.) Magic Alex asserted that our account of his scheming in India and his record as an inventor was false and defamatory.

The case was complicated under the legal rules of Great Britain and Greece. In a complete reversal of the law in the United States, where plaintiffs must prove that a statement is false, the law abroad required The Times as the publisher to prove our account of Magic Alex was true. Our lawyers gamely traveled around the U.K. and the U.S. interviewing aging rock stars and Beatle pals, hoping to find some friendly witnesses to the events of 1967. The combination of age, 40 years of passed time, and brains fogged by decades of dope-smoking proved challenging. I finally met Magic Alex a couple of years into the litigation when he and I and our small armies of Greek and English lawyers met in Athens for a mediation session to try to settle the two cases. At lunch, our hosts had planted toothpicks with tiny flags of Greece, England, and the United States in the sandwiches. The morning had been unproductive but civil enough (depending on how you feel about listening to English lawyers bicker). At lunch I learned that Magic Alex had managed to invite all of my U.K. lawyers to come visit him on his Greek isle. He had not invited me. When the afternoon session commenced, I spoke to him directly for the first time. There were often hard feelings in any litigation, I told him, we all had to accept that, but the one thing that was truly inexcusable in his case was his failure to offer me a chance to visit him on a Greek isle. It was a breakthrough moment. The tension dissipated. Progress was finally made. We reached an agreeable resolution of the Greek case and the English case—and Magic Alex assured me that I could come visit him any time I wanted in Greece.

I never made it. But I always had a soft spot for Magic Alex. His passing in the early days of 2017 made me nostalgic. Maybe it was just the craziness of his case, his magic psychedelic-sixties life, his connection to the Beatles, his wacky inventions, the thought of his armored cars blowing up in the middle of the Jordanian desert on the first test run. I don't generally expect to feel that way about the people who sue The New York Times. Magic Alex's case was difficult, but it was not freighted with political overtones or just one more skirmish in some polarizing cultural war. He was just a guy who thought we got a story wrong and felt he needed to sue to remedy that. That seemed far removed from where we were with the latest libel cases.

I am pretty certain that Bob Murray and I won't be visiting any Greek isles together any time soon.

9

Fake Fake News

Look, I want to see an honest press. When I started off today by saying that it's so important to the public to get an honest press. The
press—the public doesn't believe you people anymore. Now, maybe I
had something to do with that. I don't know.

—Donald Trump, Feb. 16, 2017

A handful of Republican operatives close to the White House are
scrambling to Trump Jr.'s defense and have begun what could be an
extensive campaign to try to discredit some of the journalists who
have been reporting on the matter.

Their plan, as one member of the team described it, is to research
the reporters' previous work, in some cases going back years, and to
exploit any mistakes or perceived biases. They intend to demand corrections, trumpet errors on social media and feed them to conservative outlets, such as Fox News.

—*Washington Post* article, July 12, 2017

MAY 23, 2017: The annual fundraising dinner for the Reporters
Committee for Freedom of the Press is a galaxy away from the evan-
gelical tent revivals that I saw pass through my tiny hometown as
a small boy in Illinois, setting up in the midst of the soybean fields
and calling the faithful to come together and believe on sweaty
August nights. The RCFP doesn't do tents and fields. It prefers the
elegant Pierre Hotel in Manhattan. The crowd is dressed up. The

alcohol flows. The waiters are in tuxes. Its religion is not born-again Christianity but freedom of the press. But in its way it is a spiritual twin to the events in those worn tents of those Illinois summers, a chance for the faithful to gather, to leave the doubting world behind and commune with fellow believers, certain of the righteousness of their common cause.

Dear Lord, did we need that in the spring of 2017.

The world beyond the Pierre and New York City often seemed like a hostile place to be a journalist, or to believe that the press was a force for good, or to think that press freedom was actually something worth preserving. Inside, no one suffered from doubt. Everyone believed. The spirit was replenished. "It's so nice to be in a crowd this big with people who think like me," a woman told me. It was in every sense a revival.

I was scheduled to give a five-minute talk to the faithful somewhere deep in the program that evening. I had come across a statistic that was making the rounds from the Gallup polling operation: "Americans' trust and confidence in the mass media 'to report the news fully, accurately and fairly' has dropped to its lowest level in Gallup polling history, with 32% saying they have a great deal or fair amount of trust in the media. This is down eight percentage points from last year." I found the statistic absurd. I laid waste to it that night in my remarks:

> Of course the question I get asked most often these days is What to do? What to do—when we have an administration that declares the working press to be the enemy of the American people, that thinks it's OK to exclude reporters it dislikes from press conferences, that bridles at the thought that reporters might actually believe that facts matter, and that longs for a country where journalists can go to jail for publishing the truth.
>
> If you are a journalist, the answer is simple: keep doing what you are doing. For all the toxic noise coming out of the White

House, I do not see journalists silencing themselves, I do not see journalists backing off. What I see is journalists asking the right questions, writing tough stories, doing what they have always done—helping the American people understand what is being done in their name.

Yes, I have seen the polls showing that only 32 percent of the American people answer yes when asked whether they trust the "mass media"—whatever "mass media" means today. TMZ or *The Financial Times*? Fox News or MSNBC? My local paper or Breitbart News? It's like this: Have you ever asked a 13-year-old boy, "How was school today?" There is only one respectable answer: "It sucked." And it is the same deal here. Ask any self-respecting, freedom-loving, institution-hating Americans a big stupid unanswerable question about what they think of the "mass media." Of course they are going to say, "It sucks."

The room loved the remarks—applause, laughter, lots of rah-rah. Which was nice. You want that at a revival. You want to connect with the believers. Except I had serious doubts about whether I was right. Maybe we did need to pay attention to the polls.

I would study the poll results over the course of 2017 as Donald Trump invited the country to dismiss the mainstream media as biased hacks serving heaping platters of fake news. Maybe the Gallup question was silly, a throwback to a time when the term "mass media" meant something to people, but no poll was cutting us much slack. I stumbled upon a Politico/Morning Consult poll that shredded the idea that all the right-wing bluster about "fake news" was just a lot of howling in the political night. The poll showed that 46 percent of voters believed that news organizations made up fake news stories about the Trump administration. Only 37 percent disagreed, with another 17 percent still trying to make up their minds. The Republican numbers were off the chart and not in a good way: More than 75 percent of the GOP voters were convinced that the media published fake news. Even 20 percent of the Democrats agreed.

In December 2017, the Poynter Media Trust Survey—which, as it turned out, probably should have been called the Poynter Media Distrust Survey—was almost as grim. Asked whether news organizations fabricated stories "more than once in a while," 44 percent of Americans answered yes. Poynter broke out the numbers: 24 percent said the fabrications occurred "about half of the time," and 14 percent weighed in with "most of the time." Maybe we were to take as good news that only 6 percent voted for "all of the time."

People in the media tried to dredge up some actual good news in the polls. It wasn't easy. There was the Reuters/Ipsos poll from September 2017. At first blush, that offered a glimmer of hope. The number of people saying they had a "great deal" or "some" confidence in the press was, yes, on the rise—all the way up to 48 percent from 39 percent over the course of a 10-month period following the election. Meanwhile, the percentage of those who said they had "hardly any" confidence in the press had dropped. That number had gone to 45 percent from 51 percent. It was easy for us in the press to latch onto the way the numbers were moving—we were making progress with the public—but you could only get there if you ignored what the poll actually showed: close to half the people still had no trust in the press.

We all knew the standard lines about what was wrong with the surveys. The disapproval numbers masked and oversimplified reactions. In some surveys, those who thought the press was too soft on Trump ended up pushed into the same number as those who thought the press was out to get him. Many people told pollsters they did not trust the media but then went out into the world relying unflinchingly on what they had just read and saw. And the questions tended to treat the press as one big monolith: from Fox News to NPR, from *The New York Times* to the (truly) failing local newspaper.

But that was just quibbling. The pattern was unmistakable. There was a fight taking place in the country for the hearts and minds of the public, a nationwide reckoning about what the press was going to be in American society. For those of us who were media lawyers, who had spent our professional lives looking out for press freedom in courtrooms and finding protection in judges' opinions, the dawning of this new reality was unsettling, and for good reason: none of it was about the law exactly. In most ways, the law protecting press freedom had never been stronger. We had won in 1964 in *Times v. Sullivan*, and we had kept winning. But that history somehow seemed almost beside the point. What this was about was something more basic: a concerted effort to undermine the standing and status of a free press in American democracy. The law can do only so much. It can give the press the freedom to matter but it can't make the press matter. Whether the press counted, whether it had a role to play, depended in the end on the will of the people. It doesn't really matter how much freedom the press has in a society if the press is not believed. A distrusted press is little different from a shackled press: It lacks the authority to mobilize public opinion against wrongdoing, corruption, and misguided policy. It has no voice to hold governments accountable. It gets ignored. And I was pretty sure that at some point a disregard for the press would translate into a disregard for the law of press freedom.

It was not a good sign that public outrage was almost nonexistent over Trump's threat to use—misuse—the power of the federal government to punish news organizations that failed to fall in line behind him. He suggested that NBC's broadcast licenses should be pulled, that The Washington Post should register as a lobbyist because it was owned by Amazon founder Jeff Bezos, and that the Justice Department should refuse to approve a merger sought by CNN's parent, Time Warner—as if the federal government were just an apparatus to address the president's personal grievances (as opposed to, say, dealing with every American justly).

Whether we liked it or not, Trump had hit a nerve with his attacks on the press. The disorienting part was that there was in fact a fake news problem in America. Actually, there were two. One was the real fake news problem—the polluting of the political ecosystem through social media with intentionally false stories designed to mislead and divide. The other was the fake fake news problem—the deployment of the term "fake news" to undermine and delegitimize those news organizations that dared to raise questions about the Trump administration.

The president was right, of course, that *The Times*, CNN, and the rest of the mainstream media and their new digital rivals made mistakes. Nothing new about that. CNN retracted a story saying that a Trump ally had met with the head of a Russian investment fund. (CNN accepted the resignations of three journalists responsible for the mistake.) ABC's Brian Ross got it wrong when he reported that Trump had directed Michael Flynn to make contact with the Russians before the election. (Ross was suspended for four weeks.) A *Washington Post* reporter posted a photo on Twitter that suggested a Trump rally had failed to draw a big crowd when in fact the photo was taken before the event started. (The reporter took the tweet down in 20 minutes and apologized.) *The Times* stumbled when we did an article saying that the administration was trying to squelch a climate change report when, as we learned too late, the report had already been made public on a website. (A clarification followed.) The reasons for those and other errors were many: plain old mental lapses, mistaken sources, sloppy editing, a failure to be thorough, a blindness that sometimes takes hold in the pursuit of a good story. Here is one thing that was not a reason: willful fabrication. The notion that the errors were intentional made no sense if you thought about it for a minute. The stories were too public. The public scrutiny too inevitable. The corrections too quick and too prominent. The competition too ready to call out the mistakes of a rival news outlet. Nobody in the mainstream press was trying to get away with a deliberate falsehood.

In other words, the president's claim of fake news in the mainstream media was itself fake news.

In 2017, The Times jumped into the fray over truth and falsity with a series of TV and internet advertisements on the theme "Truth Is Hard." In April, a set of ads featured the gripping photojournalism that *The Times* had done about the refugee crisis in Europe, the Ebola scare in Africa, the desperate times in Venezuela, and the war against ISIS. The ads ended with the taglines: "The truth is hard/ the truth is hard to know/the truth is more important than ever." Later that month, I was asked to help with a new commercial that was to focus on government secrecy and The Times's efforts to overcome it. The idea was to have it up to mark the 100th day of the Trump administration. The marketing department wanted to know whether I had some redacted government documents from our regular battles with the federal government over our right to get documents under the Freedom of Information Act. The commercial-makers needed a visual element.

They had come to the right place. I had my own personal stockpile of redacted documents. I was generally known as a connoisseur of redaction, having fought more or less daily with federal agencies over documents that our reporters wanted. FOIA is a world unto itself. In theory, reporters write sensible requests for documents, send the requests to an agency, and the agency responds by delivering the documents. It does work that way, on occasion. But, more often, the government bureaucracy takes weeks or months or years to consider the requests and then produces page after page of documents that have huge portions blacked out because the government claims that information cannot be legally released. My collection of redacted documents was impressive. I had a page from the FBI that had every word redacted except the word "propaganda" at the end of a line about two-thirds of the way down. I had a page received in response to a FOIA request to the Justice Department that came back with only the words "approved for public release" visible at the top. A request for a booklet of photos from the army was met with the production of a version of the booklet that blocked out many of the photos but left the captions. One particularly artistic redaction involved a governmental chart that was completely redacted except one cell in the dead center of the chart—and that cell was blank—creating the world's first doughnut-shaped redaction, albeit a rectangular doughnut.

The work on the commercial was not without its ironies. One of the companies assisting in the production had heard enough of the president's rants about suing everyone and everything and insisted on being assured that The Times would cover any legal expenses they might incur "for any and all claims arising from use of political references in the spot and any related materials." It was tempting to explain to the heads of the production company that they may have missed something, that the ad campaign was about the freedom to speak up without fear, that being able to speak up was the Big Idea behind America. That was why we were doing the campaign. That was the message we were going to deliver. They still wanted to be indemnified.

Then there was the actual making of the ad. Mark Mazzetti of our Washington bureau was doing the voiceover. The narrative was supposed to highlight the paper's battles with the Trump administration over secrecy. There was plenty of that to go around, even though the administration had barely had 100 days to get the hang of it. The White House visitor logs, which had previously been made public, were now kept under lock and key. Rex Tillerson, the secretary of state, had objected to having a pool of reporters on the plane with him for a foreign trip, an accommodation that had been standard practice in prior administrations. Sean Spicer had had his moment in the darkness, skirmishing with the press over his closed-down super-gaggle. The long-promised release of the Trump tax returns was all promise, no reality. There was just one problem: none of the redacted documents I possessed had anything to do with the Trump administration. They were all from earlier FOIA fights during the Obama and Bush administrations. The Trump administration was too new to have engaged in seriously ridiculous redactions (something that time would soon cure). Mark and I worried that the spot created a misimpression and left us open to criticism. It struck us as bad form to do an advertisement devoted to "the truth is hard" if the ad in question was, well, not quite the truth. Call us old school. We raised our objections, and script changes were made. "Secrecy in government is not something that came around this year," the spot now began. "We have seen secrecy grow across the years, over several administrations of two different parties."

We weren't alone among our peers in trying to make the case to the public that the truth mattered—hard as it was to believe that the point even needed to be made. Everyone struggled to find the right tone and message. *The Washington Post* wielded a sledgehammer when it posted its new slogan on its home page: "Democracy Dies in Darkness." CNN preferred the subtle and high concept— very high concept. It opted for a TV ad that featured the picture of an apple. "This is an apple," a disembodied voice announced. "Some people might try to tell you it's a banana. They might scream 'Banana, banana, banana,' over and over and over again. They might put 'banana' in all caps. You might even start to believe that this is a banana. But it's not. This is an apple." It was part of a campaign with the slogan "Facts First." NPR urged listeners to support "fact-based journalism" as if there were some other station down the dial offering fantasy-based journalism.

I knew it was important to drive home the message in sound bites, but that was also part of the problem. Trump had made the

term "fake news" the ultimate political sound bite—magic words
able to replace real thinking. The dark beauty of it was that it had
the ring of something that someone would say while deep in the
pursuit of truth. If only. Denouncing a story on CNN or in *The
Times* as "fake news" is not embracing the truth. It is just the opposite. It is asking people to skip over the analytical step of weighing what is true and what is not and instead prodding them to
simply dismiss what they don't like hearing. Trump did not try to
hide that very much: "Any negative polls are fake news, just like the
CNN, ABC, NBC polls in the election," he tweeted once. Not surprisingly, as Karen Greenberg pointed out in *The New Republic,* a
65-year-old book sold out on Amazon in the days immediately after
the election. It was *The Origins of Totalitarianism* by the social
critic Hanna Arendt. One of Arendt's themes was what Greenberg described as the "vacuum of unthinkingness"—the danger
that comes "when it no longer matters to the populace whether
something is true or not, only whether it is useful." Unthink about
that for a while.

Meanwhile, the real fake news problem harming America was
going on and on with no end in sight. In the aftermath of the election, we learned just how much the political ecosystem had been
bombarded by intentionally fabricated stories, often disguised as
real news articles, posted by a small army of online users. Some
were part of the Russian disinformation campaign. Some were
political partisans looking to harm their enemies. Some were just
guys out to make a buck, many hunkered down in places like
Macedonia, others closer to home.

Just before the inauguration, Scott Shane of *The Times* chronicled the fake news adventures of a guy named Cameron Harris.
Nothing stood out about Harris. He was a recent college graduate
living in Maryland with a passion for Republican politics. He saw
on video a Trump speech from Ohio in which the candidate said
he was hearing more and more about how the Democrats were

trying to rig the election. Harris sprang into fake news action. Sitting at the kitchen table in his apartment, he crafted a fake story headlined "BREAKING: Tens of Thousands of Fraudulent Clinton Votes Found in Ohio Warehouse." It appeared on a fake news site called ChristianTimesNewspaper.com. The picture illustrating the piece—showing stacks of ballot boxes in storage—had been pilfered from a story about a U.K. election on an English news site. Harris posted the story and within days it had been shared with six million internet users. Ohio officials, alarmed by the allegations, launched an investigation into voter fraud. Harris ultimately earned $22,000 in ad revenues for the 20 hours he invested in fabricating and posting the article.

It had been a dizzying campaign season for the wizards of fake news. Buzzfeed reported that more than 960,000 Facebook users recommended a story about the Pope's endorsement of Donald Trump. A half million people had shared a story blasting out that an FBI agent involved in the Hillary Clinton email case was found dead, the victim of a murder-suicide. The phony stories were not all Trump-centric. Hundreds of thousands of online users saw an article about how Ireland was accepting refugees from the United States in a special program for those fleeing the Trump administration. Others identified by Buzzfeed went after familiar themes and the old favorites of the grocery store tabloids: the death of Willie Nelson, Bill Clinton's filing of divorce papers, the replacement of the Jefferson Davis statue in New Orleans with one of Barack Obama. A lot of traffic made its way to a story that fell into the venerable category of "too good to be true but how I wish": it was a thrilling account of a woman who won the lottery and then got arrested for defecating on her boss's desk.

The research on the impact of fake news was inconclusive—people are complex when it comes to how they read, how much they read, what they remember, and how they make decisions like what candidate to vote for—but nobody thought that it was helping democracy to have a world in which it was more difficult than ever to decide what to believe. Facebook's initial reaction to the scandal of fake news was to act as if it had nothing to do with the problem, like the driver who slams on his brakes setting off a 100-car chain reaction crash behind him, then drives away looking in his rearview mirror, wondering what happened and why there are so many bad drivers on the road. Over time, Facebook got religion and started proposing initiatives to deal with the problem, making it less likely that random fake news posts ended up in people's news feeds and trying to flag fake news, but whether technological solutions would really work was not readily apparent.

And the legal solutions? If there were laws or lawsuits that could clean up all that duplicity on social media, nobody seemed to know exactly what they would be. It was natural in America to look to lawyers to try to fix a problem. It's in our genes. We litigate over coffee spills and sports tickets and hurt feelings. Were the courts and the legal profession really doomed to stand by idly while fake news chewed away at the fabric of democracy? The answer was, in all of its sad likelihood, yes. Here was the legal problem with fake news: It was just fake. It didn't defame anyone. It didn't defraud anyone out of money. It didn't misrepresent a product for sale. It was just lies. That was where Xavier Alvarez came in, and the lawyers went out.

No man in America has ever done more to protect the right to lie. Alvarez was a habitual liar. He claimed to have played in the National Hockey League. He said he was once married to a movie star. He told people he had won the Congressional Medal of Honor for his bravery in combat. All of that was untrue, just brazen, self-aggrandizing lying. As it turns out, though, falsely claiming to be a military medal winner is not just a lie; it's a federal crime. Alvarez managed to get himself prosecuted and convicted in federal court after he bragged about his Medal of Honor during a public meeting of a local government body in California. He took his case to the Supreme Court in 2012, carrying the banner for everyone who believed that among the sacred rights that we all possess as Americans is the right to tell big fat lies. The Supreme Court agreed. The court found that his lie was protected by the First Amendment. In the words of the court, America did not need its government to be a Ministry of Truth, sorting out what was false and what was true. The law under which he was prosecuted could not stand in the face of the First Amendment.

Alvarez's case took on special meaning early in 2016, just as the primary season was heating up. A federal appeals court used the decision to strike down an Ohio law that made it illegal to tell lies about a candidate during election campaigns. Somebody wondered whether the court feared that the law would lead to prison over-crowding, but the real issue was the First Amendment again. The court found much not to like about the Ohio law: it was too am-biguous in too many ways, about what constituted a lie, about how lying was to be policed. It seemed unlikely that any legislature anywhere could write an anti-lying law that would survive a First Amendment challenge.

This was the American deal, as maddening as it was at times: the same First Amendment that had done so much to protect the speech rights of those intent on strengthening democracy also pro-tected those who were attacking it. The message from the courts was clear: If political falsehoods were a problem, the solution in America was not more laws or more lawsuits. The remedy was the American people. It was up to them to speak up for the truth, to challenge the falsehoods, to convince others of what the facts were. It was the classic philosophical premise of a marketplace of ideas: if truth and falsity could freely compete for the public's attention, truth would ultimately win out, with no intervention needed from the government or the law.

That was how it was supposed to work, at least. It was hard in 2016 and 2017 not to have a few doubts. Facebook revealed that content generated by Russian agents reached 126 million users on Facebook alone. The Russians also managed to post more than 131,000 messages on Twitter and 1,000 YouTube videos. Somebody in Moscow was plainly betting that in the marketplace of ideas, falsity had a decent shot of coming out on top.

Meanwhile, the other fake news problem—the use of the term by the president to undermine the independent press—continued unabated. The "fake news" label got used so often and so stupidly that it became, in time, almost a laugh line. One day I was in a gift shop, and there between the handcrafted wooden cheese platters and the artsy dish towels was a stack of pennants emblazoned with the words "FAKE NEWS" in white lettering on black, as if it were somebody's favorite college football team, about to go head-to-head in a big game against the archrival REAL NEWS. But as much as I wanted to discount all the screeching about fake news as just so much noise, I couldn't escape the nagging feeling that all of Trump's trashing of the press had a darker side. Around the country, during the campaign and after, isolated incidents kept popping up with a common theme: Reporters were being abused for doing their jobs. A Trump aide assaulted a reporter at the end of a campaign rally. A reporter was physically attacked by a congressional candidate in Montana. Several journalists were arrested as they reported on the protests in Washington on Inauguration Day. A journalist covering a Trump cabinet member during a visit to West Virginia was arrested for being too persistent in trying to get his questions answered. (That is called being a reporter, by the way.) A noose was left at the door of a small newspaper in California. Three journalists reported they were physically assaulted by demonstrators at a Make America Great Again rally in California in March 2017. Ten journalists faced criminal charges stemming from their coverage of the activists protesting a pipeline in South Dakota. Maybe there was no connection between the incidents and the hostile rhetoric spewing forth from the campaign and then from the White House, but you didn't have to be paranoid to think that maybe the tone was being set from the top.

It's not that journalists have a monopoly on truth. They don't. Their methods implicitly acknowledge that the world is not thoroughly knowable. Statements are attributed to sources. Statements from the other side are presented. But journalists still proceed on the belief that truth does exist in the world and is worth pursuing. It gets proved to the best of our ability.

That was not the Trump way, as columnist Bret Stephens captured brilliantly in a speech he did honoring Daniel Pearl, *The Wall Street Journal* reporter murdered by terrorists in Pakistan. Stephens reprised how Bill O'Reilly of Fox had questioned Trump after the election about his claim that three million aliens voted illegally. Wasn't it irresponsible to say that without the data to back it up? O'Reilly wanted to know. Trump responded by saying that many people had come out and said he was right. "He isn't telling O'Reilly that he's got his facts wrong," Stephens noted. "He's saying that, as far as he is concerned, facts, as most people understand the term, don't matter: that they are indistinguishable from, and interchangeable with, opinion."

That sentiment was less elegantly captured a few weeks later by Trump aide Kellyanne Conway with her enthusiastic defense of "alternative facts." Chuck Todd of NBC had questioned her about the administration's false claims about the size of the inauguration crowd. Conway was having none of it. "You're saying it's a falsehood. And they're giving—Sean Spicer, our press secretary—gave alternative facts."

"Look, alternative facts are not facts. They're falsehoods," Todd shot back. He later prodded her about how ridiculous the whole dispute had become and wanted to know why Trump and his aides had refused to give up on the fiction about how big the crowd was. How could it matter? "I'll answer it this way," Conway said. "Think

about what you just said to your viewers. That's why we feel compelled to go out and clear the air and put alternative facts out there."

It was all of a piece, the prodding of America to see the mainstream media as fakers not worth listening to, voices to be ignored
and discounted, without having to put up any evidence or show
what was inaccurate. When Trump called reporters "disgusting
human beings" or "awful people," he summoned up the inevitable
mindlessness of spite. It was easy to descend from there into pre-
siding over a political rally in Arizona with the crowd chanting,
"CNN sucks." Trump's announcement of the Fake News Awards in
early 2018 was designed to humiliate. It was about drawing a line
around those news organizations that were doing tough reporting
on Trump and subjecting them to a little ridicule—and ridicule,
whether on the playground or in the White House (there once was
a difference), is always thought-free.

It was also politically brilliant. The administration's accusation
of false news rode on the back of the real fake news problem. It made
a hash of the line that should have been obvious between a story
fabricated by Russian agents intending to alienate and anger voters and the unintentional error of a legitimate news organization.
It nudged people to think that no one other than the government
and its allies could be trusted. It was the vacuum of unthinkingness.
It was an inversion of the central tenet of American democracy I
had grown up with in the hard-core conservative Midwest: distrust those in power.

For all of Trump's belligerent calling out of The Times for fake
news (point of pride: one of our columnists finished first in his Fake
News Awards), the relationship between Trump and The Times remained perplexing. It was, like a long bitter marriage, complicated. Trump had shown up at The Times for an on-the-record
interview shortly after Election Day. When his bungled attempt to
repeal Obamacare failed, he immediately called Maggie Haberman,

The Times's reporter who was breaking scoop after scoop about what was really going on inside the walls of the White House. Mike Schmidt of *The Times* managed to get into the dining room at Mar-a-Lago during the holidays and do an exclusive with the president. Earlier, Trump had invited him and two colleagues to do an on-the-record sit-down interview at the White House. (Schmidt's ability to gain the trust of people was legendary. He once showed me a picture from the White House session in which he was standing next to Trump and wearing a tie that extended to his thigh, just the way Trump's tie did. I didn't think the fashion decision was a coincidence.) And once upon a time, Trump, then just a real estate guy who liked to advertise his properties in the paper, did an advertisement endorsing *The Times*. "Our longstanding relationship with The New York Times will endure forever," Trump said in the 2010 ad. The ad was unearthed during the campaign by *Times* historian David Dunlap, who wrote a story about it. I am sure that Trump was tempted to label it fake news, if only he could.

And for someone who was prone to condemning *The Times* as a purveyor of fake news, Trump showed an amazing willingness to find *Times* stories Grade A 100 percent certified prime Truth when it suited his purposes. In February 2018, *The Times*'s Matt Rosenberg reported out a story about how the CIA had been negotiating with Russian intelligence agents in hopes of purchasing the much-discussed-but-never-confirmed tape of Trump frolicking with Russian prostitutes. The CIA blasted the story as inaccurate. Not Trump. He tweeted:

> According to the @nytimes, a Russian sold phony secrets on "Trump" to the U.S. Asking price was $10 million, brought down to $1 million to be paid over time. I hope people are now seeing & understanding what is going on here. It is all now starting to come out - DRAIN THE SWAMP!

Earlier in his term, he had tweeted out a *Times* story about how small businesses were feeling more confident since the election. And when *The Times* published its blockbuster stories about Harvey Weinstein, Trump did not suggest his old friend was one more victim of fake news. "I'm not at all surprised to see it," he said.

I was never convinced that there was any grand design to the seesawing way that Trump dealt with the paper, but if there were an explanation, it was most likely this: he craved *The Times*'s attention; he bridled at not being able to control *The Times*'s narrative.

And his attempt to control *The Times* was a bust. If he thought the broadsides about fake news would cow the paper into changing, he was sadly mistaken. By the time the Trump administration was settling in, *The Times* newsroom, after a period of post-election soul-searching, had a "business as usual" feel to it. People checked the box that this administration was not going to be like any other and then went about their work the way they always did. The thundering about fake news was just background noise, one or two ticks below a distraction. Jim Rutenberg, *The Times* media columnist, wrote about how, paradoxically, Trump's unprecedented approach to the art of governing spurred The Times not to throw away the playbook but to revert to the fundamentals of by-the-book journalism: "There was palpable excitement over the chance to show traditional journalism's true worth in the face of an administration that was clearly going to use misdirection, misinformation, and barbs against the press as governing tools. For as cynical a lot as there ever was, idealism rushed in," Rutenberg wrote in the *Wilson Quarterly*. The hard-edged stories that were sent to me by editors for prepublication legal review—stories about the fall of General Flynn, the financial conflicts of Jared Kushner, the spider web of ties between the Trump campaign and the Russian oligarchy—were most noteworthy for how unnoteworthy they were in their approach to reporting the news: straightforward pieces built from credible sources, told in journalism's usual dispassionate language. Maybe the best sign of all was that, as the first year of the administration rolled by, and the stories about Robert Mueller and Stormy Daniels and the Russian connections exploded across our pages, I was bypassed more and more often by the editors and reporters handling the Trump coverage. The stories went straight into the paper without a side trip through Legal. Trump's legal fuming had once injected a certain caution into the newsroom about the possibility of libel suits. By the time 2017 turned into 2018, the message had gotten through: Nobody was going to be suing anyone over our accurate coverage of the administration.

Still, it wasn't always possible to hear the "fake news" drumbeat and shrug. In the late summer of 2017, the PR person for a gun control group wrote to us with a strange cheeriness:

Morning all,

Just wanted to let you know that the NRA has released another unhinged video, this time targeting NYT. Apparently, they're "coming for you."

Happy Friday!

It was another release from NRA TV featuring its favorite over-the-top talking head, Dana Loesch, the go-to ringmistress for the group's propaganda circus. Wearing a white knit top offset by the all-black background of the NRA studio, Loesch spews out her not-quite-controlled rage about fake news, directly addressing The New York Times: "Consider this the shot across your proverbial bow. . . . We're going to laser-focus on your so-called honest pursuit of truth. . . . In short, we're coming for you."

Many people at The Times found it chilling and pressed us to respond in some way. All of that was understandable. We always had to worry about the one unbalanced (and, in this case, likely armed) person who would take the provocation to heart—nobody could pretend that we lived in some other world—and all the gun imagery was menacing and intentionally so. But I questioned whether we really wanted to give the NRA and its minions the satisfaction of knowing they had our attention. Menacing messages could at some point go too far and become illegal threats, but the First Amendment gave a lot of protection to even nasty speakers, and the NRA seemed to know how to slither right up to the line but not cross it. I recommended that we ignore the video. It had been around for months and gone largely unnoticed, which NRA TV was probably used to. Driving more traffic to NRA TV helped no one but the NRA and made us less safe, not more. As was inevitable, some of our reporters tweeted about the video and engaged in a minor internet skirmish with Loesch and her NRA enablers, but we stood down as a company. We were willing to let the hit piece fade into obscurity.

I was more than a little surprised, then, to pick up the Sunday *Times* a few months later and find spread across the Style section a glowing profile of . . . Dana Loesch. The piece crowned her "The National Rifle Association's Telegenic Warrior." For good measure the story also labeled her "wonder woman," and she and *The Times* reporter took a fun field trip to the neighborhood shooting range, the Crossfire Defense Academy & Range. The "We're Coming for You" video was neatly disposed of in a sentence that described it as "an ad in 2017 aimed at The New York Times." Dana came across as a lovely person.

I think, upon reflection, it spoke well of The Times. Loesch was a person in the news, and we write about people in the news, not just the people we agree with. I never heard whether Loesch considered the piece about her fake news, but a couple of weeks later she was once again lighting up the screen at NRA TV—literally. A new NRA video showed Loesch holding up a lighter to a print edition of *The New York Times*. "You know, I don't even have to do this.

You guys are doing a good enough job burning down your reputations all by yourselves," Loesch says in the piece.

Lovely.

But that is how the First Amendment works—part of our "profound national commitment to the principle that debate on public issues should be uninhibited, robust, and wide open," as Justice William Brennan said in *Times v. Sullivan*. Speakers are allowed to be provocative, colorful, contradictory, and wrong. It is a beautiful thing. Bizarre some days, but still beautiful.

Somewhere in the midst of the fight for America's hearts and minds, in the national conversation about the place of press freedom in a democracy, I feared the discussion was running off course. The debate was getting framed as liberal versus conservative—as if the left believed in freedom of speech and the right was against it. I thought it was a huge mistake for those of us who cared about freedom of speech to buy into that analysis. In 2010, just seven years earlier, Congress had passed its most significant law related to libel. It was called the SPEECH Act, and it was designed to protect U.S. publishers. It was addressed to a problem that had cropped up in recent years. U.S. publishers were being sued by Russian oligarchs, Saudis who were implicated in the funding of terrorism, and international businessmen suspected of corruption. Only they weren't bringing those cases in American courtrooms. They were suing in other countries that had laws that didn't adequately protect the press and made it easier for plaintiffs to win. Congress decided to draw the line by passing the SPEECH Act, which barred U.S. courts from enforcing judgments won by libel plaintiffs abroad if those plaintiffs would have lost the same case brought in the United States. And that was almost always going to be the case. So plaintiffs who had won elsewhere could not come to this country and get the courts to force U.S. publishers to pay the damages they had been awarded. The law freed U.S. publishers to continue to do tough reporting on global issues, like terrorism and international crime. When the bill came up for a vote in the House, it passed unanimously. The result in the Senate was the same; everyone voted in favor of it.

I kept thinking that in our divided times we needed to find our way back to that place. Whatever our disagreements, whatever our politics, we should be able to agree on the importance of a free press. Belief in a free press was not a liberal value—it was an American value. Couldn't we find common ground on just that one thing?

If the president's tweets were any indication, the answer appeared to be no.

10

Insecure

We respect the important role that the press plays and will give them respect, but it is not unlimited—they cannot place lives at risk with impunity.

—Attorney General Jeff Sessions, Aug. 4, 2017

U.S. intelligence officials have withheld sensitive intelligence from President Donald Trump because they are concerned it could be leaked or compromised, according to current and former officials familiar with the matter.

—*The Wall Street Journal*, Feb. 16, 2017

ON SEPTEMBER 10, 2001, I found myself in the grimy halls of Manhattan's criminal court building. It was in those days a place of unrelenting gloom, threadbare and broken. I was the newsroom lawyer for the New York Daily News then. Three teenagers had been arrested for setting fire to a homeless man in a Chelsea housing project. It was one of those stories that had mesmerized the New York City tabloids for a passing moment: three young monsters who had broken up the dead-end monotony of their lives by torching a helpless vagrant. Shortly after the teenagers' arrest, their lawyers had moved to close the pretrial proceedings. They feared the drumbeat of endless two-inch-high tabloid headlines would kill the kids' chances of getting a fair trial. It was not a crazy idea. The publicity had been brutal. Only I was there to convince a judge that nothing could be further from the truth, that the closing of the courtroom would be an affront to the Constitution, to the citizens of New York, to the very concept of justice.

The taxi that day had exited the West Side Highway just north of the World Trade Center. My brand-new paralegal, just arrived in New York from the West Coast, had never seen the towers up close. We craned our necks to take them in, the sky a deep blue behind them.

We got to court early, handed our legal papers to the attorneys in the case, and took seats in the gallery, waiting for the defendants to be led in. Their teenage girlfriends and a posse of acquaintances filled the row behind us. The defense attorneys did a page-flicking speed-read of our brief. When a side door to the courtroom swung open and the kids came shuffling in, you couldn't help but think, "These are the monsters? They're babies." Soft teenage faces, blank smiles, shell-shocked eyes doing a bad job of hiding fear and uncertainty. They gave half waves to the girls behind us.

The defense laid out its case for closing the courtroom to the judge, the usual points about how in tabloid New York it would be impossible to find 12 citizens with open minds to fairly weigh the evidence if the proceedings were held in the open. The prosecutor, Matthew Bogdanos, followed the standard playbook for the government in many such cases: The D.A. has no position on the defendants' motion to close the courtroom to the public. The court should make its own call. When my turn came around, I made the case the way I always did in those days: low-key and straightforward, methodically citing legal precedents, one dry case citation after another, each establishing that in the United States it was an extraordinary thing to have a secret criminal proceeding. This wasn't about how the *Daily News* or the *New York*

Post was covering this particular story; this was a simple matter of applying the law. Of course the temptation was there for me. Wasn't this the opportunity that someone like me lives for, to reach for some high-minded rhetoric about the people's right to know, to speak in glorious prose of the majesty of a free press? Wasn't that why I had become a First Amendment lawyer, to stand in front of a court and argue for the rights of the press and the public it serves? I let the moment pass. I was pretty sure the judge had seen the screaming headlines in the *Daily News*, convicting the kids in big block type and stoking the outrage of New Yorkers across the five boroughs.

As soon as I sat down, I noticed out of the corner of my eye some rustling at the prosecutor's table. Bogdanos, inexplicably, was on his feet again. I had apparently disappointed him. He had been hoping for something more. He started addressing the judge again. While, yes, the D.A. took no position on whether the courtroom should be closed, he would be remiss if he didn't remind the court what Thomas Jefferson had said about the importance of a free press. Bogdanos proceeded to launch into a discourse on freedom of the press in democracy and the Founding Fathers and Jefferson ("were it left to me to decide whether we should have a government without newspapers or newspapers without a government, I should not hesitate a moment to prefer the latter"). It was glorious. I wondered whether he had seen the covers of the *News* and the *Post*.

The judge took it all in and then said he needed some time to look at the law before making a decision. He directed us to come back the next morning.

I would never see those defendants or their lawyers or that judge again or even know what the court decided. Sitting in my office on 33rd Street the next morning, a friend called. A plane had crashed into the World Trade Center. I tried to get to the internet sites of all the New York broadcast outlets. Everything was frozen. I walked down the hall to the newsroom. A couple of editors stood in front of a hanging TV monitor. Michael Daly, the columnist, joined us. We watched the second plane crash into the towers. Michael dashed off, hoping to find a way to get downtown. The editors began working the phones. I walked back to my office and put away my legal papers for that morning's hearing.

The next time I heard anything about Matt Bogdanos, the assistant district attorney, it was in a front-page story in *The New York Times* dated April 24, 2004. By then, I had left the Daily News to become a lawyer for The Times. Assistant District Attorney Bogdanos was now Marine Colonel Bogdanos, an activated reservist. He was in Iraq, working at the National Museum of Iraq investigating the looting of ancient art. As he walked with a reporter through what remained of the museum, he said, "It breaks your heart. It's devastating. We're talking irreparable chapters of our history gone."

By the time I came to The Times in 2002, September 11 was a singular driving force in the work I was doing. At the Daily News, we had had repeated fights with the NYPD over access to Lower Manhattan for our reporters and photographers to cover the story of the devastation and the recovery of the dead and the clearing of the site. My only appearance ever as a defense lawyer in the state criminal courts came when I represented a *News* reporter who had wandered into a frozen zone on the West Side Highway and been arrested. In my first weeks at The Times, I sued the New York City Fire Department on behalf of the paper and columnist Jim Dwyer, seeking the secret records of the department's response on 9/11. It started a long legal journey that would end three years later at New York's highest court as we finally broke through and won the right to hundreds of pages of records documenting that unprecedented day. But in the years following the attack, the dramatic changes in legal work at The Times all centered on the global war on terrorism, GWOT. Secrecy mushroomed across the federal government, justified by the imperative of keeping the nation safe. New tools of electronic surveillance were clandestinely rolled out. A generation of reporters headed off to Iraq and Afghanistan and later Libya and Syria to cover the hostilities. The need for journalists at our Washington bureau to cover deeply the Pentagon and the intelligence agencies, with a skeptical eye toward the legal implications of their actions, had never been more urgent or more difficult. The stories of how well the government was doing in keeping the country safe and what the CIA, the NSA, and the Pentagon were doing around the world in the name of the American people could be told fully only if reporters were able to cultivate anonymous sources and get access to classified materials. To work with reporters on national security stories is to enter a dark corner of both law and journalism: hazy, sometimes treacherous, and rife with uncertainty.

In the opening weeks of the Trump presidency, we were forced to face for the first time whether national security reporting was going to be different under the new administration. Just days before the inauguration, David Sanger, the paper's national security correspondent, had dropped me an email:

> David
>
> Before we get ourselves another one of these investigations, could you give this a read? Close hold, needless to say.
>
> Best
> David

We had just spent years living with the Justice Department's investigation into General James Cartwright, one of David's sources for his reporting on the secret American cyber-warfare program to attack Iran's nuclear facilities. The whole episode, with a lengthy investigation that sowed fear among government officials, had been a searing reminder of how high the stakes were for everyone involved in national security journalism. But apart from leak investigations and the possibility that a reporter would go to jail for refusing to identify an anonymous source, there was a separate and complicated legal question that in the entire history of the U.S. had never been resolved: Could journalists be criminally charged under the Espionage Act for publishing classified information? If there were ever a president who might want to find out the answer to that question, Donald Trump seemed like the one.

In some form or other, the Espionage Act has been around for more than 100 years. It was convoluted and confusing, and what it meant was often unclear. But one thing was certain: no journalist has ever been prosecuted for possessing or publishing classified information. The legal liability, for better or worse, had always fallen on the government insider who was a source, not on the journalist. When the Supreme Court decided the Pentagon Papers, it had ruled only that the government could not stop the publication of classified information. It was a great moment for press freedom—but not the end of the court's opinion. Several justices, writing in dissents and concurrences, weighed in to say that different rules might apply after publication, and they were careful to leave open the possibility that journalists could be prosecuted under the Espionage Act.

No charges ever came, and in the decades since the Pentagon Papers, an uneasy equilibrium had set in. Journalists regularly received leaked classified information. News organizations weighed the information's value and its risks and published when it seemed like the right thing to do for their readers. The government was almost always unhappy, but brought no charges against the journalists. It worked like many things in democracy, not perfectly, but well enough, preserving freedom of the press and allowing some important information to reach the public, yet maintaining more than enough secrecy for the government's real needs. There was on both sides an appropriate dose of discretion: News organizations tried to make informed decisions about what to publish and the government stood down from finding out whether the courts would allow prosecution of reporters. In practical terms, few prosecutors relished the idea of getting into a high-profile brawl with a national news organization, especially if a story had shed light on government wrongdoing—and even more especially if the court case would put on public display just how incompetent the government was at keeping secrets.

Those of us on the media side had grown comfortable with the ambiguous legal situation, and there was little appetite for some "test case" to clarify the law—particularly if that test case happened to involve the company you worked for. But it did mean that the ultimate "what if" remained unanswered—what if the Justice Department did decide to charge a journalist? How would that play out? The statute clearly reached spies and leakers, but what about those on the outside, like reporters, who received the information and revealed it to others? A decade earlier, the government had gone after two pro-Israel lobbyists who had obtained classified information from a government source and passed it on to reporters. The wheels ultimately fell off the prosecution, but if two lobbyists could end up in the legal crosshairs, what prevented the government from going after reporters?

Most media lawyers wanted to believe that the answer to that question was the First Amendment, but few of them were completely convinced. The First Amendment argument had worked in other situations. The Supreme Court had refused to enforce a state statute that barred newspapers from printing the names of juvenile defendants and another one that prevented the media from identifying judges under investigation. In a series of cases, the court had held that only a government interest of the highest order could justify penalizing journalists for publishing the truth when they had received the information from sources and they themselves had engaged in no wrongdoing to get it. Those cases had been the backbone of my legal analysis when we published the Trump tax returns.

But the Espionage Act was not some overblown state statute protecting juvenile delinquents or shady judges or the tax returns of a presidential candidate. Who knew whether the First Amendment would carry the day in a national security case with prosecutors telling a court that the safety of the nation had been put at risk?

Attached to David's email was the first draft of the story he was writing with veteran science reporter Bill Broad. They brought to the reporting an unparalleled understanding of cyber-warfare techniques and the technical intricacies of nuclear warheads. The attached story dealt with both: it was an account of how the U.S. had attempted to use cyber-strikes and electronic warfare to sabotage the North Korean nuclear missile program. For a while, the reporting showed, the sabotage appeared to be working. All of those failed North Korean launches, with rockets falling sideways as they left the launch pad, seemed beyond coincidence or a run of particularly bad luck for Kim Jong-un and his cronies. The reporters found there was even a name for it: "Left of Launch." The idea was to sabotage launches rather than try to intercept missiles.

With the clock running down toward Inauguration Day, David and Bill had already made the trip to meet with national intelligence officials to lay out what they intended to publish. "Such conversations are always fraught," David would say later in the paper. "Understandably, government officials don't want to confirm or deny anything—in fact, they can't. But it's still important to listen to any concerns they might have about the details we are planning to publish so that we can weigh them with our editors."

I heard nothing more about the story from the newsroom. Inauguration Day came and went. The Trump administration took over in Washington. Then, on a night not long after the inauguration, Sanger called. The reporting was complete, and editors wanted to move ahead with the story. The piece had been delayed in the usual way things get backed up in the newsroom in a heavy news cycle. But now an entirely new team of national security advisors was in place in the White House. David thought we could no longer rely on the back-and-forth he and Bill had engaged in with the now-departed Obama team. They needed to reach out to Trump's advisors, let them know what we were about to report, and find out how they viewed their options with North Korea. As part of that process, the Trump White House would learn what our story intended to say. It would be a first step into the unknown with the new administration.

David and Bill set up the interviews. As David would later report in his book *The Perfect Weapon,* he sensed in his first meeting with K. T. McFarland, one of the president's national security aides, that she and the team were not yet up to speed. As he described the story we had, it appeared that she had not been briefed fully on one of the most sensitive operations launched against North Korea in recent years. Nonetheless, she assured David that she saw no national security concerns and was optimistic it would all work out. It seemed to be going by the book, more or less. At least until the next day. David and Bill were called to a meeting in the Situation Room—an unusual step seemingly designed to underscore the sensitivity of the story.

Then came the tweet. It was Valentine's Day, and President Trump was up early with his cell phone in hand, tweeting. The message from the president was impossible to ignore for those of us involved with Sanger and Broad's reporting:

> The real story here is why are there so many illegal leaks coming out of Washington? Will these leaks be happening as I deal on N. Korea etc?

The few of us inside The Times who knew about the story didn't know what to make of the random reference to North Korea. Strange coincidence? Just another round of presidential bucket-banging about one of the president's favorite topics? Something more worrisome? (Ten days later, Trump would finish up his February 24 anti-leaker Twitter tirade with the ominous: "FIND THEM.") There was no way to tell.

David, Bill, and I talked regularly over the course of February, and they filled me in on what they were hearing from the Trump team. They met with General H. R. McMaster, who had taken over following the departure of the disgraced Michael Flynn. Officials in the intelligence community were cooperating as much as they could, but none of them was prepared to say with any certainty how President Trump would react to a *Times* story built in part on classified secrets about North Korea. Lawyering is always about predicting risk, and we were left to read whatever tea leaves we could find. At one point, there had been a phone call with McMaster. He had been on the job less than a week. It was a short get-to-know-you sort of conversation, plainspoken and civil, with our reporters and editors and Arthur Sulzberger Jr. and me, but we learned nothing that would help us better gauge the likely reaction in the White House.

Other signs were worrisome. In mid-February, after David's meeting with McFarland, Donald McGahn, the White House counsel, had written a letter to us, bluntly stating that the proposed North Korea article "will compromise and/or otherwise negatively impact the national security of the United States." He wanted to set up a meeting with our publisher. The request wasn't unprecedented but it was unusual, especially coming from the White House counsel rather than someone on the national security staff—and especially coming from a White House counsel whose verb of choice was "will," not "might," not "could." Was a new administration, with less than a month in office, getting ready to turn its back on history and prove that this White House wasn't the Bush White House or, for God's sake, the Obama White House? Were Trump and his team really prepared to cross that century-old line and threaten journalists with criminal prosecution under the Espionage Act?

Most new administrations, faced with the mind-numbing complexities of the Espionage Act and the absolute certainty of a constitutional showdown for the ages, were not eager to make a sharp break with history and push forward with a criminal prosecution of reporters. The Trump administration was not most administrations.

It had been just a few weeks since Jeff Sessions testified at his confirmation hearing about how the new Trump Justice Department was going to deal with journalists and confidential sources. Senator Amy Klobuchar, the Minnesota Democrat and the daughter of a newspaper journalist, asked for a commitment from Sessions that journalists would not be jailed for "doing their job." Sessions begged off, saying he was not fully familiar with DOJ policies about the press and leaks. He understood that the department had "sensitivity to this issue," but he also believed a news organization could be a "mechanism through which unlawful intelligence is obtained."

It was gobbledygook, to be sure, but menacing gobbledygook. The press as mechanism? "Unlawful intelligence" (compared to, say, "lawful intelligence")? What did any of that mean? And had he really shown up for his confirmation hearing unaware of the issues? Nobody in Congress could have missed the media's scorched-earth coverage in 2013 of how the FBI had seized the records of journalists at Fox and the AP. The DOJ, very, very publicly and at the direction of the White House, had reworked its internal guidelines to make it harder for federal prosecutors to go after journalists' sources. Even if that was ancient history to Sessions, the issue of leaks would have been hard to miss if he was spending any time reading his boss's Twitter feed (and how could he not, given what the president was saying about the man?). Trump had regularly gone nuts about leakers and leaks, at least about those leaks revealing new developments in the investigation of his campaign's ties to Russia.

The uncertainty about whether the government would move against The Times was not an entirely new experience for me. There had been one other time when I had seriously thought that a government might finally be willing to step across the line and test the limits of the Espionage Act. That was in 2010, when The Times had received hundreds of thousands of pages of secret Pentagon and State Department documents from WikiLeaks. The disclosure was so different from anything that had come before—a massive number of documents, delivered electronically through a rogue offshore internet site, the motivation of the inside leaker unknown and unknowable. It forced us to reconsider what we knew about publishing secrets and to ask whether the old rules, forged before the internet, still applied in a digital age—whether the U.S. government was still willing to give the press a pass on publishing classified information. Obama was serious about going after leakers. It didn't take much imagination to envision him taking a second (or third) look at whether the war on leaks should be taken to the next level in a world where the digital future seemed to put all secrets at risk in ways that were novel and scary.

On June 23, 2010, I had been at the oral surgeon, and it had not gone well. Groggy, still bleeding, with a huge wad of gauze in my mouth, I stood in the waiting room trying to get clearheaded enough to make my next appointment. My cell phone rang. It was Executive Editor Bill Keller's secretary. She said Bill wanted me to come to a meeting right away. I explained to her about the oral surgery, the blood, the gauze, how things had not gone well, skipping over the part about the malpractice suit I was thinking about filing, and asked whether there might be a better time for me to meet with the executive editor, maybe a time when I didn't have a wad of gauze the size of a tennis ball in my mouth. She said that wasn't possible. Bill was pretty certain I would want to be at the meeting, and I should come to his office right away. What better place to bleed to death after oral surgery than the newsroom of *The New York Times*? I got on the N train and headed back to Midtown.

By the time I reached Keller's office, having discarded my bloody wad of gauze in the newsroom on the way through, the meeting was already going full bore, a half-dozen journalists sitting around his coffee table with more on the phone. The headline was that The Times was going to get the first batch of hundreds of thousands of pages of classified U.S. documents that had been leaked to WikiLeaks. The numbers were astonishing, as it turned out: nearly 500,000 reports on the U.S. military missions in Afghanistan and Iraq, and another 250,000 diplomatic cables from the State Department. Editors of *The Guardian* in London had enticed the founder of WikiLeaks, Julian Assange, to share the materials with *The Times* as well as *The Guardian* and *Der Spiegel*, the idea being that spreading the documents across three mainstream news organizations would magnify the force of the disclosure. Having a U.S. publisher involved, with the protections of the Pentagon Papers ruling, also made it less likely that there would be a court order that would effectively halt publication.

In Keller's office, the discussion was electric—which reporters could be called in to mine the documents, how the materials would be stored and catalogued, who could go to London to meet with Assange and The Guardian, what the documents were likely to show, what secrets were no longer going to be secret, what story lines were going to be worth pursuing. And then out of the blue, as if Keller had just then remembered I was sitting there, he turned and asked whether we could do it—"it" being publishing the largest trove of leaked classified documents in U.S. history. The conversation stopped. None of this was helping the bleeding in my mouth. I wondered whether I could get the gauze back. "I think so," I said. It hardly seemed to be the time or place, as visions of Pulitzer Prizes danced in people's heads, to start dissembling about how the law was actually completely unclear, how the Espionage Act was an impenetrable mystery, how the First Amendment had never been tested in a case like this, or any of the rest. So I went with "I think so," which is pretty much standard lawyer code for "I have no clue— let me get back to you on that."

Over the next days, my colleague Jake Goldstein and I started reading everything we could find on the Espionage Act. We tried to understand what could push us over onto the wrong side of the law. We didn't know what Assange had done to get the documents, and we supported Keller's decision to treat him as a source, not a publishing partner. (It was one of the things that would ultimately lead Assange to break off his relationship with The Times and go nuclear, including a weird scene the following year at Berkeley, where Bill and I were on a panel at the journalism school and Julian denounced The Times as he floated above us on a huge video screen, live from England, like something out of Orwell's *1984*.) Other questions couldn't be taken lightly. We looked into whether our journalists who were not U.S. citizens faced special risks and whether our board, with a legal duty to our shareholders, needed to play a role. And in the final days before the first set of stories was to be published, Jake and I became the lords of redaction, double-checking every document that *The Times* intended to post online to see what our journalists had flagged to be blacked out and to look for anything else that we thought should be removed.

The agreement among *The Guardian*, *The Times*, WikiLeaks, and the German publication *Der Spiegel* was that everyone would go live at the same time—5:00 p.m. New York time on July 25, a Sunday. I had been in upstate New York that weekend and drove back to The Times that morning. For the first (and last) time in my years at The Times, I was empowered by the editors to make the final call to publish. I stood at the foreign desk with reporters and editors who had been living with the project for nearly two months. The call was supposed to be a no-brainer: as soon as WikiLeaks posted its stories, the three publications could follow suit immediately. Five o'clock came. The WikiLeaks site showed nothing new. An editor on the desk kept hitting the refresh button. I wondered for a moment whether we had been set up by Assange and WikiLeaks. Were they trying to get the mainstream publishers to go first, so they could later make a legal argument that they were only publishing what was already public? I asked one of the journalists to try to reach WikiLeaks. We were assured that the hang-up was not devious political machinations of a shadowy offshore organization but something decidedly more mundane: a computer glitch. A few minutes later, the reports flowed from New York, England, Germany, and wherever in the world WikiLeaks existed.

In the days after our stories went live, Senator Joe Lieberman and others would urge the Justice Department to investigate whether The Times could be criminally prosecuted. But I was confident we had made the right decisions in committing to go forward with publishing. We had been selective in what we chose to use, we had gone only with those documents that shed light on U.S. policy and the conduct of U.S. military operations and diplomacy, we had redacted names of average-citizen Afghans who might be targeted by the Taliban. We had given the government a chance to comment in advance on what we intended to publish. We had made sure that the secret documents were kept securely in our possession, safe from hacking or inadvertent disclosure. (The security system put in place involved, among other things, an ever-changing password, meaning I was regularly shut out from access at critical moments and went into Unhappy Lawyer Mode as I had to track down the keeper of the key.) Our legal call was made easier, too, by the fact that a prosecution of The Times seemed unlikely when the same materials were going to be available elsewhere on the internet, thanks to Assange and the other publishers. *The Times* went on to publish two other sets of stories based on the documents, one about Iraq and a second based on State Department cables.

The legal calculation was much the same three years later with the files from the National Security Agency leaked by Edward Snowden. Snowden's disclosure had been even more breathtaking, both in its scope and in its political impact. The public was told for the first time the astonishing scope of the NSA's surveillance of Americans' communications. The Times had unhappily sat on the sidelines when the first explosive disclosures came out through *The Washington Post* and *The Guardian*.

Later, The Times would form an uneasy partnership with The Guardian to get access to materials from Snowden. The Guardian was under pressure from officials in the U.K. and wanted to make sure that the electronic files were somewhere in the U.S., where the likelihood of government action against a news organization was remote. *The Guardian* editors were right. U.K. intelligence officials showed up at The Guardian and presided over the destruction of a hard drive containing the information obtained from Snowden. The two papers continued to collaborate on stories, working from a set of electronic documents that had been brought to the U.S. by a *Times* reporter who packed a computer drive into a suitcase. And just as with WikiLeaks and with every other national security story, the government had stood down and not pursued legal charges against any journalist even as prosecutors won an indictment of Snowden, who remains in Russia.

But now, in February 2017, it was impossible to know whether the lessons of prosecutorial restraint still pertained with Trump in the White House. Over the course of later February, as David and Bill did additional reporting for the North Korea story, the editors and I read through multiple drafts of the piece (I lost count after a while), and we came to understand more fully what David had been saying all along: some of the information we intended to publish was certainly classified, but much of it wasn't truly secret. Government officials in a variety of forums had hinted—or more—at how the U.S. was attacking the North Korean missile program before the missiles were in flight. The strategy was a significant change in nuclear deterrence, and one that Americans needed to know about as they watched, and feared, the ratcheting up of tensions between the U.S. and North Korea. And it was impossible to believe that the North Korean missile scientists, for all their ineptness, were unaware of why so many of their rockets were fizzling and falling like doused fireworks. The possibility of a showdown with North Korea was made palpable in early February when the North Koreans fired off another missile, one capable of reaching North America. *The Times* headlined its article: "North Korea Fires Ballistic Missile, Challenging Trump."

All of that should have mattered to the White House in thinking about any prosecution—the prior disclosures, the public benefit, the diligent reporting—but as February turned to March I wasn't convinced that it would. In a single story, we would be delivering up a trifecta of Trump's hottest-button talking points: unchecked leaks, the hostile press, and out-of-control North Korea. The February 14 tweet, with its condemnation of leaking and the all-too-coincidental reference to North Korea, stayed with me. You could see the narrative: The New York Times, enemy of the people, aided and abetted by disloyal public servants willing to leak classified information, had endangered the country by revealing secrets to a North Korean regime that was intent on destroying all of us—even after *The Times*'s publisher was directly warned of the consequences. It would play to Trump's base and it might well play to the Sessions Justice Department.

There had been no follow-up to the White House request for a meeting with *Times* publisher Arthur Sulzberger Jr. (I took that as a good sign except in those moments when I started thinking it was a bad sign.) By the start of March, the article was ready to go. Executive editor Dean Baquet wanted to make sure that, no matter what the Trump administration was saying about the press or whatever threat hung in the air, we weren't pulling any punches. He knew his role well: "And as I always say in cases like this—easy for me to push!!!"

On March 4, the story went live: "Trump Inherits a Secret Cyberwar Against North Korean Missiles." It was made available in English, Chinese, and Korean. It was a thoroughly reported story, offering readers a sober assessment of the "imperfect options" that the Trump administration faced in staring down the North Koreans:

An examination of the Pentagon's disruption effort, based on interviews with officials of the Obama and Trump administrations as well as a review of extensive but obscure public records, found that the United States still does not have the ability to effectively counter the North Korean nuclear and missile programs. Those threats are far more resilient than many experts thought, The New York Times's reporting found, and pose such a danger that Mr. Obama, as he left office, warned President Trump they were likely to be the most urgent problem he would confront.

With the story released to the world on a Saturday morning, we waited to see how Trump would respond. In this new White House, what advisors thought didn't necessarily count for a lot. The question, inevitably, was how the president would react.

And, not long after the story went up, the presidential tweets came rushing forth—just not about our story:

Terrible! Just found out that Obama had my "wires tapped" in Trump Tower just before the victory. Nothing found. This is McCarthyism!

Is it legal for a sitting President to be "wire tapping" a race for president prior to an election? Turned down by court earlier. A NEW LOW!

I'd bet a good lawyer could make a great case out of the fact that President Obama was tapping my phones in October, just prior to Election!

How low has President Obama gone to tapp my phones during the very sacred election process. This is Nixon/Watergate. Bad (or sick) guy!

Wherever the president's attention may have been that day, the North Korea story to me was part of an important tradition in American journalism. In January 2014, in the aftermath of the Snowden disclosures, Obama had laid out in a speech the nuanced and exceptional way that the American system worked. Obama acknowledged that the Snowden materials had ignited a public discussion about what U.S. intelligence agencies should be allowed to do, and how. "One thing I'm certain of: this debate will make us stronger," Obama said. "No one expects China to have an open debate about their surveillance programs, or Russia to take the privacy concerns of citizens into account."

Then he pivoted to the uncomfortable truth that leaks created risks: "I will say that our nation's defense depends in part on the fidelity of those entrusted with our nation's secrets. If any individual who objects to government policy can take it into their own hands to publicly disclose classified information, then we will not be able to keep our people safe, or conduct foreign policy."

People would debate whether the Snowden disclosures did actual harm but implicit in Obama's remarks was a vindication of the First Amendment: publishing of the Snowden disclosures had sparked a critical public debate that would never have happened otherwise.

I understood why some people were uncomfortable with the idea that publishers should be beyond the reach of the law, even when they published classified information. It had been easier to embrace the logic of that position in a different day. Once, not that long ago, the established media organizations were truly gatekeepers—deciders with an appreciation for the responsibility that came with the job. Now everyone with an account on Twitter, Facebook, or Instagram was, in some way, a publisher. If you believed that publishers should be exempt from prosecution, you had little choice but to accept, at least in theory, that a college kid still living at home had the right to decide whether to publish classified secrets on his Facebook page and put national security at risk without fear of legal consequence.

No matter how much you wanted to hug the First Amendment, it was not easy to love that possibility: a system that placed national security in the hands of anyone who happened to receive a leak and have internet access. But there was a larger context to consider. I remembered being invited in 2012 to speak at a journalism school in Cameroon. The campus was a collection of worn-down wooden structures a few miles from downtown Yaoundé. The kids in the class were in hyperdrive, and they peppered me in French and English with questions about WikiLeaks. They lionized Julian Assange. They had studied WikiLeaks intently and for good reason. The State Department cables disclosed by Assange had provided the citizens of Cameroon for the first time a look at how their corrupt government was ripping off their country's wealth day after day, unchecked. It was an object lesson in what Americans had come to take for granted: the liberating power of information.

We as a country made a trade-off. In embracing an open system with laws that bestowed the press (and everyone else) with an astonishing level of freedom, we accepted the reality that a certain amount of risk was inevitable. That was the price we paid. Maybe the government needed to be better at identifying what really needed to be secret and keeping those secrets truly secret. Maybe we needed to be better at inculcating all citizens—now all potential publishers—with a sense of social responsibility. Maybe we could draw a sensible legal line between the publishing done by *The New York Times* and that spewing forth from the 20-year-old in the bathrobe, although how we could do that under the First Amendment was not obvious, especially with a Supreme Court that had ruled the free speech rights of the press were identical to the rights of individuals. But I continued to believe that the risks that came with freedom were worth the price.

I also believed *The Times* had been right, in its North Korea reporting and other sensitive national security stories, to give the government a chance to respond before publication. Many readers saw that process as a surrender. Snowden specifically turned to Glenn Greenwald and Laura Poitras to get his purloined NSA data published, knowing they would not hesitate to publish first and let the government find out what was up at the same time as millions of readers around the world. And sometimes we got burned by those who decided to play by different rules. In August 2013 the State Department had issued an emergency order temporarily closing 19 embassies without saying why. The government asked that *The Times* not publish one detail that our reporters had uncovered: the closure decision had been made after U.S. intelligence agents intercepted communications between two senior al-Qaeda leaders. *The Times* editors killed that detail from the story, only to be taken aback—actually, they were furious—the next day when the McClatchy newspapers told the whole story, including disclosures about the interception. McClatchy had decided not to check with the government. Relations between the two news organizations were not improved eight weeks later when *The Times* ran a story saying that the McClatchy story had led the terrorists to change their method of communication. McClatchy found the report preposterous.

Even in the newsroom, the issue was still a hot-button topic in some corners. The Times had been widely criticized after it held for more than a year the blockbuster story by Eric Lichtblau and Jim Risen of how U.S. intelligence operatives were illegally conducting surveillance on Americans' telephone calls. The decision to hold the story had come under pressure from the White House, which claimed the disclosure would undermine critical anti-terrorism efforts. The spiking of the story came on the eve of the 2004 election. When the story finally ran in late 2005 with additional reporting, many people were convinced that our decision to stand down had helped George Bush win reelection. In their minds, the very people engaged in wrongdoing had been allowed to veto the story.

It was important to debate whether The Times had been too timid then or at other times, but context was important: our newsroom has regularly decided that the government's objections were too abstract, not believable, insufficiently weighty, or given by officials too far down the food chain to know, and our editors have then resolved to move ahead with publishing. But it's not a science. Editors sometimes get it wrong. National security is intrinsically the hardest of the calls they have to make. They understand the risk that any given disclosures might prove lethal, and they never have enough information to act with absolute certainty. Which is why hearing what the government has to say is not handing over a veto but giving editors a better shot at making a decent decision. If we were ever forced to defend against a criminal charge, I wanted our legal narrative to be one of responsibility, serious deliberation, and a demonstrable concern about the public's best interests.

If the administration had any legal concerns about the North Korea story post-publication, we never heard about them. But in October, Jeff Sessions was back in front of a Senate committee to talk about press freedom. It was not particularly reassuring. Senator Klobuchar was still looking for answers to her question about how he and the DOJ were going to protect the rights of the press.

KLOBUCHAR: Will you commit to not putting reporters in jail for doing their jobs?

SESSIONS: Well, I don't know that I can make a blanket commitment to that effect. But I would say this: We have not taken any aggressive action against the media at this point. But we have matters that involve the most serious national security issues, that put our country at risk, and we will utilize the authorities that we have, legally and constitutionally, if we have to. Maybe we—we always try to find an alternative way, as you probably know, Senator Klobuchar, to directly confronting a media person. But that's not a total, blanket protection.

Nobody inside The Times needed a translation of Sessions-speak: journalists might go to jail for, yes, doing their jobs.

By then, *Times* reporters had learned more about what the president had been up to on Valentine's Day, when he had begun his morning with the tweet harangue about leaks and North Korea. Later that day, he had met with FBI director James Comey. After Comey was fired, Mike Schmidt of *The Times* tracked down a source who knew what had happened at the Valentine's Day meeting, thanks to a memo Comey had written. "Alone in the Oval Office," Schmidt reported, "Mr. Trump began the discussion by condemning leaks to the news media, saying that Mr. Comey should consider putting reporters in prison for publishing classified information, according to one of Mr. Comey's associates."

It was just as well we didn't know that in real time.

11

Weinstein & Co.

I wanted to do something inspirational for my children.

—Harvey Weinstein, June 17, 2014
(at the launch of *Finding Neverland*)

I came of age in the '60s and '70s when all the rules about behavior and workplaces were different.

—Harvey Weinstein, Oct. 5, 2017
(opening statement to his public apology for sexual misconduct)

IT WAS A pleasant June evening in New York, and I was at JFK waiting for a flight to Paris when I remembered that Jodi Kantor was looking for me. I got her by cell, and she told me that she was starting work on what she described as an explosive story about Harvey Weinstein and what he had done to women in Hollywood. She wanted me to know that what she was hearing was extraordinary and grotesque, and we were probably going to get sued because it was the kind of story that could destroy Harvey and The Weinstein Company. I had just spent the better part of a year working with Mike Schmidt and Emily Steel as they tracked down the series of confidential settlements entered into by Bill O'Reilly when he was repeatedly accused of mistreating women at his Fox talk show. I knew the drill for these sorts of stories. We could expect Harvey to ratchet up the pressure, bring in a battalion of lawyers, threaten the accusers, and tell our executives that he was pulling his company's advertising from the paper. We would print some credible allegations, he would deny them, lawyer letters would be exchanged, life would go on. This is not going to be all that big of a deal, I thought as I paced the JFK waiting area. I told Jodi she should keep me posted.

The Bill O'Reilly saga had started nine months earlier, in September 2016. O'Reilly's lawyer, Fred Newman, had called and asked to come to talk to me. Fred is the anti-O'Reilly. He is everything Bill is not: understated, drama-free, ever polite. Client-attorney relationships are like some marriages: a mystery to the world beyond, leaving everyone to wonder how these two people ever got together and how they kept it going. It must have worked for Bill and Fred. Over the next 18 months, Emily and Mike pushed forward with a series of articles, finally knocking down the incredible story that O'Reilly had paid $32 million to settle a threatened suit by one of the show's contributors, barely two weeks after her last appearance on the air. Fred remained O'Reilly's go-to guy through it all, calling me, meeting with me, sending emails. He did what he could to explain away each of the women's stories and justify settlements as expedient ways for Bill to resolve dubious claims, all the while asking pointed questions about how Mike and Emily were going about their reporting. But his client hadn't dealt him much of a hand. Some $45 million had been paid to settle six separate claims. The last article, detailing the $32 million payment, landed two weeks after *The Times* broke the Weinstein story, sentencing O'Reilly to be linked forever in the public's mind with the Weinstein scandal.

When Fred first called me in September 2016, I didn't know anything about any story being done about O'Reilly. As I put it in an email to Emily, "O'Reilly's lawyer got in touch with me today, concerned about a story they imagine you are doing. Completely polite meeting and I just listened to what the guy had to say. But let's talk when you have a chance."

That was my tentative and largely clueless step into the reporting that would help give rise to the #MeToo movement. Over the next year, Emily and Mike (working on the O'Reilly stories) and Jodi and Megan Twohey (covering Weinstein) would break story after story about the sexual misconduct of the two media megacelebrities. Those stories would, in turn, ignite reporting at *The Times* and elsewhere that swept across a patchwork of America's most iconic industries—art, theater, academia, music, fashion, the news media (including The Times itself)—exposing the sexual misconduct of men in power who harassed, mauled, and assaulted their colleagues, students, and employees. The stories quickly went international—France, India, Italy, Japan, England (where the deeply apt and all-purpose term "sex pest" was the label of choice). I spent countless hours talking to reporters about troubling journalistic and legal questions: how they could protect their sources, what might happen to women who would violate the nondisclosure clauses in their settlement agreements if they talked to us, what the reporters could do to push their reporting a little further and make sure their stories were beyond challenge—and, of course, how likely it was that one of the accused men would sue us for libel if we had something wrong (or even if we didn't).

Before it was all over, I would be dragged into one of the messy dark corners of the Weinstein scandal when *The New Yorker* magazine reported that a law firm we sometimes used, Boies, Schiller and Flexner, had hired sleazy private eyes on behalf of Weinstein to follow our reporters and try to stop *The Times* from writing about Weinstein.

Much of what I had to do on our sexual misconduct reporting had surprisingly little to do with the intricacies of the law. The review of the stories was routine—the sort of thing a newspaper lawyer would do with stories about financial fraud or badly made products or mistreatment at nursing homes. These stories just happened to be about sexual abuse. With few exceptions, when lawyers for the accused called me, they were not citing legal cases or threatening litigation but just trying whatever they could to get us not to publish a story, hoping to gin up some doubts about the facts or the sources or the motivation for the story. "*The New York Times* wouldn't have done this story a year ago, and my guy will lose his job," a lawyer told me late one evening in a call to my office. His client was an executive who had a pattern of making inappropriate comments about women's appearances and touching them at the office or at parties in ways that were unwelcome. I'd never heard of him before, but in his industry he was a major player. At least that's what I was being told. I couldn't help the lawyer. He was right. It would not have been a story a year earlier. The conduct was boorish and wrong but sadly common; the guy was pretty much an unknown to the general public. Being unfamous and unexceptional would have meant no coverage in the past. None of that mattered now. The world had turned. And I was not the commissar of newsworthiness or the crown prince of fairness. I told him he needed to have his client get on the phone and make the case to our reporter and her editors. That didn't seem likely, the lawyer told me. His client was going to lose his job, he repeated. He was right again. The story went up on our website the next morning. A couple hours later the guy was gone.

Other lawyers tried different approaches, novel tactics. I lost track of how many lawyers told me, "He's not Harvey Weinstein!" One attorney showed up at my office with what he claimed were naked pictures of the woman who was accusing his client of sexual misconduct. He wanted to show them to me. He thought they proved that whatever happened between his client and the woman was voluntary and consensual. I thought they proved that we had a long, long way to go. I didn't need to see any pictures. Later, as Megan and Jodi were doing a sweeping follow-up story about Harvey Weinstein and those who were complicit in covering up his misconduct, they heard reports that Weinstein had made a female

Weinstein Company employee procur his erectile dysfunction medicine. I never imagined that I would have to have a serious dialogue with other lawyers about how penile injections work, whether the reports made sense from the standpoint of medical science, and what damage it would do to Harvey's reputation if that account was reported. I guess that was where the reputational line was drawn for Weinstein. Not at stories about showing up naked in a bathrobe for business meetings. Not at stories about making young female actors watch him shower. Not at accounts of his groping or exposing himself or sexually attacking women. Getting help with erectile dysfunction? No, that was going too far.

Harvey Weinstein was one of the few to go into full-threat lawyer mode, and even then that came late, long after *The Times* already had the reporting that would take him down. In September 2017, before the Weinstein sex stories had been published, Megan Twohey got onto a strange story about how Weinstein had used an AIDS nonprofit he supported to raise money for a nonprofit theater company in Boston. The theater happened to be producing a Weinstein production, *Finding Neverland*. The idea was that Weinstein would arrange to get items for the charity auction of the AIDS nonprofit, but part of the money collected would go to the theater. The theater, in turn, would pay Weinstein and other investors back money they had fronted it to get the show up and running. Weinstein's failure to disclose the funding arrangement had fractured the board of the AIDS charity, and some board members were seeking a state investigation. Megan and her editor, Rebecca Corbett, wanted to know whether I thought, from a legal perspective, it was a story. I have been around newsrooms long enough to have very good instincts about at least one very important thing: I know when editors and reporters are having a disagreement about a story and think I should be enlisted to take someone's side. That is an invitation to get blown up. I went into Full Platitude Mode. I liked the story. The funding arrangement seemed dodgy to me. I had served on nonprofit boards, and I had never seen anything like it. On the other hand . . . maybe you had to be a lawyer to care about the technicalities of nonprofit law. Maybe it was too deep in the legal weeds. At one point, Rebecca stepped out of the conference room, and I privately assured Megan that the funding of the theater had to be some sort of problem, something that needed to be written about. Rebecca, the guiding hand behind our Weinstein coverage, called me later, concerned about how we were going to explain the legal complexity in the story. I agreed with her, too.

A couple of days later the charity story was published. It helped to push forward an investigation by the New York State attorney general. But Megan and Jodi always thought it did something more significant: it showed women who were reluctant to speak about Weinstein's sexual misconduct that The New York Times was not scared to take him on.

By the beginning of October, Weinstein had surrounded himself with a collection of lawyers—and, as time would show, it was more collection than team. Heavy-hitter lawyers from Kirkland & Ellis were in charge of challenging our reporting on the charity story. There was also David Boies, maybe America's most famous lawyer, although he was playing more Friend of Harvey than legal counsel. Then there was Lisa Bloom, who had made her name suing sexual harassers but had somehow bolted to the dark side. Lanny Davis, a former lawyer in the Clinton White House, was handling press relations. Charles Harder, who had represented Hulk Hogan in the Gawker case, was waiting in the wings. The draft story of Weinstein's sexual predations had been in development for days, with various versions coming to my desk day after day. The reporting was solid but the story remained a work in progress. We knew that certain Weinstein employees and others had made accusations and then settled or gone silent or issued supportive statements. I went through a late draft in the first days of October, raising questions about how we were presenting the sometimes ambiguous accounts and whether we were overplaying certain incidents. I was concerned that our language in places may have implied more than we knew on the record. At one point in the story I had five substantive questions in the span of seven paragraphs. Megan called me later with answers. She then told me that everything was going to be fine and I should hold off until I saw the latest version. Ashley Judd had decided to go on the record, she said. I knew right then it was over for Harvey Weinstein.

Maybe Harvey did, too. In talking to the reporters on October 3, he said that he needed at least 48 hours to answer the questions they had posed. The next day, Weinstein unleashed Harder to write a knuckle-dragging letter to *The Times*, threatening a libel suit, demanding that his client needed two weeks to answer questions, and closing out the letter with pages of demands that we preserve all documents, since litigation was imminent. (A year later, when Harder was representing Donald Trump and threatening Michael Wolff with a libel suit over his scorched-earth account of the White House, *Fire and Fury*, I learned that the same document-preservation demands were cut and pasted into his letter to Wolff's publisher.) The idea that Harvey needed two weeks to remember whether he had sexually abused women was absurd. I caucused in an eighth-floor conference room with the reporters, Dean Baquet, and other editors. Harvey had said he needed 48 hours; we weren't giving him more. In the middle of the meeting, Megan's phone rang. It was Lanny Davis calling, trying once more to do some damage control for Weinstein. Dean took the phone and told him, in so many words, that we were done having one Weinstein toady tell us one thing and having another Weinstein toady tell us something else. He may have used more colorful phrasing than "toady."

I went back upstairs to write a response to Harder when I was intercepted by our publisher, Arthur Sulzberger. He wanted me to brief him and his son, A. G., then the deputy publisher, about the Harder letter. We huddled in the Churchill Room, a meeting room on the sixteenth floor that housed Winston Churchill memorabilia, including a painting that Churchill had given to The Times. I assured them that we had the story cold and I would do my best to fend off the Weinstein legal team.

I quickly typed up a letter to Harder, telling him we were giving Weinstein the 48 hours he had asked for, nothing more. Being of the fight-fire-with-fire school, I also included a demand that Harvey and his various functionaries make sure that they preserved their documents, especially their texts and emails. I knew what some of those communications would show: that people in Weinstein's camp had not toed the company line in talking to our reporters. My document demand was barely two paragraphs long—a shadow of what Harder had cranked out and sent to us, but enough to make my point. A short time later, my letter, bizarrely, became the subject of a story in the *Los Angeles Times*. Harder had forwarded the letter to Harvey and his associates at The Weinstein Company (with a note suggesting that they be careful with their emailing) but mistakenly added to the address list an *LAT* reporter.

Our editors were aiming to publish the piece on Thursday, October 5. On Wednesday, Harder was back at it, threatening us again and decrying the unfairness of giving Harvey only two days to respond when the story had been in the works for months. Two things remained unclear to me: why Weinstein had said 48 hours if he needed more time and what exactly he intended to do for those two weeks if he got the extra time—check his appointment book and search his email in hopes of jogging his memory about which women he had assaulted when? We refused to budge from our deadline. We were also aware that downtown at *The New Yorker* the writer Ronan Farrow was chasing the same story, and we didn't want to get beat.

On Wednesday evening, the Weinstein crew appeared to go

with the oldest trick in the media-relations book: strategically helping out on a preemptive story in another news outlet. That often works if the subject of the story is going to have to admit to wrongdoing anyway. Better to have another publication tell the story in a shallow way and scoop the bigger, more pointed story that is coming later. "Harvey Weinstein Lawyers Up for Bombshell New York Times, New Yorker Stories," the *Variety* headline screamed. Weinstein apparently didn't get the memo about how to do preemptive stories—especially the part about how the strategy only works if the target is going to admit to some things. Without that, the strategic leak becomes something entirely different: a traffic-driving advertisement for the blockbuster story that the other publication is about to publish. Not that Weinstein exactly denied the allegations to *Variety*. "I've not been aware of this," he said. "I don't know what you're talking about, honestly." He let it be known that he was too engaged in making movies to fret:

> When asked if the publications had called him for comment, Weinstein replied that he was too busy in the editing room working on *The Current War,* an upcoming historical drama, to know the answer to that question, adding that he'd had a "crazy day."

Later, he did get around to giving a comment: "The story sounds so good I want to buy the movie rights." And lawyer Lisa Bloom got to play the slightly menacing legal heavy: "Harvey Weinstein is obviously excellent at assembling a legal team." A week later, you couldn't read those comments without wondering what they were thinking.

On Thursday, with Harvey's 48-hour deadline ticking down to the last minutes and the story ready to launch, the team at The Times waited for whatever response he would give. Harvey's statement finally appeared, reading as if it had been delivered by express mail straight from Crazytown:

I came of age in the '60s and '70s, when all the rules about behavior and workplaces were different. That was the culture then.

I have since learned it's not an excuse, in the office—or out of
it. To anyone.

I realized some time ago that I needed to be a better person
and my interactions with the people I work with have changed.

I appreciate the way I've behaved with colleagues in the past
has caused a lot of pain, and I sincerely apologize for it.

Though I'm trying to do better, I know I have a long way to
go. That is my commitment. My journey now will be to learn
about myself and conquer my demons.

There was more—a botched quotation from Jay-Z, some wacky
mention of throwing a retirement party for the head of the National
Rifle Association ("I'm going to do it at the same place I had my
Bar Mitzvah"), an announcement he was going to take a leave
of absence—but the part that interested me was all at the top: He
was apologizing. He didn't say a word about suing. He never once
hinted at there being any factual error in our piece. That was not
the statement of a man who was about to turn around and sue The
New York Times.

At least that was how I read it. Not Charles Harder, Harvey's
defamation guy. He was still manning the Weinstein legal barricades, proclaiming that his apology-spewing, pain-causing, leave-
taking, committed-to-becoming-a-better-man client was going to
sue The New York Times for libel. In press accounts, Harder chided
the paper for ignoring evidence and relying on "hearsay accounts."
He solemnly vowed that "we are preparing the lawsuit now," and
just in case anyone happened to think that Harvey was a greedy,
moneygrubbing Hollywood mogul lacking a social conscience,
Harder assured the world that all proceeds from the suit would be
donated to women's organizations.

Back at The Times, we were caught up in the story about the

story. Our PR team was encountering a blizzard of requests for comment from other news organizations wanting to know what we thought about Weinstein's statement, what we were doing about Harder's litigation threat, and what we had to say about Weinstein's complaint that he had not been given a fair chance to respond. The usual playbook when litigation is threatened is to say as little as possible. Detailed statements can only come back to haunt you in court someday if it turns out that the statement was wrong on the particulars, or out of context, or missing important facts. But this was different, a bet-the-farm story that had our reputation on the line, and I knew from working with Jodi and Megan that we had only scratched the surface of Weinstein's terrorizing of women. I wasn't about to let us lose this one in the court of public opinion. I drafted our response:

> Mr. Weinstein and his lawyer have confirmed the essential points of the story. Mr. Weinstein has not pointed to any errors or challenged any facts in our story. Also, Mr. Weinstein should publicly waive the NDAs in the women's agreements so they can tell their stories. As a supporter of women, he must support their right to speak openly about these issues of gender and power.

We shot it out to all the reporters seeking comments. Jodi sent me one of the best emails I could ever receive as a lawyer. "This brought tears to my eyes," said the subject line. She had pasted the statement into the body of the email and boldfaced the bit about how Weinstein should waive the nondisclosure agreements and prove he was a supporter of women. At the bottom Jodi wrote, "I cannot wait to tweet the hell out of that."

In the first 24 hours after the story went live, I was inundated with all things Weinstein. Every columnist in The Times's universe seemed to be cranking out Harvey-focused pieces. The social media team was promoting the story all over the web. In the newsroom, follow-up coverage was being rolled out. All of it needed lawyering. And for all the buffoonery of Harvey's statement, I couldn't ignore Harder's letter and our duty to preserve documents. My associate Christina Koningisor and I started sending out emails to anyone at The Times who was likely to have emails or texts or story drafts related to Weinstein. It was the least exclusive club the newsroom had ever known.

I was in the midst of all that when a reporter asked, "Did you hear about Lisa Bloom's interview?" I wasn't sure what he was talking about. Bloom, who had spent her professional life defending women who were harassed, had somehow ended up in Harvey's legal camp, where, among other things, she was supposed to be helping him behave better. The day our story ran, she seemed to be in some sort of weird competition with her client to see who could issue the most inappropriate public statement. She initially characterized Weinstein as nothing more than an "old dinosaur learning new ways." Among those who were questioning what Bloom was doing was her mother, Gloria Allred, the crusading plaintiffs' lawyer, who told *Variety* that she was ready to help Weinstein's accusers: "While I would not represent Mr. Weinstein, I would consider representing anyone who accused Mr. Weinstein of sexual harassment, even if it meant that my daughter was the opposing counsel." Bloom scrambled for the higher ground, retorting that she would never take a case in which her lawyer mother or her lawyer daughter was on the other side because "I believe in family before business." Thanksgiving with the Allreds and Blooms was going to be interesting this year. The morning after the story ran, Bloom began tiptoeing toward the exit. She had gone on national television with George Stephanopolous and conceded that Weinstein had engaged in "illegal" conduct.

None of it made sense to us. Wasn't her legal teammate Harder preparing his big *Weinstein v. The New York Times Company* lawsuit? Hadn't he said that *The Times*'s story was "saturated with false and defamatory statements" (making it sound as if we were not just wrong but a danger to our readers' cholesterol)? I know well that law is unpredictable, but it was starting to seem very unlikely that women's organizations around the country were going to be hauling in huge buckets of money from Harvey's plan to win a suit against The Times and donate the winnings.

By Saturday, Lisa Bloom had quit working for Weinstein. Lanny Davis quit, too. Harder hung around for a few more days and then exited. In the post-O.J. world of lawyering, it was rare indeed to find a client so odious that his own lawyers wanted nothing to do with him. By the time Harder's departure was made public, *The New Yorker* and *The Times* had published more explosive details about Weinstein's abuse, and The Weinstein Company had fired Harvey, who was purportedly off to rehab.

The floodgates had opened, and accounts of sexual misconduct by Weinstein and then others became a staple of our coverage in October. Reporters came to me and walked through the accounts they were hearing from victims. I read their drafts. Most of what was getting covered were incidents with no witnesses. We developed an unofficial protocol of finding out whether the woman had talked to a friend or family member or colleague contemporaneously with the events, and then interviewing the other people. That shored up the credibility of the accounts. I also realized that with most stories, the legal threat was more likely to come not from the perpetrator but from the minor characters in the pieces—the HR directors who did nothing, the agents who knew what was going on, the supervisors who apparently protected the predator. I wanted to be sure we had those details buttoned up.

At first, it was disconcerting to hear how badly men behaved in so many companies in so many different ways. After a while, for better or worse, with so much repetition of accounts of perverse, hostile, or simply gross behavior, with so much discussion of the bizarre facts and grotesque circumstances, I became more inured to the precise details of the misconduct. An editor called me as I was sitting on a plane at LaGuardia and wanted my take on whether—legally—masturbating on someone was the same as or different from masturbating in front of someone. "I never thought I would have to ask anyone this question," he began. And I never thought I would have to give a legal opinion about it.

In the background that October, there was some good legal news for the paper and for me, news that had nothing to do with Weinstein—until it did. We had spent the past year dealing with a very difficult libel case brought by a New Jersey mother whose adult daughter had accused her in a *Times* article of being abusive when she was growing up. The daughter was featured in a piece on her efforts to bounce back from years of drug abuse, prostitution, and crime. The mother had not been interviewed before publication and then sued us, saying there had been no abuse, just caring and love for a very troubled and challenging teenager. Sorting out what happened in the confines of anyone's home a decade earlier is never easy in a libel case, and the daughter's checkered past made her an easy mark for attacks on her credibility. Somehow, our very capable outside lawyer, Peter Skinner, had built a compelling case for us, leaving the mother's lawyers with no option but to withdraw the lawsuit. Peter was a junior partner at Boies, Schiller and Flexner, the firm founded and led by David Boies.

When it had first surfaced that David was representing Weinstein, I was put in an awkward position. The Boies firm had handled occasional matters for The Times for 20 years, beginning before my time in Legal. The firm's lawyers also represented some of the worst characters in the world: the corrupt leader of Malaysia, ethically suspect Chinese businessmen, Russian oligarchs. They had never sued The Times (they had sued others for libel), but they occasionally wrote us threatening letters when our reporters were doing stories about someone in their rogues' gallery of clients. David's approach to lawyering was always a little puzzling. He and his firm had done noble work on behalf of sex-trafficking victims, and he had become famous decades ago representing CBS and *60 Minutes* when General William Westmoreland sued for libel over a story accusing the general of lying about how well the Vietnam War was going. I had seen him speak at the NYU law school's graduation in 2013 when he talked movingly of how, at the end of the day, the source of a lawyer's power was his or her reputation and how important it was for lawyers to protect that. Getting threatening letters from his firm was irritating, especially given the sketchy clients that the firm was usually fronting for, and other media lawyers couldn't understand why we maintained a relationship with the firm, but I felt that the connection to Boies Schiller usually worked in our favor, keeping a line of communication open when a Boies Schiller client had a complaint about our reporting.

We were wrapping up the paperwork for ending the mother's libel case late in the day on November 6 when a Hollywood reporter contacted me and wanted to know whether I had a comment on the breaking piece in *The New Yorker* titled "Harvey Weinstein's Army of Spies." One section of it, the reporter told me, dealt with how David Boies had hired private investigators to help derail our reporting on Weinstein. I hadn't seen the story, but what I was being told didn't strike me as particularly worrisome. I had on a couple of occasions hired private investigators. They are sometimes helpful in finding out background information on people who are suing us. I assumed that was what David had done, hired private eyes to investigate Weinstein's accusers, and, not to gloat, but that strategy had failed miserably, hadn't it? I was pleased to see Harvey Weinstein waste his money. Our editors were not worked up about that part of the story either. They were worked up more about getting scooped by Ronan Farrow of *The New Yorker*, who had uncovered some shocking new details about the Weinstein scandal.

Then I got an email from a friend and former colleague, Deirdre Sullivan, who had worked with Boies Schiller attorneys when she was at The Times. She wanted to make sure I had seen the *New Yorker* piece. She was disappointed by the firm's double-dealing— Boies had been sending out people to spy on our reporters at the same time we were sending his firm big checks to pay legal fees. I told her I wasn't sure what the investigators had done or not done. Her response stopped me: "Fwiw, I think I saw mention of a success fee if the article was not published in whole or part."

I went online and was able to find a leaked copy of the contract that Boies had signed with the investigators, a slimy outfit known as Black Cube, whose leaders bill themselves as veterans of the Israeli intelligence service. It was like no investigator contract I had ever seen before. It was not aimed at merely finding out information about Harvey's accusers, but was an open invitation for Black Cube's operatives to do whatever it could to kill our Weinstein story before it saw the light of day. Black Cube, which was not even licensed to work in New York State, was to be paid $200,000 for starters. Then Clause 16 added, "In the event in which Black Cube provides intelligence which will directly contribute to efforts to completely stop the Article from being published at all, in any shape or form, Black Cube will be paid a success fee of USD $300,000." David Boies would later tell me that Black Cube was just trying to get at the truth so that Weinstein and his cohorts could present our reporters with information that would show our reporting was wrong. Maybe David believed that. Somehow that high-minded concept never made its way into the contract. Black Cube was to get the $300,000 bonus if the story got killed, no matter how that was achieved. The contract specified that Black Cube was to hire someone to pretend to be a journalist, apparently as a cover to get information. We later learned that someone else posing as a women's rights advocate contacted Jodi seeking a meeting. Another Black Cube dirty trick. (She didn't fall for it.)

It was impossible to read the contract as anything other than a strong-armed attempt by Harvey Weinstein to keep the truth from ever seeing the light of day. At the bottom of the contract was David Boies's signature and the date: July 11, 2017. On that day, as David Boies was signing a contract with the aim of interfering with our core work as a newspaper, one of his partners was contacting me about setting up a time for a meeting with our CEO about a business matter the firm was handling for The Times. On the same day, Pete Skinner and I were going back and forth about details of a deposition that had taken place in the libel suit. David would later publicly point out that in hiring his firm we had agreed that his lawyers could take on matters in which they might be adverse to us and that we waived whatever conflict that might present. That was true. We did that at times with big firms with lots of clients. The waiver provision envisions that the firm will file a public suit that names us as a party or is contrary to our interests or will contact us on behalf of a client who has issues with us. At that point we would be free to decide whether to continue with the Boies firm or walk away. That was not what the Black Cube deal was about. It was secret, and it sanctioned interference with our business through an investigative firm whose calling card was duplicity and dishonesty. Don't talk to me about the conflicts rules that apply to legal representation. Let's talk about what's right and wrong.

On the evening of November 6, as *The New Yorker* story was breaking, we had issued a mild-mannered comment, noting that David Boies had not represented us but that we had matters with other lawyers in his firm. As I sat in my office reading the Black Cube contract, I knew we were about to get killed in the media unless we did something. We were going to look as if we were fine with what Boies had done and this was all just business as usual in New York law circles. I madly typed out a statement and asked our communications people to start pushing it out. It read:

We learned today that the law firm of Boies Schiller and Flexner secretly worked to stop our reporting on Harvey Weinstein at the same time as the firm's lawyers were representing us in other matters. We consider this intolerable conduct, a grave betrayal of trust, and a breach of the basic professional standards that all lawyers are required to observe. It is inexcusable, and we will be pursuing appropriate remedies.

By 10:30 that night, I was on the phone with Jim Rutenberg, our media columnist. The newsroom decided that *The Times* couldn't ignore the escalating Boies-Times fight, which was cascading across social media. Jim's story went up later that night.

Early the next morning, Arthur Sulzberger Jr. called me into his office to talk about what had happened. I fumbled around trying to explain how we got ourselves into this messy sideshow. It was my fault. I knew we were playing with fire when we hired the Boies firm. I thought I could make it work. I shouldn't have done it. Arthur wasn't really interested in assigning blame. He wanted to make sure that I realized we needed to end our relationship with Boies Schiller. I shifted on his couch. Of course, I said, but there was just one problem. It was the libel case by the New Jersey mother. We were waiting for her lawyers to send us the papers withdrawing the suit. The papers were supposed to come that morning. If we fired our attorneys now, it could get complicated and give the other side an incentive not to go through with the withdrawal. Maybe we could wait a few hours and terminate the firm later once we had the papers in hand?

So we waited, caught up in the red tape and minor strategic decisions of litigation, awkwardly sidestepping press inquiries about whether we intended to dump the Boies firm. It was pretty clear that people were looking for some big Trumpian moment from us in which we would instantly proclaim, "You're fired!" We weren't going to be able to give them the satisfaction. I felt bad for Pete Skinner, our lawyer at Boies Schiller who had done such a tremendous job on the libel case and was just collateral damage of The Times's skirmish with his boss. The withdrawal papers from the mother's lawyers showed up early in the afternoon, I fired Boies Schiller, I entered the case as the new counsel of record, I filed the papers, and the case was over a few minutes later.

Maybe I should have spent some time at that point contemplating what lessons were to be learned from the whole sorry episode with Boies—what it taught me about hiring lawyers, and being a lawyer, and the moral ambiguities of practicing law. But one of our editors in the culture department needed to talk to me urgently. We had learned that the comedian Louis C. K. liked to masturbate in front of women who worked with him. There were new stories coming and legal questions that needed to be answered.

12

Alice in FOIA-land

Secrecy, being an instrument of conspiracy, ought never to be the system of regular government.

—Jeremy Bentham, nineteenth-century philosopher

The federal government censored, withheld or said it couldn't find records sought by citizens, journalists and others more often last year than at any point in the past decade.

—News article about the state of the Freedom of Information Act from the Associated Press, March 12, 2018

IT FELT INEVITABLE: the Trump presidency was barely a half-year old, and I was suing the administration over a tweet.

It began in the early evening of July 24, 2017. That was when the president tweeted: "The Amazon Washington Post fabricated the facts on my ending massive, dangerous, and wasteful payments to Syrian rebels fighting Assad. . . ." The tweet was intriguing in many ways. One was the timing: It came at 7:23 p.m. It was not part of one of those early morning presidential tweet storms. Then there was the reference to the "Amazon Washington Post." *The Washington Post* has not changed its name, and it is not owned by Amazon. It is owned personally by Jeff Bezos, who also happens to be the founder of Amazon and the richest man in the world. But there was more: the payments to Syrian rebels mentioned by the president? That CIA program was a classified national security secret. So was the president's decision to end the payments. Nobody without a security clearance was supposed to know anything about it. The president, armed with his cell phone, had just leaked national security secrets to his tens of millions of Twitter followers and everyone else in the world.

The tweet had come in response to a *Washington Post* story five days earlier in which *The Post* reported—based on confidential sources—that CIA director Mike Pompeo and National Security Advisor H. R. McMaster had recommended that the covert program be shut down, and the president agreed. *The Post* reported that the decision "will be welcomed by Moscow" and—not to put too fine a point on it—quoted an anonymous government official as saying that "Putin won in Syria." The CIA had reportedly spent over a billion dollars training and arming Syrian rebels.

With the tweet still fresh, *Times* reporter Matt Rosenberg quickly shot off a Freedom of Information Act request to the CIA, asking for all documents about the funding of the rebels and the president's decision to cut off the payments. Now that the president had confirmed the existence of the program and his decision to stop the funding, there was no secret left to protect, and, as we saw it, the CIA had to provide documents about the program under FOIA. Spoiler alert: the CIA didn't exactly see it that way.

From the start, the idea behind FOIA was simple: Average-Joe citizen writes to federal agency and asks for documents. Agency sends Average-Joe citizen documents. Democracy thrives. Maybe Lyndon Johnson actually believed it would happen that way when he signed FOIA into law in 1966. It was the Fourth of July, a good day to be signing a bill that had "freedom" in its name. Johnson was no particular fan of the legislation, but members of Congress loved the idea—once they exempted themselves so they would never have to turn over a piece of paper under the new law—and Johnson caved after some exemptions were written into the law to protect a few things that needed to remain secret. It was a big deal in its way. Up to that point, as scholar Michael Schudson has documented, the government had been run on the philosophy that the American people, including members of Congress, were out of luck if they wanted to get information from a federal agency unless the agency just decided to give it up, which an agency was not all that prone to do. There was no right to know; there was a right to know nothing. FOIA was meant to change all of that.

But it wasn't long before Ralph Nader, consumer advocate and regular bearer of bad news, rode onto the scene to let people know just how the new law was working out. He gave the climax away in the title of the article he wrote: "The Freedom from Information Act." He had sent a bunch of young associates out to test the new law. Federal bureaucrats may get a bad rap for lacking a certain creativity, but that was not the case when it came to figuring out ways to cripple the brand-spanking-new Freedom of Information Act. Nader's people found that agencies were resorting to "primitive responses"—losing documents, lying about the existence of records, showing favoritism to corporate requesters. And in just a matter of months, the agencies had become masters at invoking FOIA's exemptions to make sure that the public rarely laid eyes on the really interesting documents. The bureaucrats also showed an inherent knack for dragging their feet. It was a dismal picture that Nader painted.

Fifty years later, if the FOIA system had changed, it had changed mostly for the worse. Absurd delays? Check. Runaway exemptions used by agencies to keep documents secret? Check. Pages so redacted they looked like abstract art from the late Soviet era? Check. True, the process sometimes worked the way Johnson envisioned at that Fourth of July signing ceremony. Documents requested; documents obtained. But here was how the FOIA story often unfolded. In 2002, The Times sent a FOIA request to the De-

partment of Labor asking the agency to identify the most dangerous places to work in the United States. The department had
published a list of 13,000 companies that had excessive rates of injuries and deaths in the workplace, a veritable honor roll of the worst
places to work in America. But the department refused to say who
was number 1 and who was number 12,999. If you happened to be
looking for a factory job, it probably mattered to you whether you
were signing on to work at the top place in the country to be dis-
membered or killed or just showing up at one of the modestly lethal
factories where you still had a decent chance of making it through
the week with all your fingers. The Labor Department didn't exactly
deny our FOIA request. It responded that it would need 15 work
years—that is, one person working 30,290 hours—before department officials could get back to us with a complete response and let
us know which part, if any, of the information could be released. As
I read the department's letter laying all this out, I tried to envision
that lonely government worker reporting for work day after day for
a decade and a half doing nothing more than laboring over our
request. Week after dreary week, year after dreary year, there he
would be, trudging home each evening after putting in another
eight of his 30,290 hours, to regale his spouse over dinner about
his huge career working on The New York Times's FOIA request.

I sensed that our reporters probably didn't want to wait quite
that long, crossing off the days on a big calendar for 15 years, like
an inmate serving a prison term. I also knew something else: FOIA,
as written, required a response in 20 days. We sued.

Like me, the judge, Shira Scheindlin, wanted to know how a
20-day response deadline set by Congress and signed into law by
the president could be refashioned by an agency into a 15-year
slow walk. The Labor Department was not helped when its
lawyer tried to tell the judge that the lawsuit had to be dismissed
because—here comes the genius part—The Times's request had
never been denied. See, the Department of Labor was actually in

the midst of responding and, once we got the response—in 15 years—if we were still dissatisfied (and alive), then we could come to court and complain. Judge Scheindlin ordered the Labor Department to get us the information. What happened next was no surprise in the upside-down world that is FOIA: The department didn't really need 15 years to handle our request. It was closer to 15 days once a federal judge told Labor to get moving.

That was the beginning of my career as a FOIA litigator at The Times. Most news organizations stopped doing FOIA litigation in the early 2000s. There was no budget for it, the industry was being racked by the loss of advertising revenues, and FOIA had become synonymous with delay and frustration. It didn't seem worth the bother to most news organizations. The Times decided to go the opposite direction. With libel litigation on the decline and secrecy becoming epidemic after 9/11, it made sense for us to switch focus, to start going to court and trying to get judges to join us in the fight against the excesses of secrecy. It was often going to be frustrating, and we were going to lose a lot, but I thought about FOIA lawsuits the way public defenders often think about criminal defense work. In the criminal justice system, the enormous power of the government is being used to prosecute and imprison an individual. Shouldn't someone be standing up in court and making sure that the law was being followed, that individual rights were being protected? We weren't doing anything as consequential as defending the accused, but I saw a parallel. If every time an agency turned down a request for documents, the citizen-requester just shrugged and walked away, there was no check on the government's power to be the final arbiter of what was secret (a lot) and what was public (not enough).

Over the eight years of the Obama administration, I filed more than 30 FOIA suits on behalf of *Times* journalists. In that same period, our nearest competitors in the news media were Fox News with five suits and the Associated Press with three. We kept going once the new administration came into office when our requests were either denied or ignored. We sued to get the visitors' log from the Trump transition office, we sued to get the daily calendar of the EPA administrator, we sued for access to the memos written by James Comey about his meetings with the president, we sued for documents showing whether there had been changes in how the president's daily security briefing was being prepared, we sued for information about the decision to reduce the size of Bears Ears National Monument, we sued for the legal memos prepared by the Department of Justice explaining how the nepotism rules applied to Jared Kushner and Ivanka Trump, we sued to find out whether the White House was trying to influence decisions about high-speed trains that went near Trump properties—and we sued over that Syrian-rebel tweet.

When the CIA failed to respond to Matt Rosenberg's FOIA request about the Syrian program, we drafted a complaint and went into court in New York. While the case moved forward, the CIA did finally get around to sending a response. The agency said in a letter that it could neither confirm nor deny whether it had documents. It was what is known in FOIA-land as a "Glomar response," when an agency takes the legal position that even acknowledging the existence or nonexistence of documents would itself reveal a national security secret. In the pretzel logic that is FOIA, agencies give Glomar responses even when there are no documents, believing that in the parallel universe in which they exist, the fact that a program doesn't exist is a secret, too. A couple of years ago, an unwell individual named Michael Taylor sued the National Security Agency in Georgia wanting to get all documents showing how the NSA had planted electrode monitors in his brain. Now, you might think that even at a hard-ass agency like the NSA, some soft-hearted soul might have drafted a response to Mr. Taylor saying in so many words, "Dear Mr. Taylor, we don't have any documents pertaining to those electrodes in your brain because, frankly, there are no electrodes in your brain, and have you considered getting some competent mental health care?" You might think that, and you would be wrong. The NSA responded by telling Mr. Taylor they could neither confirm nor deny the existence of documents about those electrodes in his head. That's about as cruel as your federal government gets.

The attorney assigned to defend the CIA in our case got in touch with me and my associate, Christina Koningisor. He was pleasant but forthright. He had considered our papers, and we had one problem: we didn't understand President Trump's syntax.

I am usually pretty skeptical of what opposing counsel has to say, but this time it was hard to argue. Not understand the president's syntax? That made Christina and me not so very different from hundreds of millions of English-speaking people around the globe. But what did that have to do with our lawsuit? The attorney explained that we were misreading the tweet, that the tweet actually denied that there was a Syrian arms program. That was plain from the text of the tweet itself. The president said *The Post* had "fabricated the facts" about the president's decision to end the program. That, the attorney assured us, meant that the president was neither denying nor confirming that the program existed or that it had been ended or any other fact in the real, nonfabricated world. The president was just engaged in—I don't know—a little freestyle criticism of journalism.

Christina and I were puzzled. Between the two of us we had better-than-average reading-comprehension skills. So—seriously—when the president described the payments to the rebels as "massive, dangerous, and wasteful," he was talking about a program that didn't actually exist? It was a massive, dangerous, wasteful—and nonexistent—program? I don't have all that much experience with nonexistent things, but when I do, they tend not to be massive, dangerous, and wasteful or anything else—just not real.

We decided to take another shot at explaining ourselves: the president's complaint that *The Post* had engaged in fabrication was not aimed at the parts of the story that revealed the funding program and the decision to end it, but at the incendiary theme of *The Post*'s story—that Trump's decision was made to suck up to the Russians, who were supporting the Syrian government in the fight with the rebels. In our minds, the president—whether he knew it or not—had declassified the program when he hit the send button. Maybe the CIA had some other legal grounds on which to withhold the documents, but the agency could not seriously claim that the program was a national security secret and hand us a Glomar response when the president was complaining about how massive and expensive and dangerous the program was. Could it?

It could. It did. So a case based on 140 syntactically challenged characters was going to have to be decided by a federal judge.

FOIA is a dull, dull knife for cutting through all the unnecessary secrecy that is invoked daily in the name of national security. Technically, the government has the burden of proof. It is supposed to show the court that the secrecy is necessary. In the real world, few judges want to second-guess the CIA or NSA or any other intelligence agency about what needs to be secret and what doesn't. It is disheartening to see the judiciary surrender its power to the executive branch. Only judges are in a position to be a check on the executive branch if the intelligence agencies are cynically misusing the law to keep the American public in the dark. But it isn't always cynical, I know. Sometimes the agencies just seem indifferent to the public. Sometimes they seem incompetent. It doesn't really matter what the root cause is. Information that the public should have is never going to see the light of day.

If you spent enough time working the FOIA beat, there was a certain risk you assumed—the risk that you would get so caught up in playing the government's secrecy game that you lost sight of just how twisted it was. You came to accept that you would be litigating cases in which you never got to see the government's factual arguments, which themselves were treated as national security secrets. They were presented to the court in secret filings. That meant you lost lawsuits without ever knowing why. In a FOIA case we had before the Second Circuit Court of Appeals, the government's lawyers were permitted to meet privately with the court and make their case for an hour before the court heard from us. We later learned that the government lawyers had brought to the secret session a mystery man who refused to identify himself fully to the court. The judges, in a much-later opinion, said they were unhappy about that and warned the government about doing it again, but the secret session had gone forward. It was apparently lost on the government that in democracies we don't have secret minders monitoring our judges.

Truth often floated away from the courtrooms where FOIA cases were heard. The government's lawyers would deny the existence of facts that had been widely reported in *The Times* and elsewhere. Until those facts were officially acknowledged by the government, they did not exist, as far as the government was concerned. In one of our cases, Judge Colleen McMahon described the government's position as something straight out of *Alice in Wonderland*. The government lawyers were doing what they typically did in such cases: insisting on declaring secret what wasn't secret and shouldn't be secret but pretending it was secret and asking us and the court to go along for the ride. The sad part was that the law more often than not let the government do exactly that.

Secrecy breeds absurdity. That is never truer than in litigating against those masters of secrecy run amok, the CIA. It's a bizarre dance. We sued the CIA a few years ago for documents about injuries sustained by U.S. troops as they cleared munitions dumps left behind by the Saddam Hussein government in Iraq. Our reporter

Chris Chivers and others were doing a series of stories about how U.S. troops were left unprepared and unprotected as they stumbled upon and detonated old chemical weapons after the invasion of Iraq. The Pentagon then decided to cover up the injuries for political reasons. To assist Chris's efforts, we filed a FOIA request for three documents. The CIA, on cue, said it could neither confirm nor deny that the documents even existed. That was a little awkward. We had asked for the three documents by their actual titles. And by date. (It makes a difference to have reporters with good sources.) So off we went to court, with me writing briefs premised on the idea that there was no question that the documents existed and the CIA responding with briefs that pretended it had no idea what I was talking about. The judge was not impressed by the CIA's double-talk, and in the end we obtained documents about the program. The CIA also had to pay us $51,000 to compensate for the time I had spent fighting off the agency's undue secrecy.

I also declined to play along with the government and pretend that two dead men did not have names. They did. Their names were Gul Rahman and Manadel al-Jamadi. They died while being detained by agents of the U.S. government, one in Iraq, the other in Afghanistan. But as we litigated a case with the Justice Department for documents about the torture of detainees, the government's lawyers refused to mention the names. They claimed it was a matter of protecting the men's privacy. We thought it was a matter of dehumanizing two victims. It was also nonsensical. As our case was grinding its way through the courts, the CIA inspector general released a report about the Rahman case. It showed that Rahman, an Afghan suspected of ties to terrorist groups, was alternately defiant and fatigued, hurling death threats at his guards and throwing his food and defecation bucket at them. He was shackled using a technique known as "short chaining" that forced him to remain seated on a cold concrete floor while naked below the waist. Rahman was found dead from hypothermia the next day.

That was all in the CIA report. But, in our case, the DOJ had been telling us and the court that nothing could be disclosed about Rahman, not even his name.

Maybe the names should not have been such a big deal to me, but the government's refusal to say the names out loud spoke to so much of what was wrong in the culture of secrecy. That particular FOIA case was an important one. Our reporter Charlie Savage was seeking the release of the secret Justice Department memos that had recommended that no CIA operative be charged with a crime for abusing detainees in the aftermath of 9/11. Justice had appointed John Durham, a veteran prosecutor, to look into 101 reports of possible torture, including the cases of the two men who had died in custody. Maybe Durham had made the right legal call, maybe no one should have been held legally responsible, but why were the American people not given a chance to see the memos and decide for themselves? That seemed like Democracy 101, except to the government. The Justice Department dug in and said that not a word from the memos could be released, even as the DOJ's top officials, including Attorney General Eric Holder, praised the thorough and compelling legal work that Durham had done.

A few days after Holder left office—and therefore was now powerless to do anything about secrecy—he told a gathering of media lawyers and journalists that he hoped the Durham memos would someday be released because the public would benefit from seeing Durham's careful work. That is how it goes in FOIA-land: everyone is on your side except when it matters. Well, that wasn't exactly true. Judge Paul Oetken of the Southern District of New York, after a briefing that stretched over two years, ultimately ordered that five of the memos be released in redacted form to The Times. The government appealed. The wheels of FOIA turned some more, slowly.

Not surprisingly, our standoffs over secrecy with the government occasionally played out in shades of surrealism. In the summer of 2015, the government as part of a FOIA suit had agreed to turn over certain documents to us about the NSA's massive operation to collect data about Americans' phone calls. A batch of those documents came in by email late one afternoon. I immediately forwarded them to Charlie Savage, the reporter behind the FOIA request—standard operating procedure for us to avoid getting scooped if the agency is delivering the same documents to others. Charlie called me at home that night and wanted to know whether I had noticed, just by chance, that in the midst of the documents were pages that the government had not intended to give us. They were still marked classified. They showed some never-disclosed and important details about the NSA program, and Charlie wanted to report on them. I knew that as soon as Charlie called the NSA for comment the next morning, my day was going to take a serious turn for the worse.

By 9:30 that morning, the government's lawyers were calling me and insisting we return the classified pages. I said I wouldn't do that unless a federal judge told The Times it had to. If the First Amendment protected the news media when documents were leaked—think the Pentagon Papers, WikiLeaks, Snowden—how could there be any obligation to return these documents, and not report on them, when they were given to us officially and voluntarily by the government itself? Was I supposed to tell our reporters to pretend they had never seen the words on those secret pages? I felt bad for the government lawyers. They were good attorneys and good guys, and I knew someone was in deep, deep trouble somewhere on the government side, but I couldn't be part of hiding the truth, at least not without getting a chance to first make my case to a federal judge. Then one of the government lawyers played his trump card: "When this happened with the ACLU, they gave the documents back," he said.

Seriously? The ACLU? Those ultimate outsiders, forever standing up for truth, at constant war with the government—that ACLU?

Was he really trying to tell me that the ACLU lawyers had backed down and politely returned to the government classified documents that were mistakenly released to them voluntarily under FOIA?

I was immediately on the phone to my friends downtown at ACLU headquarters. It was true, sort of, they said. A few years earlier, the government had inadvertently produced some classified materials as part of a FOIA case. The documents hadn't been all that interesting, and the ACLU decided it didn't make much sense strategically to get into a huge legal fight over them. They agreed to keep the documents confidential until the judge in the case could rule on whether the ACLU had a right to have them. The judge ruled in favor of the government and the documents were officially secret again.

Nothing about that phone call was making me feel good. The ACLU had voluntarily stood down. A federal judge had ruled that the First Amendment did not apply. And 15 floors below me at The New York Times, editors were moving ahead with Charlie's story. I consulted with some First Amendment lawyers, looking to get bucked up in my position that, by God, the documents were ours. They were not in a bucking-up sort of mood apparently. Maybe the First Amendment applied in leak cases, but these documents were being produced as part of a FOIA lawsuit. Maybe I as an attorney (and therefore an officer of the court) had a duty to notify the court of what had happened and to maintain the status quo until the judge could decide what to do. I didn't relish the thought of having to go down to the newsroom and tell the editors that, on second thought, maybe we couldn't do the story after all, maybe the First Amendment didn't stretch that far. I knew they would think the First Amendment easily stretched that far and even further. In fact, in most journalists' minds, it was pretty close to boundless.

The government lawyers called me again. They were waiting for authorization from their superiors to go to court. I should stand by. I told them I would.

And that is when things got even stranger. Charlie and his editors were already reaching out to officials at the NSA, seeking comment. I was certain that the NSA would not be happy to know we had the secret material and would inevitably ask us not to publish. The NSA decided not to comment. As often happens with national security stories, our editors considered whether to refrain from publishing or to withhold some information. In the end, they decided to go ahead with a story disclosing new details about the NSA's ties to the phone companies. By 5:00, as I continued to wait for word from the government's attorneys, the story had gone up on our website. The lawyers called a few minutes later just to update me. They were still waiting for authorization to go to court. I suggested they take a quick read of nytimes.com. It seemed a little late for a huddle with a judge, maybe a lot late. They told me they'd call back.

We never saw a judge. Later that week I got a letter from the government lawyers asking for the documents back and citing cases that supported the government's position. I wrote a letter in response citing the First Amendment, the Pentagon Papers, and other decisions. Charlie still has the classified documents.

All of us who do FOIA cases are, at heart, hope junkies, believing that the next case, or maybe the one after that one, will bring us back to Lyndon Johnson's promised land. We keep going because we do sometimes surprise even ourselves and win. In 2011, a CIA drone attack killed the radical cleric Anwar al-Awlaki, a jihadist who was living in Yemen. A second drone strike killed his son. They were both American citizens. Our reporters, Charlie Savage and Scott Shane, knew that the Department of Justice had given legal clearance for the attacks—in essence, found that it was legal to kill an American citizen away from the field of battle without traditional due process. Scott and Charlie filed FOIA requests and got nowhere. They were told that even the legal analysis was classified. It struck us as absurd, no matter what the memos said. Why did national security require the government to keep the American people in the dark about the legal basis for the extraordinary use of U.S. force against individual citizens?

I called a lawyer with expertise in national security and asked what he thought our chances were of winning a lawsuit. "Not completely hopeless," he said. In many of our cases, that was about as encouraging as things got. We sued, and the ACLU filed a similar suit not long after. A year later, Judge McMahon released her *Alice in Wonderland* decision, which spent pages hammering away at the government's dubious position that it was legally free to kill Americans abroad without a hint of due process. But in the end, she said, there was nothing she could do about our FOIA requests. The government had met its burden for imposing secrecy.

We pressed on. On October 1, 2013, the Second Circuit Court of Appeals took up the two cases. The rest of the government had closed at noon because Congress had been unable to pass a budget. The courtroom was packed with court employees who had been rendered unemployed a couple hours earlier and had nothing better to do that afternoon than watch The New York Times and the ACLU get slapped around by the government and the judges. I sat at the counsel table with my associate Victoria Baranetsky and the team from the ACLU, waiting for the court to convene. Jameel Jaffer, the lead lawyer for the ACLU, leaned over. "Could you not do that argument about the ACLU today?" he asked. I knew what he was talking about. The ACLU had been smart and generous allies, but in every brief we had done in the case, we had included a few sentences pointing out how the ACLU was making a sweeping request for all sorts of documents while The Times, that picture of reasonableness and restraint, was seeking only the legal memos. We were bad at being subtle: the clear message to the court was that the ACLU had gone ape-mad nuts, and the court shouldn't confuse our perfectly rational and respectful request with theirs. It was the worst sort of legal strategy: disingenuous and not working. I pretended to cross out the first two pages of my argument outline.

With no other cases on the docket, the court kept us there for the better part of two hours. We pinned much of our argument on the repeated assurances the Obama administration had made in public forums that the strikes had been vetted by the Justice Department and were found to be legal. We believed the government could not have it both ways: bragging to the public about the savvy legal analysis and dropping hints about the legal justification but refusing to level with the American people about what the legal memos actually said. While the case was pending, DOJ had also released a "white paper" setting out the legal case for permitting drone strikes.

When the court ruled in favor of The Times and the ACLU six months later, the judges not only held that the main legal memo had to be released (with certain details about CIA operations redacted) but took the extraordinary step of releasing the memo as part of the decision. No federal appeals court had ever done that before in a national security case. The court found that the Obama administration's many public statements about the legal case for targeted killing had crossed a line and waived whatever objections the government may have had to releasing the memo.

As it turned out, the court's decision in the drone case would be an important component of our argument four years later in the Trump tweet case. Judge Andrew Carter had called the lawyers into the courtroom so they could discuss their respective legal positions. I was able to say, with adequate lawyerly gravitas (but it wasn't easy), "The government believes we don't understand the president's syntax." The CIA's lawyer stood his ground, working his way through the syntax puzzle and then denying that anything had been declassified by the tweet. That led to one of those house-of-mirrors moments when Judge Carter asked an obvious question: Why was the program still a secret if it had been discontinued? The CIA's lawyer had to explain that, because of national security, he couldn't say whether the program had been ended because he couldn't say whether the program ever began, and so whether the program had ended or hadn't ended or existed or never existed at all, he really couldn't answer the judge's question. The judge set a schedule for our written briefs.

When the CIA's brief was filed with the court a few weeks later, it was exactly what we expected: the agency clung to its Glomar response. The existence or nonexistence of the Syrian rebel funding program was a classified secret, and the presidential tweet had not changed that. The CIA's lawyer was in a tricky position. The government had to acknowledge that the president inherently had the authority to declassify information at any time for any reason—that was a necessary component of a president's power in the event of a national emergency—but the government was not exactly keen to give a huge thumbs up to the idea of Declassification by Tweet. More discussion of presidential syntax followed. We responded with a brief diving deep into the law surrounding a president's authority to declassify information (there was, we had to concede, precious little case law on Declassification by Tweet) and we offered up a compelling discussion of how the government had waived its right to invoke secrecy, just the way it had done in the drone case. We giddily worked our way back to the Aspen Security Forum—the one where General Thomas had done his loose-lipped acknowledgment of the rebel arms program. To us, that was further proof that the big CIA secret was no secret. We also provided our own by now well-honed analysis of the president's syntax.

A few months later, the judge issued his opinion: he was dismissing our case. The government, he said, had shown that the information was still a classified secret. It was disappointing, but not surprising. FOIA cases are rarely easy. We filed our appeal, looking to take our chances in the Second Circuit.

When I think about all that is wrong with FOIA—and what is right about it—I think about Sergio Florez's case. Sergio is an editor at *The Times* who was seeking the CIA files about his late father, Dr. Armando Florez. Dr. Florez had been a high-profile Cuban diplomat in the 1960s before defecting to the U.S. He had been ill and died before Sergio could fully find out about his remarkable life—from his role in the Castro government and his time as the chargé d'affaires at the Cuban embassy in Washington to his brave decision to defect in the late 1960s during a visit to Spain. Victoria Baranetsky, our First Amendment fellow, had heard Sergio's story and convinced me we should start a FOIA case for Sergio pro bono. We sued the CIA for the documents. Forget that 50 years had passed, that spycraft was completely different, that the relationship between Cuba and the United States had evolved and then evolved again. The CIA refused to release anything. It said it could not even disclose whether or not it had any documents about Dr. Florez.

That proved to not be completely accurate. One of our Yale Law student interns went into the CIA's electronic reading room—a repository of declassified documents online—and promptly found two CIA reports mentioning Dr. Florez. It was an energizing moment for our team—but it was not to last. The district court dismissed our case, finding that the CIA had justified its decision to not say whether other documents existed. National security required it.

Sergio showed up at my office and wanted to know whether we would appeal. I hemmed and hawed as my associate Jeremy Kutner looked on, wondering how big a pushover I was going to be. It was going to be a lot of work, I began, and the Second Circuit Court of Appeals was not likely to reverse the district court. It was FOIA; it was national security. An appeals court was not going to dig into the facts. We'd almost surely lose.

So I told him we would do it. That's how it works: the client gets to decide even when the lawyers are sentencing themselves to more misery.

Shortly before the case was to be heard by the Second Circuit, one of those small litigation miracles occurred. The FBI, in response to a separate FOIA request, released dozens of pages of formerly classified documents about Sergio's father. They offered a telling look into his work for the Cubans, his defection, and the government's initial suspicions that the defection might be the trick of a double agent. When we appeared for oral argument, the appeals court pounded the government's lawyer with questions about how the CIA's recalcitrance could possibly be squared with all the disclosures just made by the FBI. The court ruled in our favor, and the CIA ultimately settled with Sergio, giving him a few documents (which he should have received years earlier) and paying our legal fees. The day I argued the case in the Second Circuit, Sergio brought his family to watch. It had been a big deal to him, the child of Cuban immigrants, that in America there could be a case called *Sergio Florez v. The Central Intelligence Agency*— and the second highest court in the land would hear it. For all the cynicism that got baked into FOIA—the delays, the unnecessary secrecy, the lame excuses that the agencies expected you to believe, the slow drip of justice you were treated to when you finally went to court—there was still something right about a system where you had a chance to stand up to your government in a court of law, whether you were The New York Times or just a guy trying to find out about his father. Sergio's wife told me he had worn his father's tie to court that day.

13

A World of Trouble

[The Committee to Protect Journalists] annual report shows record # of journalists imprisoned worldwide in 2017, including 21 on "fake news" charges. @POTUS must understand his harmful rhetoric only empowers repressive regimes to jail reporters & silence the truth.

—Senator John McCain, Dec. 13, 2017

IT BEGAN IN the quiet way so many stories do, with information passed along to a reporter from a confidential source. Only this one was destined to be trouble from the start. It was a story about Egypt, and the information included a set of secret recordings. The recordings were proof that the Egyptian government was engaged in a two-faced foreign policy, publicly condemning the U.S. for the decision to move its embassy to Jerusalem while secretly supporting the Trump administration's plan. An Egyptian intelligence officer could be heard calling some of the country's most popular broadcast hosts and delivering a message: encourage the Egyptian people to accept the embassy move. David Kirkpatrick of *The Times* got the recordings in the final days of 2017. *The Times* went live with his story in the first week of the new year.

The blowback was immediate. David worked in London after many years in Egypt. He was out of harm's way. Not so for The Times staff who continued to man our bureau in Cairo. They were a soft target, employees of a foreign news organization that had dared to take on Egypt's supreme leadership. An Egyptian lawyer filed official papers demanding that the authorities begin a criminal investigation of The Times. The story had done the intolerable, he said, it had created an atmosphere of "instability and anxiety." It was clear to him and his allies that The Times was nothing more, and nothing less, than a tool of the Muslim Brotherhood. By the next day, the vitriol aimed at The Times had seeped into Parliament. The Speaker claimed to have proof that The Times was funded by Qatar, a longtime Egyptian nemesis. (If you happen to be a conspiracy theorist, here's something to pick over: our advertising department had managed to sell some ad space to the Qatari government shortly before our story.) Others joined in the campaign of intimidation. Pictures of our reporters were plastered in local newspapers, and a second member of Parliament weighed in, denouncing the story as evidence that the foreign media was waging a war against Egypt. From where I sat, the situation seemed to be exactly the opposite.

Soon the inevitable came: the accusation that we were trafficking in "fake news"—a term that since January 20, 2017, had become the slur-in-waiting for the world's authoritarians every time they were unhappy about having the truth disclosed. By the start of 2018, the Egyptians were masters at deploying it, wielding it both as a weapon to silence and a way to link arms and curry favor with the new press-hating American administration. Ten months into the Trump administration, we knew better than to think that the U.S. embassy could have some constructive role to play in easing a tense and escalating situation that threatened an American news organization and put in jeopardy Americans' ability to get real journalism about a country that mattered in the world's most volatile region.

Within days of the story's appearance, our Egyptian lawyer

called: the state prosecutors were moving ahead with the criminal investigation of The Times.

It was never clear to me whether *Times* readers understood how isolated American news organizations and their journalists had become in many foreign outposts. The economic downturn in the newspaper industry had blown a hole in international coverage. Most large-city American newspapers had shuttered their foreign bureaus and retreated to their home bases, leaving the increasingly perilous business of covering the world from an American perspective to a handful of big players like the Associated Press, *The Wall Street Journal*, *The Washington Post*, and *The Times*, helped along by a few gritty and crazy-brave freelancers. For those news organizations that remained in the world's hardest places, journalists had become easier targets for hostile regimes. It was just math: silencing one voice wasn't much of a lift for governments used to locking down their own people whenever they dared to resist, especially if no one was there to witness it.

Back in New York, *The Times*'s international editor Michael Slackman and I tried to get a handle on what was happening in Cairo. In one sense, none of this was new. Michael and I had worked our way through threats to journalists in too many places over the years: Pakistan, Venezuela, Afghanistan, Turkey, Ethiopia, Cuba, Jordan, Mexico, Iran. That was just the short list. But no matter how often we had done this drill, the learning curve always seemed to start anew with the next call or next email about fresh troubles somewhere. There were too many variables, most of them out of our control or hidden from view: the shifting political climate, the on-the-ground sensitivities of a particular story, the strength of a reporter's connections in a country, a regime's appetite for bringing more attention to a damaging piece of reporting. Everything worth knowing was unknowable. And in many places we didn't have many options anyway, which meant we were inevitably circling back to a first-order question: was it time to move our people out of the country?

I had sat through too many pitches from security firms that specialize in providing protection to American workers abroad, and they tried to impress me by how quickly they had moved their clients out of countries that had imploded with public unrest or terrorist attacks or the onset of war. I had little interest in any of that. I needed to know how good they were at keeping safe the people who planned to stay behind and run toward the fire. We were a news organization, not an oil company. We were in the world to be a witness to its troubles. And that was what made the calculation of deciding when to pull people so much more complicated. No one wanted to be the person who encouraged reporters to stay, only to watch from the warm safety of New York when they were detained by the authorities or worse. That was not abstract or hypothetical, at least not in Egypt, where American aid workers and Al Jazeera reporters had been arrested in recent years. On the other hand, to pull out could send the absolutely wrong message to a regime's leaders: that they had the power to rid themselves of Western reporters by bullying them in the courts or in the streets. And there was always one more consideration: the reporters got a say. More often than not, they wanted to stay no matter what, to continue their reporting, to stand up to oppressive governments, to prove they weren't going to be intimidated.

I had never set out to be The Times's go-to person on security. It began in November 2008 when I received a call from Bill Schmidt, one of our editors, letting me know that our reporter David Rohde had been kidnapped in Afghanistan. David had set up a communications plan with our Kabul bureau and then driven with two Afghan colleagues to interview a Taliban leader who had previously met with Western reporters. After David missed a phone check-in, someone at our Kabul bureau had called his cell phone and learned that the three of them had been seized after driving into a trap set by the guy they were meeting. Three years earlier, I had been the drafter of the company's kidnap response plan. I had worked with a committee and a consultant, we had convened several meetings, we issued our plan, and it was quickly tucked away in a drawer and essentially forgotten. That, it turned out, was enough to put me in charge of managing our response to David's kidnapping three years later. I had only the vaguest idea of what we were supposed to do. A group of editors and I sat in a conference room that first afternoon trying to find out what we could from Carlotta Gall, our bureau chief in Kabul. I knew we had crisis consultants we could call, but we had never done that before; nobody at The Times had communicated with them in the years since the response plan was laid to rest in the drawer. Somebody mentioned that David was also working on a book about Afghanistan. Maybe we should find out what his publisher could do to help us, someone else suggested.

I stepped out of the room and tracked down the number for the publisher's general counsel. When I got through, I explained how David Rohde was writing a book for his company and how David had just been kidnapped by the Taliban. He agreed with me that it was a terrible situation. "I'm glad you're involved," he said. "We wouldn't know what to do."

For the next seven months, my life would be consumed by David's kidnapping. I would go to the FBI's New York operations center with our editor Bill Keller to watch hostage videos released by David's captors. I was on the phone or in meetings every day with David's wife, Kristen, and his brother, Lee, as we tried to figure out how to get David and his two Afghan colleagues back home. Reporters at The Times with connections deep into the intelligence services gave us information that was always interesting but could never be verified. I worked with two outside security consulting firms. One was The Times's regular consulting firm for crisis management. The other, introduced to us by a friend of David's relatives, was run by a former Green Beret, whose top operations person was a former CIA agent. The CIA guy had already been convicted of a felony; his boss would be convicted a few years later of defrauding the government on defense contracts. They came filled with promises of cowboy missions and deep-state intelligence. They conjured up one crazy scheme after another. They gave code names to people who they said were in Pakistan, where David was being held, and who were providing them with firsthand information on David's captors. They came up with mind-boggling plans to bribe Taliban guards, have them overpower the others, and spirit David and the two Afghans off into the night—going where and how . . . who knew? The details were not part of their game. At one point, Kristen, Lee, and I were summoned on a Sunday afternoon to a New York hotel lobby to meet with a guy who claimed to work undercover for the CIA and was willing to go into Pakistan and bring David out. We sat in an isolated corner as he whispered about his plans and swept his eyes around the nearly empty room. We had no idea what was real and what was phony, what would work and what wouldn't. Somehow I had stumbled into this life, filled every day with Langley rejects, real and pretend spooks, and the occasional con artist, the bountiful reward for having once upon a time written a crisis management plan for my buttoned-up corporate employer.

It didn't help that the U.S. government was mostly an enigma to us. The FBI is the lead agency when an American gets kidnapped—even in a distant war zone like Afghanistan, where the CIA and the U.S. military and the State Department know far more about what is going on and seem not very interested in sharing with others, especially out-of-their-depth FBI types. FBI agents would lecture us on the illegality of paying ransoms, and then an agent would call me later and tell me that I shouldn't be an idiot: these things got solved by money more often than not. Every so often, I would get invited down to the FBI operations center in the Chelsea neighborhood of Manhattan so agents could complain that I wasn't sharing information, and then I could complain that they weren't telling me and David's family anything, and then we would talk about sports. The FBI was unhappy that we had our own private security team working on the kidnapping, no matter how bungling that team might have been, no matter how little we actually knew about what the security consultants were doing, no matter how sketchy they were. At times, individual FBI agents and U.S. officials went out of their way to be helpful, reaching out directly to Kristen and David's family and meeting with them in Washington. Others put on their game faces, revealing nothing and, I suspected after a while, knowing nothing. There would be very occasional contact from the kidnappers, always seeking money or the release of detainees. At one point David was able to make a call to his wife. The recording of it was heart-wrenching, and a testament to the strength of both of them, especially Kristen, who was composed and poised under circumstances I couldn't imagine living through. Another time, the Red Cross showed up with a letter for Kristen from David. We spent seven months working blind, searching for some reason to hope, but never knowing what was really going on, not even with the people who were supposed to be helping us.

The Times also managed to keep the kidnapping out of the press. It was a controversial decision, one of those things that cut hard against our DNA as a news organization. Most kidnapping experts tell companies and families that they are better off not having the kidnapping in the papers. Little good can come from publicity. Worrying about what is going to be said and whether it could provoke the kidnappers to harm the victim or make more absurd demands is one more stressor in a situation that is, minute by minute, day in and day out, a slow burn of tension. When so little is under your control, it makes no sense to bring on one more out-of-control factor. At the request of David's family, Keller and our corporate PR people asked other news outlets to stand down and not report what they knew about the kidnapping. It was awkward—we were in the business of disclosing information, not hiding it—but lives were at stake, and we extended the same consideration to others who were kidnapped when we were asked. In April 2009, David, while still in captivity, was part of a group of *Times* reporters who won the Pulitzer Prize for reporting on Afghanistan and Pakistan. We expected the story of the kidnapping to break then, and we prepared for the media blitz we anticipated. It seemed too good of a story for others to pass on—the Pulitzer Prize winner who was at that very moment being held by kidnappers, seized doing the coverage that was being recognized by the Pulitzer committee. The day came and went. No stories were written. At one point in the kidnapping, Al Jazeera obtained a staged Taliban video of David and his two Afghan colleagues marching through the mountains with their captors and put it on the air. Keller got on the phone to AJ editors and was able to get them to pull the piece. It was never broadcast again.

On a summer Friday evening in June 2009, seven months in, I was in a car with Susan Chira, our foreign editor, heading to a dinner party Susan was hosting when Kristen called my cell phone. "David just called my mother. He's escaped and he needs help," she said. I tried to make sense of what she was saying (beginning with the idea that a man held captive by terrorists for seven months would, first thing out of the box, call his mother-in-law). Kristen had gone out to dinner with a college friend, and her mother, who was at Kristen's apartment, had picked up the phone when it had rung. David and Tahir, his Afghan colleague, had escaped by using a car tow rope to lower themselves from a roof to the ground below and made their way through the town of Miranshah to a nearby Pakistani military garrison. They had persuaded the Pakistani sentries and the military officer in charge to let them in (after they removed their shirts to show they were not rigged with suicide vests), but it didn't mean they were safe. In the lawless tribal areas of northwestern Pakistan, where the Taliban held sway and the Pakistani government maintained only a nominal presence, there was no guarantee that they wouldn't be handed back to their captors.

From the sidewalk outside Susan's apartment, I called our security consultants. No one knew anything about the escape, and, after months of bravado and wild plans, they had no ideas about what we should do in the much-too-real situation that was unfolding before me. Susan and I had stopped outside her building, the two of us on the sidewalk making calls to Times people in Pakistan and Afghanistan and anyone else who might be able to help. I told her she needed to blow off her guests and come downtown with me to Kristen's apartment. I didn't make it sound like a choice. She and I dashed past her arriving guests and flagged down a cab. In the car, I called the U.S. embassy in Kabul, talked my way past the switchboard while sounding only marginally crazed, and finally got through to an official there. It was not yet daybreak on the other side of the world. I explained everything I knew so far, which wasn't much. I could hear the embassy guy taking notes. He asked me for some basic information. And then he said, "Be assured, Mr. McCraw, we will do nothing to stand in the way of your operation." I was in a cab on the West Side of New York. I was a media lawyer who had once written a corporate kidnap response plan. I was trying to get two kidnap victims out of the tribal areas of northwestern Pakistan. This guy on the phone was, as far as I was concerned, the U.S. government. "I don't have an operation," I said. "I need you to have an operation." He went off to find an operation, never to be heard from again.

We worked through the night calling everyone that Kristen, Lee, and I knew in the Obama administration, asking for their assistance. The calling was frantic, and it got to the point that someone at the Pentagon finally told Lee we needed to shut it down because everybody was spending valuable minutes answering phone calls from the officials we had called rather than doing something useful to get David out. The plan, as it evolved over the early morning hours, was to have a Pakistani military helicopter fly into Miranshah, pick up David and Tahir, and transport them to Islamabad, the Pakistani capital. An FBI agent had shown up at Kristen's apartment, and his colleagues were on the phone with me throughout the night and into the morning. After their spotty performance over the prior months, they were, at least for one night, true stars. Around 3:00 in the morning, we learned that the Pakistani intelligence service was insisting on having someone onboard the helicopter. That was not good news. The Inter-Services Intelligence, popularly known as the ISI, was the clandestine ally and sponsor of the Haqqanis, the Taliban family that had held David. The following year, the ISI would be accused of paying the Haqqanis $200,000 to carry out an attack that killed seven Americans at a CIA compound in Afghanistan. My FBI contact in New York told me that it was beyond his pay grade to do anything about the ISI's involvement and suggested I call the U.S. ambassador in Pakistan, Anne Patterson. I reached her shortly before dawn, working on adrenaline after being up for 23 hours, and gave an almost cogent explanation of my problem with the ISI. What could the ISI contribute to any of this? What did the ISI agents intend to do? We needed to get David out. We didn't need the ISI to do that. The ambassador listened patiently and then told me I was completely missing what was actually going on. David's family and I had managed to rattle the entire U.S. government, which had in turn rattled the entire Pakistani government. Everybody was watching to make sure the mission went off without a hitch. If I needed something real to worry about, she said, maybe I should stop worrying about the ISI and start worrying about the weather—it was terrible in the north—or how nervous that Pakistani helicopter crew must be with so many people from two governments monitoring the crew's every move.

A few hours later, I received word that David and Tahir had made it to Islamabad, then been flown to Bagram Air Base in Afghanistan before David would return to America. Because David had largely worked overseas, I had never met him before, never talked to him on the phone, never sent an email to him during his years at The Times. We met one morning for the first time in the Dean & DeLuca restaurant on the ground floor of The Times building a couple of weeks after he got home. It was odd to feel such a bond to someone I had never met but who had been such an outsized part of my life day in and day out. There was so much to say, so many notes to compare about what we had been hearing back in the U.S. and what was really going on during his captivity, but a first meeting in a coffee shop was hardly the time or place. We settled for some polite conversation. Over the following weeks, I was welcomed into his family, embraced actually, and one day in the fall we all went to Fenway Park for a Red Sox game. Around the fourth inning, David and Kristen pulled out sonograms and handed them to me. They were expecting their first child. The passing out of sonograms (like crying) is not really allowed in baseball—I can't help it; I'm a traditionalist—but it reframed for me a year of my life right then and there.

At the time it was happening, David's kidnapping seemed like a one-off. It was in fact more of a beginning. Security became part of my day-to-day life (complete with obsessive checking of my cell phone to see if someone had wandered into harm's way and needed help). Three months after David returned, I received a call on a Saturday morning outside a suburban grocery store. Reporter Steve Farrell and an Afghan journalist who worked for the paper, Sultan Munadi, had been taken by the Taliban in Afghanistan. It started all over again: making the difficult calls to family members, connecting with the right people in government, collecting whatever information we could about the reporting trip they had been on, seeking out advice from the consultants (although we were done with cowboys). Four days later, British paratroopers staged a night raid on the house where they were being held. Steve was rescued. Sultan was killed in the battle, as was a British soldier. In David's case, the American government had told David's family that it would advise them if a military raid was being considered. Steve's kidnapping was being handled by the U.K. government because he was a British citizen. The first time I knew of the military operation was when my contact at the Foreign and Commonwealth Office called me as the helicopters were bringing Steve back to Kabul.

And David's kidnapping never quite went away. Rumors spread that The Times or the family had paid a ransom. We hadn't. If someone else paid—the Saudis, the ISI, the U.S. government, persons unknown—we never knew about it, and the idea seemed particularly preposterous based on what was verifiable and known. David and Tahir showed up at a military garrison unannounced and had to plead to be let inside. There was no plan in place to get them out of the Pakistan tribal areas and to safety, not until David's family and I prompted the U.S. government to do something after Kristen's call to me in the car. None of that would make sense if someone had paid millions to arrange for the release. It would be irrational and illogical to leave such critical loose ends. Ransom-payers don't want to have to pay twice. Plus I had heard David's and Tahir's story of the escape often enough to have no doubts about it. They said no one had told them to try to escape, and no one helped them. And I had every reason to believe that some of our cowboy consultants, eager to get a little credit for freeing David, and at the time embroiled in a billing dispute with us, knew something about how the rumors got started, although they always denied it.

By 2014, when the world was horrified by ISIS's brutal executions of journalists James Foley and Stephen Sotloff (along with two aid workers), we had resolved to do better in protecting the safety of our journalists. The age of the swashbuckling foreign correspondent who drank hard, smoked to excess, and moved about the world with reckless abandon to track down The Story as the bombs fell and the bullets flew was over (if it ever existed at all). New security protocols were put in place, requiring journalists heading for dangerous places to provide us with copies of passports, basic information about their families, and a security memo to be signed off on by our incomparable in-house security advisor, Tug Wilson. Scheduled phone check-ins became commonplace. Reporters at times traveled with security advisors. We occasionally pulled people out of countries when the personal risk became unacceptable. Inside the news industry, I became one of the people who was called when other journalists were in trouble overseas: photographers who disappeared in Libya; Foley and the others taken by ISIS; Austin Tice, the freelance journalist and law student who disappeared inside Syria; reporters in trouble in Turkey.

One Sunday morning in January 2014, Karam Shoumali, a young Syrian working for us in Turkey, was given a picture of Theo Curtis, a freelancer who had been taken by al-Qaeda in Syria. Over the next 12 hours, Karam and I, along with our longtime foreign correspondent Chris Chivers, worked with Theo's family to establish contact with a sheik from Kuwait who was behind the transmittal of the picture and was offering to help. In the end, we arranged for Theo's mother, Nancy, to travel from Boston to Istanbul for a meeting, set up by Karam. It led nowhere (the all-too-usual story in every kidnapping), although the Curtis family told us it was empowering to, at last, be doing something directly to try to help Theo. Most days in a kidnapping are spent just waiting, feeling helpless, worrying without knowing a thing. We knew in helping Nancy we were going far beyond anything we were paid to do by The Times or supposed to do. We were putting The Times in the uncomfortable position of being part of a story, not reporting on it. But after what we had been through with our own journalists, I was unwilling to hand off the photo to Theo's family and turn away if there was something we could do.

And maybe more was behind it, at least for me. Theo had been held for a time with a freelance American photographer named Matt Schrier. They were imprisoned in a basement in Syria and after weeks of being there were able to get a high small window open. Theo boosted Matt up and he wiggled through. Matt made an effort to get Theo out, but then dashed to freedom when Theo could not get up and through. When Matt got back to the states, both CNN and *The Times* interviewed him about the escape and mentioned that Matt had been aided by a second American prisoner. I somehow missed the reference as I reviewed our story before publication. I have never regretted anything more in my work for the paper. When Theo was later freed, he acknowledged what I had feared: he had been brutalized after his captors learned of his role in Schrier's escape, apparently from the media accounts. Much later, I was invited by Theo's family to a screening of a documentary about his time in captivity. It was hard to sit there in that darkened theater and watch the part about CNN and *The Times* and be reminded of what had happened to Theo afterward.

After the incident with Steve and Sultan, we had no more kidnappings, but other crises kept coming. Anthony Shadid died while on a reporting trip inside Syria; Alissa Rubin was seriously injured in a helicopter crash on Mount Sinjar in Iraq; a freelancer was detained in Ethiopia; two other freelancers were jailed while reporting from the Sinai Peninsula; one of our stringers in the Democratic Republic of Congo had to be relocated to Kenya; and we were in a more or less constant showdown with the authorities in Turkey as the Erdogan government took a hard turn toward authoritarianism. The dark turn of the Turkish government was particularly saddening for me. When four of our journalists disappeared in Libya during the war there in 2011, it was the Turkish embassy we turned to for help. The U.S. diplomatic corps had left the country, but the Turks had stayed and were instrumental in getting our people back home. They stood up for the journalists and for human rights in a way that now with Turkey seems unfathomable.

The four—Tyler Hicks, Anthony Shadid, Lynsey Addario, and Steve Farrell—had vanished one afternoon, along with their driver

Mohamed Shaglouf, as they covered the war from the rebels' side. About the only useful bit of information we had in the first hours was that they had been carrying a satellite phone. And we knew that for as long as the phone was on, it would be transmitting their geographical location—the longitude and latitude of where they were. It would be a critical clue to finding them. There was just one problem: the sat phone company wouldn't give us the data from the phone. Our tech people kept calling; the phone company kept refusing. The most important lesson I had learned from dealing with foreign crises was to be persistent, to keep trying, anything and everything, no matter how hopeless. The company was head-quartered in the Middle East, and I finally got a senior executive to come to the phone. It was early in the morning in New York, and I sat in my office, alone on my floor, making the plea. I explained that we needed the geographic coordinates, that it was a matter of life and death. The executive was warm and courteous, courtly al-most, but nothing I said could move him. He said it was illegal to give me the information. But it was our data, I protested. No, he said, that was wrong. The data did not belong to The Times, and it did not belong to his company. It belonged to the land that was Libya, to the planet earth. It was nonsensical, utterly stupid, and so around and around we went. I was exasperated.

Then the executive's tone shifted unexpectedly. "Oh, Mr. David," he said, "I hear what you are saying. You know sometimes a person's head speaks and sometimes his heart speaks. And my head, it is saying I cannot legally give you this. I am so sorry. But, Mr. David, you know, my heart is saying something else, it is saying that you should type into Google right now . . ."

It was true. The guy was giving me the coordinates. I wrote the numbers down feverishly, hung up the phone, turned to my com-puter, and typed in the coordinates.

Some obscure location in the middle of Poland popped up.

I was pretty certain that Tyler and the others were not in

Poland. I was pretty certain the Qaddafi regime had not surreptitiously transported them to Europe when we weren't looking. I was pretty certain I'd written the numbers down wrong. So I took a deep breath and dialed back. "Can you go back to that part, the one where your heart is doing the talking?"

We learned over the next day that the journalists had been rounded up during a fight between the rebels and Qaddafi's military at a checkpoint. In New York, I was working 16 hours a day trying to get them freed, knowing that the U.S. and its allies were about to start bombing Qaddafi's strongholds and everything would be more complicated when that happened. Chris Chivers left his home in Rhode Island and showed up to assist. We were joined by one of our outside security consultants. The three of us sat hour after hour in my office brainstorming on how we could reach the Qaddafi government. Every morning and afternoon, I gave regularly scheduled updates to the four families. We sorted through Twitter trying to figure out which way the war was going. Four days into the crisis I learned of two people in New York who knew Qaddafi personally. I got them on the phone and convinced them to call the Libyan leader even as the bombing of Tripoli started. (I was told that Qaddafi said The New York Times could go fuck itself.) I cajoled and pressed my contact in the State Department to do more to help us get to the right people in the Libyan government. We'd learned that our journalists had been mistreated, and we needed the government to do more, faster.

In the strange way these things unfold, I ended up on the phone one afternoon with a Libyan government official who was in the same room with not just the four *Times* journalists being held but also David Kirkpatrick. David was covering the war for us from Tripoli, while at the same time working tirelessly to help his imprisoned colleagues, and he had been permitted to come see them. The official told me everything could be resolved if I got in touch with an American named "Jose." Jose had always known how to get things done whenever there was a problem involving the U.S. government. He was the man to speak to. The Libyan official gave me Jose's cell phone number. Jose, it turned out, was the CIA's clandestine contact person in Libya. The State Department was not pleased that I had his number.

Five days into the standoff, the Libyans finally committed to handing the four over to Turkish diplomats. A time was set, arrangements were made, and the Turks began traveling through the streets of Tripoli to the pickup point. And then the bombing resumed. The Libyans said the transfer could not go forward. It was late at night in New York. Chris and I closed down my office and came dragging back in at 4:00 in the morning, when the Turks were to try again. Shortly after dawn, we got the news that the ordeal was over. Our journalists had been handed over. The Turks had come through. They escorted the four to the Tunisia border and freedom.

There remained one task undone. Mohamed Shaglouf, the driver, had disappeared after the car was stopped at the checkpoint. He had worked for The Times for exactly one day, hired that morning to take *The Times* journalists to report on a hospital in a village near the front. Prodded by Chivers, a former marine, I knew we had to help his family as they tried to find out what had happened to him. By then, Libya was attempting to pick up the pieces after the fall of Qaddafi and the rebels' victory. Mohamed's family had tried to sort through rumors and hazy reports of his whereabouts. Someone recalled hearing his name called out at a Qaddafi detention facility. That proved to be untrue. In fact, he had been shot and died at the checkpoint. (Chris and Tyler Hicks later traveled back to Libya to meet with the family and pay their respects.) Not far from where he had died, a Libyan man had created a carefully tended cemetery of unmarked graves for those whose bodies had been left behind in battle. He had taken pictures of the interred in the hopes that, later, families might be able to identify their loved ones. Shane

Bell, one of our security advisors in country, volunteered to travel into the heart of Libya to get DNA samples from Mohamed's family and from a body that appeared to be his. I set about trying to find a lab anywhere in the Middle East that could do the DNA testing quickly. I got nowhere. Shane was due to take home leave, so he packed the samples in his suitcase and carried them halfway around the world to Australia, where he found a lab that did DNA work. The samples were not in good shape, and the lab told me it would be hard to do a proper analysis, but the technicians there finally managed to pull it off. They sent me the results. There was no chance that the body in the unmarked grave was Mohamed.

I carefully typed up an email to the Shaglouf family, hoping to cushion what I knew would be the harsh blow of learning that they had not found their son and brother. They had studied pictures of the corpse and they were convinced that the DNA would confirm the identity. I expressed my regrets as best I could and hit the send button. I had been in regular contact with the family for months, I knew their grief, and I knew there was nothing more I could do. No response came. I feared that I had offended them in some way with my email. I felt cowardly about having not called. At the same time, I worried they would come back and ask for me to do something more in what I knew was now a hopeless situation.

Months passed, and the whole ordeal of Libya finally faded for me, until one morning when I woke up and checked my email. At the top of the inbox was the name of Mohamed's brother. I could only imagine what the family wanted now, and I dreaded being asked. I clicked on the email and read: "Mr. David, we have heard about the storm Sandy in New York City. We hope you and your family are safe."

Throughout the course of the kidnappings and the detentions and the random mayhem our reporters encountered, I didn't always love the way we were treated by our government, but that was usually in the details—disagreements about what could be done reasonably and what could not. My experience had been that when an American reporter was in trouble, somebody in the U.S. government would come to the phone. Whatever unhappiness an administration may have had with our coverage, it got set aside. I also knew that as part of the core American diplomatic mission, under Bush and under Obama, the foreign service made a point to advocate for a freer press in countries struggling to find democracy. The Bush State Department, no fan of *The Times,* had sent me to speak in Jordan, Yemen, Kuwait, Bahrain, and various countries of the old Soviet bloc about how press freedom worked in the U.S. It was part of spreading the secular American gospel of freedom.

The first time we had a problem in the Middle East during the Trump administration, someone in the State Department called one of our editors. He wasn't authorized to speak, but he needed to tell us about a threat that was looming for one of our reporters who had offended the local government. The official had made the call on his own because he wasn't convinced that in the new State Department we would be able to count on anyone at the local embassies to help us out. I was told by people at other news organizations with reporters in trouble that the Trump State Department had continued to be helpful, but I was not looking forward to finding out for myself the first time we really needed the backing of the U.S. government in the midst of a crisis.

Then there was the president's obsessive denouncing of the U.S. mainstream media as "fake news." It was corrosive inside our borders. Beyond them, it was dangerous. The calculus for the world's worst autocrats was simple: if the American president could denounce independent news organizations in his country as enemies of the people and work to undermine a free press, there was no reason they should not deal with their own local journalists in exactly the same way. By the second year of the Trump administration, autocratic nations like Malaysia were enacting laws banning fake news, barely hiding what was really going on: there would now be another tool available for authoritarians to control the media and keep unpleasant truths from their people. The situation was also bleak for those American news organizations that happened to be working in repressive nations. When autocrats harassed or brought charges against American news organizations over stories that displeased a regime, they undoubtedly assumed they were ingratiating themselves with the government in Washington.

Steven Erlanger of *The Times* reported on how infectious the president's "fake news" diatribe had been among the world's worst leaders. Syrian president Bashar al-Assad, responding to reports of human rights abuses, said, "We are living in a fake-news era." President Nicolás Maduro of Venezuela echoed his sentiments. In Myanmar, where the government turned a blind eye to the military's savage killing of Rohingya Muslims, an official said it was all fake news. Others joined the chorus in Poland, Hungary, Libya, Russia, and Somalia. Steve offered a chilling example from the *People's Daily*, the government propaganda organ of China, which wrote:

> If the president of the United States claims that his nation's leading media outlets are a stain on America, then negative news about China and other countries should be taken with a grain of salt, since it is likely that bias and political agendas are distorting the real picture.

America had often held itself as a model when it was out promoting democracy to the world. The authoritarians of the world didn't seem much interested in following our lead in those days. But now? They were suddenly eager to sign on to be like this new America.

In the summer of 2018, A. G. Sulzberger, our new publisher, traveled to the White House and raised directly with President Trump how dangerous his attacks on the press were, how easily they could prompt violence against journalists. In tweeting about the meeting, the president never mentioned anything about that, and within days he was back out doing campaign-style rallies, denouncing journalists as always.

The situation in Egypt after David Kirkpatrick's story continued to perplex us. We were told by our local lawyers that the investigation of The Times was going forward, but what the investigators were doing and how seriously they were doing it remained secret. The lawyers advised us that our reporters in Cairo should continue carrying on, doing what they always did—writing stories about what was going on in that critical country and how the complicated relationships that laced the Middle East remained in uneasy flux. The criminal investigation would have to exist for us as a shadow in the background, not quite visible but not going away.

A few weeks after we broke Kirkpatrick's story about the broadcast hosts, Michael Slackman got in touch with me. Our reporters were working on a new story out of Egypt, this one about how the Egyptian authorities were secretly letting Israel conduct air strikes inside Egypt's borders aimed at destroying terrorist encampments. The timing was all wrong for us. We were under criminal investigation for our critical reporting on the government, and here was another story that would cast doubts on the honesty and trustworthiness of Egypt's leaders. It would show again the government's clandestine alliance with the demonized state of Israel. It was easy to predict what the reaction from the Egyptian government would be.

Michael and I talked through our options, but we both knew what the truth was: there was no way for *The New York Times* not to publish a story that important.

14

One Morning a Letter

A letter is a worthwhile communication tool only if the recipient understands, and is receptive to, its content. Knowing this, the conscientious lawyer tailors the letter to meet the characteristics of the person to whom the letter is directed.

—Gretchen Viney, "101: Writing a Professional Letter," *Wisconsin Lawyer* magazine, June 2013

Don't use value judgments designed to make readers feel bad about past mistakes. Instead, try to motivate your reader to improve behavior in the future.

—Gary Blake, "A Few Tips on Writing to Opposing Attorneys," International Risk Management Institute, Jan. 2004

The writing is clear while at the same time being legally precise. . . . It's also perhaps the first time in legal history in which "libel per se" and "piece of ass" were used in the same document.

—Brian Carroll, *Writing and Editing for Digital Media* (2017)

TWO YEARS LATER, after Sean Spicer and alternative facts, after the endless insults about the "enemy of the American people" and fake news, after James Comey and Anonymous and Stormy Daniels and Bob Mueller, after the flood of White House leaks, after Harvey Weinstein and #MeToo, I sometimes thought back to October 2016 with something akin to nostalgia. For all the intensity and zaniness and viciousness of the 2016 presidential campaign, there was a certain simplicity to those days; at least that is how it seemed in retrospect. It was a crazy time, yes, but the craziness seemed more sheet cake than layer cake.

Do we need to respond? my boss wanted to know, as we looked over a letter from Candidate Trump's attorneys one October morning. The letter was about a story we had just run in which two women said Trump had groped them years earlier. It was a huff-and-puff, blow-your-house-down sort of lawyer letter. It had nothing of substance to say. It didn't offer any proof. Donald Trump was not likely to sue The New York Times for printing the story. Hadn't he just been all over TV and the internet bragging about grabbing women by the pussy? What was the point of spending time writing a letter that would either be ignored or just fuel some infuriatingly pointless back-and-forth with Team Trump?

I don't know, I said. There had been so much attention already to the letter. Our PR people were being hounded about what we had to say and whether we intended to respond. Our readers don't understand how these things work. They don't understand that these fire-breathing letters come in all the time and then the lawyers are never heard from again. Won't a non-response be read as a sign we're worried or intimidated or have doubts about our own story, and maybe all three? And wasn't it just a little outrageous that Donald Trump was blaming *us* for his crappy reputation for treating women badly? Maybe I should try to bang out something later that morning and then we could decide. We were already late for a meeting.

The night before, Twitter had been ablaze (as it often is when nothing real is actually happening). Trump's lawyers had written us a letter even before we published the story saying we would be sued if we went ahead with publication. We printed the story. It detailed the women's accounts of two separate incidents. Immediately, Trump campaign aides were telling anyone who would listen that there was going to be a lawsuit. "Assume you will tell us if we receive anything tonight," Eileen Murphy, the head of Corporate Communications, wrote to me at 10:30 that night. "It's a hot topic and the Trump people are saying they're preparing a lawsuit for delivery tonight." That struck me as a particularly unlikely event. A real summons and complaint, which are needed to start any lawsuit, had to be filed in court before the papers could be served on us, and as far as I knew, about the only court open late for business was the night arraignment part in the Bronx Criminal Court. The judges there see some wickedly crazy stuff, night in and night out, but, as far as I knew, they didn't handle a lot of after-hours libel suits from presidential candidates.

An hour later, as midnight approached, a lawyer at one of the country's biggest law firms wrote me: "If Trump really does sue, you have got to give me a shot." "I hear you," I wrote back, "but I might have to go with someone with a bigger groping law practice." I went to bed.

I woke up to an email from Dean Baquet. There was no message, just the subject line "After Midnight." (I would later get some seriously indignant mail from *Times* readers/music purists when I referred to "After Midnight" as an Eric Clapton song in an article I wrote. Everybody knows it's a J. J. Cale song. Clapton stole it and ruined it. Only a hopeless corporate puke would think it was a Clapton song.) Attached to Dean's email was the late-night letter from Trump's lawyers demanding a retraction:

> We represent Donald J. Trump. We write in response to the libelous article published October 12, 2015 by The New York Times entitled Two Women Say Donald Trump Touched Them Inappropriately.
>
> Your article is reckless, defamatory and constitutes libel per se. It is apparent from, among other things, the timing of the ar-

ticle, that it is nothing more than a politically motivated effort to defeat Mr. Trump's candidacy. That is why you apparently performed an entirely inadequate investigation to test the veracity of these false and malicious allegations, including why these two individuals waited, in one case, 11 years, and, in another case, more than three decades, before deciding to come forward with these false and defamatory statements. Clearly, The New York Times is willing to provide a platform to anyone wishing to smear Mr. Trump's name and reputation prior to the election irrespective of whether the alleged statements have any basis in fact.

We hereby demand that you immediately cease any further publication of this article, remove it from your website and issue a full and immediate retraction and apology. Failure to do so will leave my client with no option but to pursue all available actions and remedies.

It was not yet 6:00 in the morning when I read the letter, and I immediately did what lawyers do when someone puts a client on notice of a possible suit. I typed out an email to everyone who had been involved in the story. We needed to make sure no one in the company was saying anything off message that might complicate the company's legal position later if a lawsuit did actually come. I suggested we needed to have only one person speak for the company. It made sense to have that be Eileen Murphy in Corporate Communications. Could we agree on that? I hit send.

I heard straight away from reporter Michael Barbaro: "We are headed to do CBS This Morning," he wrote. Then his reporting partner Megan Twohey weighed in: "I just did NPR. We're scheduled to do CBS morning news at 730."

The sound I heard was the litigation playbook being chucked out the window.

I did think there was some chance that Trump might sue. Not

right away, of course, but after his inevitable upcoming loss in the election. What was the incentive for him not to sue then? He had the money to come after The Times, and he would no doubt blame us for his defeat. He had chased author Tim O'Brien around for years with his unwinnable libel lawsuit over nothing more than how much he was worth. Why wouldn't he do the same thing this time? He had no realistic chance of winning a suit that I could see, and I trusted our journalists' reporting, but lawyers are paid to prepare for the worst. I didn't know how the two women would stand up as witnesses if they were suddenly dragged into a libel suit. Why had they been silent for so many years? Why were they coming forward now? Let's guess who had their votes in the election.

Eileen wanted to know whether we should head off further interviews. She was worried that pulling out of the TV news spots would send the wrong message. She was right. There was no turning back. This was going to be a public brawl. Al DeVivo, head of our security desk, sent out an email letting everyone know that the news trucks were already lined up outside the building. And because the day was not shaping up to be strange enough, a news alert blinked across my computer screen: Bob Dylan had just won the Nobel Prize for Literature.

When my meeting wrapped up, I headed down the hall to write a response to Trump's attorneys. I only had 45 minutes. Later, I was always amused that the number of people who said "That letter must have written itself" was more or less equal to the number of people who said "You must have had somebody write it for you." Great to learn that the people who knew me best thought the letter was either ridiculously easy or way, way beyond my abilities.

I typed away, took a conference call, and then, shortly before noon, got a group of colleagues together to do a joint read of the draft—our general counsel, Ken Richieri, his deputy, Diane Brayton, and our new First Amendment fellow, Ian MacDougall. By then, everyone was onboard with doing a strong response, but I wasn't sure I had it right. We went around for about 30 minutes, talking about whether the overall point and tone were right, whether words should be tweaked, whether the ending was too much. I went online to double-check the facts. We tried to gauge the likely public reaction. I made some minor edits. There was some uneasiness in the room about the second paragraph:

> The essence of a libel claim, of course, is that a statement lowers the good reputation of another in the eyes of his community. Mr. Trump has bragged about his non-consensual sexual touching of women. He has bragged about intruding on naked beauty pageant contestants in their dressing rooms. He acquiesced to a radio host's request to discuss his own daughter as a "piece of ass." Multiple women not mentioned in our article have publicly come forward to report on Mr. Trump's unwanted advances. Nothing in our article has had the slightest effect on the reputation that Mr. Trump, through his own words and actions, has already created for himself.

It made sense legally—a person whose reputation is already in the dumper cannot claim that a story harmed his reputation further—but even as lawyer letters go, the paragraph was more sledgehammer than surgical knife. It also contained the somewhat less than lawyerly and decidedly non-*Times*ian phrase "piece of ass." And then there was that ending:

> It would have been a disservice not just to our readers but to democracy itself to silence their voices. We did what the law allows: We published important information about a subject of deep public concern. If Mr. Trump disagrees, if he believes that American citizens had no right to hear what these women had to

say and that the law of this country forces us and those who would dare to criticize him to stand silent or be punished, we welcome the opportunity to have a court set him straight.

Welcome the opportunity? Really? Maybe something more like "we are prepared to vigorously defend any claim," I suggested, lapsing back into full-lawyer mode. I typed out some possible new endings so we could all look at the words. We tried something more on the theme of "such a case would be unsuccessful." I typed some more. Nothing quite carried the message as well as the original. We decided to go with it.

Like lots of lawyers, I write dozens of lawyer letters every year. They tend to have an audience of one. An attorney writes to the paper unhappy with something we have done. I write back. More often than not, nothing more is ever heard. We take no offense. We're lawyers, not novelists.

And I had learned early on in my career at The Times that there is almost a direct correlation between the speciousness of the complaint and the level of audacious self-righteousness contained in the letters I receive. Lawyers who write to complain about The Times's coverage can't seem to help themselves. Words like "malicious," "deliberate falsehood," "impugn," "utterly lacking," and "reckless disregard" must be hot-keyed on their laptops. Never mind the client's recent indictment. Never mind the videotape, the recordings, the documentary evidence, the 27 sources, the federal investigation, or the damning admissions. Never mind the First Amendment. I once got an impassioned letter from a lawyer complaining about how one of our local newspapers had covered the arrest of his client. Outrage poured forth, interspersed with protestations of his client's innocence. What was odd—or perhaps telling—was that the lawyer never once mentioned exactly what his client had been arrested for. I tracked the article down. It was a routine police story based on the police logs. The client had been accused of masturbating while his car was stopped at a red light next to a vehicle driven by a woman. When the police caught up with him, he assured them that it was all a tragic mistake. Nothing like that had happened. He was, he told the cops, just checking for tick bites.

I also knew a little about how letter-to-letter combat plays out in public. Earlier in 2016, The Times found itself in a very public standoff with the National Football League. We had run a story tracing how the NFL's response to research on concussions resembled the tobacco industry's response to research linking smoking to cancer, and we reported on some of the connections between the tobacco industry and the NFL. The league posted a long lawyer letter saying it intended to sue us unless we retracted the story and took it down from the internet. I responded with a letter of my own, pushing back on the league for—as I saw it—trying to silence critics and keep fans in the dark. Sports being sports and lawyers being lawyers, the internet loved the exchange. It was the first time I ever found my work being handicapped by both legal blogs and sports columnists. I had been struck by the letters from the NFL's lawyers, in particular a reference to how "odious" the tobacco industry was. For The Times to associate the NFL with such corporate pariahs was outrageous, the lawyers said. No decent business would want to be associated with the likes of Big Tobacco. Only then I remembered that a few years earlier the same law firm had represented one of the big tobacco companies in the famous lawsuit brought by the Department of Justice over the tobacco industry's misrepresentations of smoking's health risks. Yes, the firm disputing our reporting that links existed between tobacco and football represented tobacco and football. I couldn't let it pass. After pages of legal argument, I moved to the conclusion: "While your earlier letter to The Times called the tobacco industry 'perhaps the most odious industry in American history,' you somehow fail to mention in either letter that it was your firm that represented Philip Morris in that RICO case."

I knew the Trump letter would go public, too. The Trump campaign had distributed the threat letter on the internet overnight. The morning news shows were leading with it. Still, when all the political hyperventilating ceased, my letter was just a lawyer letter. "Stand by your Twitter accounts. We are about to go live," I wrote to my colleagues in the Legal Department. I intended it to be a joke. In the first 90 minutes, I had 90 emails from readers. Then the pace picked up.

Hundreds of emails poured in. They came from Tanzania, the Northern Mariana Islands, England, Sri Lanka, Australia, and all over the U.S. Someone asked to translate the letter into Spanish. Most of the emails were from strangers, many from lawyers, but also from a nurse and a doctor, retired people, the founder of a nonprofit, law school students, parents whose kids had seen the letter online at college, journalists from other news organizations. I heard from students I had taught 30 years ago when I was a college professor, former colleagues, law school classmates I hadn't seen in two decades, my brother's high school girlfriend, a person who says we met at a wedding 10 years ago, my ex-wife.

One person took issue with my comma usage. Somebody suggested I be disbarred. I was made aware of a raging online debate set off by the letter over whether there should be two spaces or one after a period. (It ended when a young woman asked people to knock off the carping about the double spaces in my letter because, well, that was just how old people write.)

By Friday night, more than a million people would come to *The Times* website to read the letter. Hundreds of thousands of others were reading it on other sites. On Saturday, two days after the letter went public, it still topped the "most emailed" and "most viewed" list on nytimes.com. A reporter was in a downtown bar that weekend and heard a table of twentysomethings quoting the letter from memory as they drank beers. Two women proposed to me online.

Someone asked what it was like to be the guy who "broke the internet." I was pretty sure I was not yet in Kardashian territory. Plus there was this: My day job didn't care how I was doing on Twitter. A photo editor wanted me to help a freelancer who was running into problems getting access to a college campus. Our bureau in Hong Kong was doing a sensitive story about the Thai royal family, and we were once again dealing with Thailand's oppressive *lèse-majesté* laws, which bar any criticism of the monarchs. A lawyer got in touch with me to try to resolve (once again) a never-ending contract dispute over delivery routes in the city of Boston. I spent a big chunk of the day deep in the misery of producing documents and data for a class-action suit we were facing over our marketing materials in the state of California. Meanwhile, the emails about the letter kept pouring in. At night, I would sit up late and reply to them, dozens and dozens every night. People had taken the time to write. I thought they deserved a response. Totally Midwestern. I still correspond with a 90-year-old woman named Rusty who wrote to me then and, every couple of weeks, lets me know what the world looks like from the vantage point of Colorado and all those years.

A year before the #MeToo movement would rise up, the notes from women who had experienced harassment in their own lives were moving. "I felt you were also speaking . . . for all of the women that have been bullied after reporting sexual harassment/assault/abuse. For that I sincerely thank you," one wrote. Another said, "I don't know one woman who has not experienced some level of this sort of aggressive, entitled behavior over the course of her life. Yet so many of us just try to bury it and move on, while arguing within ourselves whether we weren't partially to blame. Perhaps this new discussion will help bring about meaningful change. Thank you for helping bring this into sharp relief." Someone else tried to capture the discouraging reality of what women went through on the job.

"I know more women than I can count on both my hands and feet who have had similar experiences to my own. The number of said women who had the courage to push against these more powerful men can be, sadly, counted on one hand alone. . . . I thank the New York Times for standing strong."

Other people simply wanted to express their appreciation. A guy wrote to say that it made him proud to have gone to the same high school as I did—unless I was some other David McCraw. "Even if you are not an MHS grad—I still admire what you did." "Sending you the highest of fives," wrote another reader, although she predicted my spam filter would end up snagging her email. A couple in California said they had opened a bottle of wine and toasted the letter. A New Yorker said he wanted to be the "289,000th human being to say thank you." The best email was the one that ended: "As my sister put it, 'I've never wanted to hang a paragraph from a lawyer on my fridge before.'"

Then there was the note from the lawyer in California. He said he had spent his entire career working for a movie studio, which meant that he had spent a lifetime writing polite responses to all the jerks in his industry. You must be lucky, he said, to work at a company where they let you respond by saying what you really think and believe.

His email hinted at what many people wanted to know. Did the senior management of The New York Times really let me write a letter like that? That would be a letter that not only said "please sue us" but also contained that choice phrase "piece of ass." In those days I had a glass office, and about 10 minutes after the letter went up I found out one of the not-so-great things about having a glass office. One of the not-so-great things is that you can see when the CEO of your company is walking toward your office with a certain look on his face and certain letter in one hand. In that instance, you begin to wonder whether it was such a super-great idea to send a "bring it on" letter to the next president of the United States without first checking with senior management. Our CEO, Mark Thompson, is an Englishman. He walked right in and he was direct. He held the letter up in front of me. "Brilliant letter," he said, "but there's one thing I'll never understand. Why do you Americans insist on capitalizing after a colon?"

That could have turned out much worse.

In the months after the letter went viral, I became one of the faces of the press freedom movement, speaking on campuses about the Trump presidency and the war the president was waging against independent media. Inevitably, people wanted to know whether The Times ever got a response. I had heard from thousands of people about my letter. The one person I didn't hear from was the actual recipient of the letter, Trump's lawyer. In time I stopped looking for a response. The election was over. Trump had won. The threat of any suit faded into an afterthought.

Then one night in February 2017, as I sat eating dinner at another endless meeting in a law firm conference room, an email showed up in my inbox. Checking my phone under the table, I recognized the sender immediately. It was the lawyer. There was nothing on the subject line. Just his name and a blank space. I hesitated for a moment, then I clicked.

At the bottom of the email was a brief news item about a commencement speech I had been invited to give at a law school. Above that was a simple message: "I think it's about time that you began cutting me in on your honorariums, don't you think? Congratulations. Hope you are well."

I couldn't resist. "I completely agree," I wrote back. "But being the enemy of the people doesn't pay the way it used to. I think I am up to $900 total." Two lawyers treating each other as professional colleagues? As human beings? Normal stuff. Maybe there was hope for America after all.

The responses that mattered most to me, though, were the ones that came from journalists. Inside *The Times* newsroom, the re-action had been bracing. Reporters circulated the report that I got a standing ovation as I walked into the room on the day after the letter was sent, and pretty soon that anecdote was in media ac-counts. As sometimes is the case in journalism, the truth was a little more complicated. I did get an ovation. And some of the jour-nalists were standing around when I came into the room. I leave it to others to decide whether that constitutes a standing ovation.

But elsewhere journalists had reservations about what I had done, especially the paragraph about Trump's reputation for inap-propriate behavior toward women. In the fall of 2017, during an in-terview at an NPR station in St. Paul, Minnesota, the host drilled down on that paragraph, wanting to know why I had included it. The questioning was sharp and smart. I explained that my letter was a lawyer letter, that I was setting out the legal argument we would make in court. That is how these letters go. You let the other side know what your case is going to look like if they are foolish enough to run into court. It was, I tried to say, just garden-variety lawyering: laying out the law and applying it to the facts. I didn't sound all that convincing—face it: the paragraph was a take-no-prisoners volley—and I wasn't looking forward to the NPR host's follow-up. Then, suddenly, behind me someone in the control room signaled that President Trump was going live with an ad-dress to the nation. The station was cutting away from my inter-view to cover it. I turned and saw on a hanging TV monitor Trump heading for a lectern at the White House. I had never been so happy to see the guy. The interview was over.

Even at the time the letter came out, there were dissenting voices. Mark Halperin, then a highly regarded political correspondent at Bloomberg, said the letter had veered into partisanship. "To put that letter in public making those accusations. . . . If my news organ-ization did that, I would be uncomfortable," he said. He saw the

ONE MORNING A LETTER   269

letter as an "ad hominem" attack and said The Times "should do their speaking in the paper" and "do their arguing in court if necessary."

Some of what Halperin had to say didn't track. Was The Times supposed to not respond to a demand for a retraction from lawyers that the Trump campaign had released publicly? If we did respond, were we then supposed to hide the fact that we had done so? Erik Wemple in *The Washington Post* came to The Times's defense: "A word to Halperin: If Trump wants to make noise about legal action, the New York Times may deploy its lawyers to provide a response. Releasing it to the public is merely an act of transparency that merits the support of journalists, not a silly and faux-ethical condemnation."

Still, I could understand the discomfort of some journalists. My role is to defend The Times's work and, more often than not, to advocate for a single position: that we got the story right, we were within our legal rights to do it, and the person threatening us or suing is wrong. It is impossible in that situation not to be adversarial, even if our reporters can't be and shouldn't be. But I knew, for the paper's own good, there was a line somewhere out there not to be crossed. I tried to be careful to build my case from facts we had reported and to have my judgments be legal opinions, not political ones. In an article in *The Times* after the letter, I expressed my own uneasiness with people who wanted to embrace the letter as one part of some anti-Trump offensive. That was not how I saw it. My role was to take on anyone who was trying to silence the truth or wrap the government in secrecy. When people attempted to bully us or when officials were trying to conceal what the public deserved to know, it didn't matter to me what their political views were. I fought with New York's arrogant Democratic leaders, I sued the Obama administration more than 30 times for withholding information, and I took on the Republicans whenever they were trying to make America a less transparent nation. My job didn't change with the administrations. My job was to do whatever I could to make sure our reporters had a chance to pursue the truth and tell it the best they could.

I was glad that Clarence Jones was there to remind me of that in October 2016.

Clarence was in his mid-80s. In the early 1960s he was Martin Luther King's personal lawyer. *Times v. Sullivan* had arisen from an ad placed in *The Times* by Dr. King's supporters detailing the violence and abuse that civil rights protesters had endured in Montgomery, Alabama. Sullivan was a local police official in Alabama, and all across the South power brokers were using libel suits to intimidate news organizations like The Times that were trying to tell the world about the civil rights movement.

Clarence Jones wrote to me in October 2016 to remind me that when The Times and the Sulzberger family had stood up for the newspaper in the *Sullivan* case, they were also standing up for the civil rights leaders who had published the ad. "All of my then 31-year-old self advised Dr. King and The Times that Sullivan's suit was an effort to silence the Times and decapitate the leadership of the Southern Civil Rights Movement," he said. "We and the Times had no choice but to fight it. We were fighting for our survival."

Clarence Jones was right then, and he is right now. Fifty-five years after *Sullivan*, there is still no choice to be made but to fight.

The First Amendment Is Dead:
A Love Story

The King is dead, long live The King!
— Traditional expression, uttered on the passing of the monarch

OF COURSE, IT isn't really dead. In some ways the First Amendment has never been more alive. If you want to produce videos depicting animal cruelty, parade around with homophobic signs at the funerals of dead soldiers, or donate your vast wealth to elect someone to a job that pays $150,000, the First Amendment has embraced you in its loving arms in recent years and held you tight. All of those cases have come to the Supreme Court in recent times, and every time the court has jumped to the defense of those claiming a right to express themselves. And even in more pedestrian ways the First Amendment remains central to our culture. It is the fertile ground on which every Facebook post is planted and every tweet comes to blossom, to be cast into the cyber winds of the internet.

I see that. I have spent 16 years as The New York Times's newsroom lawyer. I have overseen dozens of libel suits, filed more FOIA suits than any other mainstream media attorney in the country, and stood up to countless legal threats by people unhappy with the things we have said about them. Did the First Amendment make that easier for me? Every day.

But over those 16 years I have come to see how silent the First Amendment has been on so many of the real challenges that journalists face today in covering a dangerous world and a blisteringly divided country. The great awakening of press freedom occurred in this country 50 years ago. In a country torn by racism and administrations that had lied their way from Vietnam to Watergate, the First Amendment responded, interpreted by a Supreme Court that understood that courageous and important journalism would be possible only if the press felt free from legal peril. *Times v. Sullivan*, in 1964, revolutionized libel law, throwing significant obstacles in the way of those public officials who wanted to use libel suits to silence criticism. But context mattered: it was a case about the right of civil rights leaders in the South to be heard and a decision designed to protect the right of Northern reporters to travel into Mississippi and Alabama and the rest of the Deep South to expose injustice. Seven years later, in 1971, in the Pentagon Papers, the court drew the line on prior restraints, effectively reining in the power of the government to go to court and stop the press from reporting. But context again mattered. It was not just a sensitive story, but a story about the duplicity of the government in conducting the war in Vietnam. There was a story that needed to be told, and the First Amendment made it possible to hear the voices of those journalists courageous enough and enterprising enough to go after the secrets that the government held close.

Today, the existential threats to the press—the mainstream media that remains democracy's best hope of delivering the truth and checking the inevitable overreach of the powerful—are of a different scope and shape: the proliferation of fake news, an administration that devotes a breathtaking amount of time to delegitimizing a free press ("the enemy of the American people"), the unchecked reach of government surveillance programs that threaten report-ers' ability to have sources, the failure of the law to provide mean-ingful protection to confidential sources for the most sensitive and most important stories that the press does, the perilous reality faced by foreign correspondents in large stretches of the world, and the fractured media environment that has created two realities, a red reality and a blue reality, Fox and Breitbart over there, The Times and The Post over here, a divergence that makes sensible de-mocracy regularly impossible. And in the background these past 16 years has been a technological revolution that disrupted the economic model that supported journalism and the singularity of voice that gave news organizations their authority and power. The First Amendment has largely nothing to say about how to fix any of that. A press threatened, a democracy in need of truth. Five de-cades ago, press freedom was an indelible part of the solution. Five decades later, the press has often failed to respond meaningfully, and in some ways it has fostered the very problems that now threaten our democracy.

Still . . . this has been a love story. A story about what it has been like to experience all that change as a lawyer and—to use the throw-back term of a different era—as a Timesman, to find in the law and in lawyering a way to protect a journalism that is worth protect-ing. As a small boy, I started my morning reading the *Decatur Herald* alongside my father. It spoke to Decatur, Illinois—an im-possibly exotic place 30 miles away from my tiny town—but also to the possibilities of an unimaginable world far beyond our lives deep in the Illinois heartland.

And it has been a love story about the First Amendment, filled as any good love story is with a nostalgia for the bright shiny mo-ments of the past and a hope, without naivety and without illusion, for some future in which it will be part of the answer.

I never once lost sight of the fact that it was a privilege to call myself a lawyer for The New York Times. I have been there, behind the scenes, as *The Times* reported and wrote stories that changed so much about who we are as a nation: the aftermath of 9/11, WikiLeaks, the war on terrorism, the Arab Spring, the mayhem in Iraq and Syria and Afghanistan, the rise of Trump, the tsunami of sexual reckoning loosed by the Harvey Weinstein revelations.

But as much as we celebrate that deep and consequential reporting and know intuitively that it would not be possible in a place without press freedom, there is that gnawing other reality that we can't easily ignore: that the First Amendment also gives succor to those who spew hate speech online, who use the internet as a high-powered weapon of revenge, who actively work to distract an already unsteady nation, who obscure the line between truth and falsity, and who rally Twitter mobs to diminish the lives of those they find different, unacceptable, too outspoken, or even just too homely. Tim Wu, a Columbia law professor, published an essay in *The Times* in October 2017 called "How Twitter Killed the First Amendment." It began: "You need not be a media historian to notice that we live in a golden age of press harassment, domestic propaganda and coercive efforts to control political debate." Meanwhile, way over on the other side of the political spectrum, a president declares all unpleasant truths "fake news" and invites the parts of America that follow him to close their eyes and turn their hatred toward a press that dares to not fall in line.

They are not unrelated, the runaway internet and the anti-press president with autocratic impulses. The genius, stable or otherwise, of Donald Trump is some intuitive knowledge of that relationship. The First Amendment is at base a belief in the idea of a marketplace of ideas where truth and falsity compete and an engaged citizenry can discern the difference without coaching from the government. The internet should be democracy's engine, breaking down all the barriers that have in the past prevented those who want to speak and those who want to hear from participating meaningfully in that mythical marketplace. Instead, a technology that has the potential to make us smarter, better informed, less isolated, more empathetic regularly achieves precisely the opposite. There has never been a more important moment in history to demand that Americans discern, question, and doubt, but in the cacophony of our breached politics, many people will do the easy opposite: believe and ignore. That the president should want to hide the truth, and hide from it, should surprise no one. We all have our inconvenient truths. But the surprise is this: how many Americans are willing to stand with him in that dark place. The demonized Other—the dishonest and corrupt mainstream media—is not to be believed. The Other abuses its power, misuses the First Amendment, stands in the way, destroys. It is the enemy.

The reason that sort of demagoguery is so corrosive for democracy is this: the First Amendment story is, in the end, not about law but about hearts and minds. It doesn't really matter how much freedom journalists have if no one believes them. A discredited press plays no role in shaping democracy and holding power accountable. And a public that finds a press contemptible holds no stake in defending First Amendment values and standing up for press freedom. Why would it? The civic instinct is to do just the opposite. It is a very short half-step from not believing the press to not believing in press freedom.

The national consensus has frayed. It is hard to recognize in the breach of modern democracy that this is a country of people who have historically stood together to protect the free speech rights of those they disagreed with. And it is understandable that those who seek to shut down hate speech, end bullying online, and curtail the power of falsity on the internet see the First Amendment as an impediment, part of the problem, not part of the solution.

But, as I said, this is a love story. It is about the love for an idea. The authors of the First Amendment were not naive. They understood from hard-edged experience that lies were inevitable, the urge to deceive grounded in human nature. But democracy's remedy was an informed citizenry that, in the fullness of time, would pull the lever for truth over falsity. The alternative—a government that used its power to decide who spoke and who was silent, what was real and what was fake—was untenable. We come closer and closer to learning that every day.

The First Amendment is not really dead but it will live long only if the American people fall in love with it again. It is no effortless romance. It requires hard work: to not just embrace the right of everyone to speak, but to care about the truth, to listen and hear, to discern as best we can, and to believe that, for all of its gobsmacking craziness in our digital present and future, the marketplace of ideas is still a better idea than anything anyone else has dreamed up. None of this is to say that The Times and everyone else in the news business get it right every day. We don't. Journalism is more art than science. But were we to actually nail it day after day, get it perfectly right, that alone would still not be enough to make democracy great again. The only path to that sort of greatness runs through the hearts and minds of the American public.

It is impossible not to wonder about whether the First Amendment can find a new life, can embolden a flagging democracy, can be to our current troubles what it was to civil rights and Vietnam and Watergate. Despite everything, I still believe it can and it should. The belief carries on. That is how it is with love.

ACKNOWLEDGMENTS

The accounts and opinions set forth in this book are solely mine, but I am deeply indebted to the people who generously took time to read sections of my manuscript and then provided invaluable counsel and editing: Drane Brayton, Susanne Craig, David Rohde, Kristen Mulvihill, David Sanger, Jodi Kantor, Megan Twohey, Sergio Florez, Mike Schmidt, Michael Slackman, and Christina Koningisor. Suzanne Daley reimagined the opening chapters and inspired everything that came after. Mark McCraw was a ruthless, and maddeningly right, fact-checker. Neil Swidey, Susan Crawford, Karen Greenberg, and Chris Chivers, all friends who have written their own books, offered advice and encouragement at critical moments. Michael Pollak was a deft copy editor for me. At The Times, General Counsel Diane Brayton supported this project from the start and was instrumental in setting up a leave so I could finish writing. Her predecessor, Ken Richieri, helped shape my thinking about the book when I first began talking about it in the fall of 2016. The senior leadership at The Times, Arthur Sulzberger Jr., A. G. Sulzberger,

Mark Thompson, and Dean Baquet, enthusiastically embraced the idea that a Times lawyer should, and maybe even could, write a book. It was the literary agent Kim Witherspoon who first raised the idea of the book when we met in October 2016, and she has been a guiding hand ever since. I am also indebted to the team at St. Martin's—Adam Bellow, Kevin Reilly, Alan Bradshaw, and their coworkers, who turned a manuscript into a book and made it better at every step.

INDEX